CHINESE SCHOOLS
IN PENINSULAR MALAYSIA

The **Institute of Southeast Asian Studies (ISEAS)** was established as an autonomous organization in 1968. It is a regional centre dedicated to the study of socio-political, security and economic trends and developments in Southeast Asia and its wider geostrategic and economic environment. The Institute's research programmes are the Regional Economic Studies (RES, including ASEAN and APEC), Regional Strategic and Political Studies (RSPS), and Regional Social and Cultural Studies (RSCS).

ISEAS Publishing, an established academic press, has issued more than 2,000 books and journals. It is the largest scholarly publisher of research about Southeast Asia from within the region. ISEAS Publishing works with many other academic and trade publishers and distributors to disseminate important research and analyses from and about Southeast Asia to the rest of the world.

CHINESE SCHOOLS
IN PENINSULAR MALAYSIA
The Struggle for Survival

LEE TING HUI

ISEAS

INSTITUTE OF SOUTHEAST ASIAN STUDIES
Singapore

First published in Singapore in 2011 by
ISEAS Publishing
Institute of Southeast Asian Studies
30 Heng Mui Keng Terrace
Pasir Panjang Road
Singapore 119614

Internet e-mail: publish@iseas.edu.sg
World Wide Web: <http://bookshop.iseas.edu.sg>

The responsibility for facts and opinions expressed in this publication rests exclusively with the author and his interpretations do not necessarily reflect the views or the policy of the Institute, or its supporters.

ISEAS Library Cataloguing-in-Publication Data

Lee, Ting Hui, 1931-
    Chinese schools in Peninsular Malaysia : the struggle for survival.
    1.   Schools, Chinese—Malaysia.
    2.   Schools, Chinese—Government policy—Malaysia.
    3.   Chinese—Education—Malaysia.
    4.   Education and state—Malaysia.
    I.   Title.
LC3089 M3L481   2011

ISBN 978-981-4279-21-5 (soft cover)
ISBN 978-981-4279-22-2 (E-book PDF)

Cover photo (top): The Wufu Shuyuan [The Academy of Five Blessings] in Penang, founded in 1819.
Cover photo (bottom): The New Era College established by Dong Jiao Zong (UCSCA and UCSTA) and Merdeka University Ltd. Co. in 1998.
Photo credits: Both photos are reproduced with kind permission of United Chinese School Committees' Association (UCSCA).

Typeset by International Typesetters Pte Ltd
Printed in Singapore by Utopia Press Pte Ltd

CONTENTS

ACKNOWLEDGEMENTS

It was Dr Leon Comber of the Monash Asia Institute, Monash University, Australia, who suggested to Ambassador Kesavapany, Director of the Institute of Southeast Asian Studies, that I do this study on Chinese schools in Malaysia. I am very thankful to Dr Comber for having made the suggestion and to Ambassador Kesavapany for having accepted the book proposal.

The Lee Foundation helped to finance this work partially. My heartfelt thanks are due to the foundation for extending the assistance.

While doing my research, I obtained substantial help from Mr Choong Woei Chuan, Director of the Information Bureau of the United Chinese School Committees' Association, and Mr Yap Hon Kait, Executive Secretary of the United Chinese School Teachers' Association (UCSTA). Mr Choong afforded me the opportunity to consult Malaysia's annual reports on education and the various educational acts. Mr Yap provided access to information on Chinese primary schools that has been collected over the years by the Education Research Centre of the association. He also kindly presented me with copies of the association's work reports of recent years. To both Mr Choong and Mr Yap, I extend my profound gratitude.

I also wish to thank Mr Loot Ting Yee, Advisor to the UCSTA. Mr Loot generously and enthusiastically gave me a number of items from his collection of publications on Chinese education.

In the course of my research and writing, I was privileged to have the comments and opinions of many seniors and colleagues in the field of Chinese education. I am greatly indebted to them. Because of their help, I have been able to produce this objective history of the Chinese schools in Malaysia.

Last but not least, I wish to thank a close friend who rendered me substantial research assistance but who wishes not to be named.

Lee Ting Hui
Singapore
May 2009

ABBREVIATIONS

DAP	Democratic Action Party
FMC	Federal Malayan Certificate
Gerakan	Gerakan Rakyat Malaysia
HSC	Higher School Certificate
LCE	Lower Certificate of Education
MCA	Malayan Chinese Association
MCACECC	Malayan Chinese Association Chinese Education Central Committee
MCE	Malaysia Certificate of Education
MIC	Malayan Indian Congress
MNP	Malayan National Party
PAS	Parti Islamic SeMalaysia (*Islamic Party of Malaysia*)
PKR	Parti Keadilan Rakyat (*People's Justice Party*)
PMR	Penilaian Menengah Rendah (*Junior Secondary Assessment*)
PPP	People's Progressive Party
PR	Pakatan Rakyat (*People's Alliance*)
SC	School Certificate
SJK (C)	Sekolah Jenis Kebangsaan (Cina) (*National-Type Chinese Primary School*)
SJK (T)	Sekolah Jenis Kebangsaan (Tamil) (*National-Type Tamil Primary School*)
SK	Sekolah Kebangsaan (*National Primary School*)
SMJK	Sekolah Menengah Jenis Kebangsaan (*National-Type Secondary School*)
SMK	Sekolah Menengah Kebangsaan (*National Secondary School*)

SPM	Sijil Pelajaran Malaysia (*Malaysian Certificate of Education*)
SRJK (C)	Sekolah Rendah Jenis Kebangsaan (Cina) (*National-Type Chinese Primary School*)
SRJK (T)	Sekolah Rendah Jenis Kebangsaan (Tamil) (*National-Type Tamil Primary School*)
SRK	Sekolah Rendah Kebangsaan (*National Primary School*)
SRP	Sijil Rendah Pelajaran (*Lower Certificate of Educaiton*)
STPM	Sijil Tinggi Persekolahan Malaysia (*Malaysian Higher School Certificate*)
Three-M	Membaca, Menulis, Mengira (*Reading, Writing, Counting*)
UCSCA	United Chinese School Committees' Association
UCSTA	United Chinese School Teachers' Association
UDP	United Democratic Party
UMNO	United Malay National Organisation
UPSR	Ujian Penilaian Sekolah Rendah (*Primary School Assessment*)

NOTES ON
COVERAGE AND NAMES

Our account is mainly about events in Peninsular Malaysia, which was commonly referred to as the Malay Peninsula or Malaya before 1963 when it formed Malaysia with Singapore, Sarawak, and Sabah. However, the narrative also covers developments in Singapore before 1965 when the island broke off from Malaysia and became an independent country.

Chinese names, whether of persons, schools, or organizations, are retained in their original spellings. Names with spellings which cannot be ascertained are transliterated with *hanyu pinyin*. All these, in addition to appearing in the text, are tabulated in the Glossaries, together with their Chinese characters.

All translations into English from Chinese or Malay sources are the authors' work, unless otherwise stipulated.

All currency references are to the Malayan dollar before the formation of Malaysia in 1963, and to the Malaysian ringgit afterwards.

INTRODUCTION

This book attempts to give an account of how Chinese schools in Peninsular Malaysia struggled to survive and develop between 1786 and 2003, a period spanning more than two hundred years. The overriding consideration is to see how the various governments of the country over these years posed challenges to them and how they responded to these challenges.

In the years before the Pacific War, the British colonial government left the Chinese schools alone. However, when they caused harm to the country's economy by their political activities, the colonial government adopted legislation to control them.

During the years of the Pacific War, when the Japanese who ruled the country closed all the Chinese schools, they had no means of responding.

After the Pacific War, the British were back in the country. Because of the China orientation of the Chinese schools, they sought to transform them into English schools between 1945 and 1955. The Chinese schools responded by reorientating themselves to Malaya and escaped transformation.

From 1955, the country came under the rule — at first partially, but then fully from 1957 — of a Malay government. The new government sought to achieve their "ultimate objective" in education, which was to have all schools use the Malay language as their main medium of instruction. From then until now, this was the challenge posed to Chinese schools, which put in their best effort to meet this challenge.

Our story is divided into seven chapters. Chapter 1 covers the years from 1786 to 1941, from the first arrival of the British in Malaya to when the British lost it to the Japanese in the Pacific War. The focus of this chapter will be on the founding of modern Chinese schools in Malaya in the twentieth century. Like those in China, these schools were instruments for the modernization of China. As such, they were highly politicized. Soon their political activities became injurious to the economy of the country. As a consequence, the British colonial government adopted legislation to curb their activities. The challenge of the British action, however, did not affect their growth.

Chapter 2 spans the years from 1942 to 1955. The year 1942 was when the country fell completely to the Japanese, and 1955 was when the British returned partial control of the country to the Malays. The Japanese ruled the country until 1945 when they surrendered it back to the British. While the Japanese were here, they promoted only education through the Japanese language. As a result, all Chinese schools were closed down as they failed to meet the Japanese challenge.

The Chinese schools were revived after 1945. The second part of Chapter 2 narrates how between 1946 and 1955 the British took steps to try to transform the Chinese schools into English schools. The British did this because the Chinese schools placed their loyalty with China instead of Malaya. Eventually, the Chinese schools reorientated themselves and were not forced to change as they met the British challenge successfully. This period also saw the founding of Chinese educational organizations which became defenders of Chinese education.

Chapter 3 covers the period from 1956 to 1969. The year 1956 was when the "ultimate objective" in education was first enunciated, and 1969 was when racial riots broke out between the Malays and the Chinese. The highlight of this period of development was the enunciation of this "ultimate objective" through the Razak Report. Another highlight was the release of the Talib Report in 1960, and the passing of an Education Act based on that report the following year. While the Razak Report did not seek the immediate realization of the "ultimate objective", the Talib Report and the consequent Education Act did take the first step towards that goal. Under the latter, Chinese primary schools were allowed to continue and receive government aid, but Chinese secondary schools were forced to change to using English instead of Chinese as their main medium of instruction. Or they could choose to remain as they were, but would receive no government assistance. They would thus become independent schools. The chapter also accounts for other but lesser challenges posed by the government to Chinese schools during this period. On the whole, Chinese schools managed to survive.

Developments in the 1970s are covered in Chapter 4. The most significant event during these years was that the government took further steps to bring about the realization of the "ultimate objective". First, English educational institutions in the country had to change to Malay. Next were those Chinese secondary schools which had earlier changed to using English instead of Chinese as their main medium of instruction to change again, this time to using Malay as their main medium of instruction. During that time, the government also came out with a Cabinet Report, 1979, to seek the improvement of the whole educational system in the country, but the report paid scant attention to Chinese schools. Other lesser challenges to Chinese schools are also covered in the chapter. Both Chinese primary schools and independent Chinese secondary schools faced serious problems during this period, but a campaign to revive Chinese education proved successful.

Chapter 5 chronicles the events of the 1980s. The push towards the "ultimate objective" on the part of the government persisted. Eventually, a series of events catapulted the government's drive to a climax in 1987. This was followed by the government launching "Operation Lalang" in which elements opposed to the government, especially prominent Chinese educationists, were arrested and sent to jail. Disputes such as the 3-M Issue are also discussed in this chapter.

Chapter 6 covers the period from the 1990s until 2003, which was when the then prime minister resigned. The period was dominated by what was called Vision 2020. This vision brought both joy and disappointment to the Chinese schools. For instance, the transformation of existing schools into "Smart Schools" was a development welcomed by them, but the conversion of existing schools into "Vision Schools" upset them.

Chapter 7, which concludes the book, summarizes the highlights of events discussed in all the foregoing chapters, examines problems faced by Chinese schools in recent years from 2004 to early 2009, and tries to anticipate what is in store for them in the immediate future.

1

THE YEARS BEFORE THE PACIFIC WAR

To understand why there were and still are Chinese schools in the Malay Peninsula, we need to know how the land became a British dependency between the eighteenth and twentieth centuries for there were few Chinese living there before the British arrived and even fewer Chinese schools worth noting. The Chinese followed in the wake of the British, arriving to seek a better living which the British could provide. The British initiated vast economic developments which necessitated extensive utilization of manpower. In addition to the attractiveness of the land under British rule, China, from where the Chinese came, was ravaged by wars with foreign powers as well as civil conflicts from about the middle of the nineteenth century, which made life very difficult for ordinary people.

The first Chinese to come to the Malay Peninsula actually arrived in the fifteenth century during the days of the Malacca sultanate, but they were insignificant in numbers compared with those arriving later. Francis Light and Stamford Raffles set up trading stations in Penang and Singapore in 1786 and 1819 respectively, and these stations became great magnets for Chinese traders as well as labourers. In 1826, the British also acquired Malacca from the Dutch and used it for trading. This former sultanate had fallen to Portuguese rule in the fifteenth century and then to the Dutch. Penang, Singapore, and Malacca were then formed into one administrative unit named the Straits Settlements. Then, beginning from 1874, the British moved northwards from Singapore into the hinterland, to the states of Perak, Selangor, Negeri Sembilan and Pahang which they formed into a federation called the Federated Malay States in 1896. The metal, tin, was found to be abundant in Perak and Selangor, and this was what drew the British northwards. In 1909, the British and the Thais reached an agreement to divide between themselves some Malay states straddling the present border between the peninsula and Thailand, and so the British also took over Kedah, Perlis, Kelantan and Trengganu. Later, another state just north of Singapore, Johor, was also acquired. All these later acquisitions became collectively known as the Unfederated Malay States. By that time, the Malay Peninsula had come to be known as a land especially suitable for the cultivation of rubber. Thus, by the early years of the twentieth century, the whole peninsula had been taken over by the British.

Penang, Singapore, and Malacca attracted Chinese immigrants because of trade. The rest of the peninsula became interesting to them because of tin and rubber. Drawn by these attractions and pushed by the difficulties of life in China, they emigrated to the Malay Peninsula in ever greater numbers after the British moved into the mainland. Along with their arrival was the establishment of education for their children.

Table 1.1 shows the influx of Chinese immigrants into the Malay Peninsula from 1871 to 1941, and the percentage of these immigrants of the total population in the country over those years.

Table 1.1
Chinese Immigration into the Malay Peninsula, 1871–1941[1]

Year	Total Population	Chinese Population	% of Chinese
1871*	308,097	104,615	34
1891	910,123	391,418	43
1901	1,227,195	583,396	48
1911	2,644,489	914,143	35
1921	3,338,545	1,179,551	35
1931	4,345,503	1,703,528	39
1941	5,545,173	2,418,615	44

Note: '1871*': This line refers only to the Straits Settlements.
Source: See note 1.

EARLY EDUCATIONAL INSTITUTIONS

In the early days, there were three kinds of institutions which afforded Chinese children an opportunity to learn their mother tongue. The first were those established by the Chinese settlers themselves and which may be called old-style schools. The second were those founded by Christian missionaries, and the third were what came to be called the free schools.

Old-Style Schools

An old-style school was known in Chinese terminology as a *sishu*. It was modelled after what prevailed in China during the days of the Manchu Dynasty.

An old-style school could be started by a family hiring a tutor to come to the house to teach its children. Or it could be started by a single person, quite often a family tutor breaking off from his employer to start his own establishment as an independent teacher in his own house, to make a better living. Something on a larger scale than either of the above would spring up when community leaders gathered a larger number of children in the whole community into an ordinary or ancestral temple to begin an institution. Sometimes when the number of students in such a place increased significantly, the school would be moved to a clan or district association where space would be more ample. And on further increases in student intake, the new recruits might be accommodated again in an ordinary or ancestral temple as a branch school. The Wufu Shuyuan [Academy of Five Blessings] in Penang, believed to be the earliest *sishu*, was founded in 1819.[2]

According to some sources, in 1815, there were nine such establishments in Malacca; in 1829, there were three in Singapore; and in the 1830s, there were three, and even one for girls, in Penang.[3] By 1884, the statistics had become twelve in Malacca, fifty-one in Singapore, and fifty-two in Penang.[4] And it was also reported that in 1901, about 2,000 students attended old-style schools in Perak, Selangor, Negri Sembilan, and Pahang.[5]

An interesting question is what the students were taught in such institutions. As was well-known, they first learnt the *San Zi Jing* (Trimetrical Classic), the *Bai Jia Xing* (Century of Surnames), the *Qian Zi Wen* (Millenary Classic), and the *You Xue Qiong Lin* (Odes for Children). Later on, they would learn the *Xiao Jing* (Canon of Filial Piety) and then the *Si Shu* (Four Books) which consisted of the *Da Xue* (Great Learning), the *Zhong Yong* (Golden Means), the *Lun Yu* (Analects), and the *Meng Zi* (Book of Mencius).

Next, the more advanced among the pupils would study the *Wu Jing* (Five Classics) which were the *Shi Jing* (Book of Odes), the *Shu Jing* (Book of History), the *Yi Jing* (Book of Changes), the *Li Ji* (Book of Rites), and the *Chun Qiu* (Spring and Autumn Annals). The important point to note about these compilations is that they were all vehicles of Confucianism, and the primary virtues the students were expected to imbibe from them were *zhong* and *xiao*. *Zhong* was loyalty to the ruler of the country, and *xiao* was to be filial to one's parents and ancestors. These were the pillars which upheld traditional Chinese society.[6]

It had been noted that students in the old-style schools could range, in age, from as young as five or six to as old as about twenty. Presumably, the age of any particular student was an indication of which level of the books mentioned he had reached.[7]

Christian Missionary Schools

The first Christian mission to set up schools in the Malay Peninsula was the London Missionary Society, a Protestant organization. The primary aim of this society was to spread Christianity in China. However, the government of the day in that country, the Manchu Dynasty, did not welcome Christian evangelization. So the London Missionary Society decided to set up a station in a place near China to prepare the ground, especially to train Chinese church workers, for the day when China would alter its attitude, open its doors, and would no longer bar Christian activities.

So, in 1815, at the suggestion of Dr R. Morrison, who was the person who originated the idea of the China evangelization project, Dr W. Milne began such a station in Malacca. Later on, similar stations were also opened in Penang and Singapore. For us, the pertinent point to note was that these stations ran schools for children where both the English and Chinese languages were taught, among other things. The mission was to top these institutions with the founding of an Anglo-Chinese College in 1818 in Malacca which would embark upon both cultural and evangelical dissemination at a higher level.[8]

A newspaper in Singapore, the *Singapore Free Press*, reported on 16 December 1823 on the aspirations of these educational establishments:[9]

> [The institutions'] immediate object is to impart a thorough education, making religious knowledge an essential part of it, to a select number of

Chinese lads, and the plan is to instruct them well in English, in addition to their own language, as the medium of studying the higher branches of education and acquiring an acquaintance with English literature and the arts and sciences of Europe. The more remote object is to secure, by the blessing of God and the diligent use of proper means, a body of native agency to co-operate hereafter in the more extensive plans of diffusing religious as well as useful and scientific knowledge among their countrymen.

The newspaper was very clear about the purposes of the London Missionary Society's educational efforts in the peninsula.

Another Protestant organization to found evangelical stations and schools for children in the Malay Peninsula in those early days was the American Board of Commissioners for Foreign Missions. This took place in Singapore and Penang in the 1830s.[10]

The establishments of both the British and the American missions, as expected, really turned out to be ephemeral. When China was open to Christian evangelization after its defeat in a war with the British, the Opium War of 1839–42, they were all closed except for one girls' school belonging to the British. Both Christian groups moved the loci of their activities to China.[11]

The Roman Catholics followed in the footsteps of the Protestants. It was reported that in the 1870s and the 1880s, they managed schools not only in the Straits Settlements, but also in Kuala Lumpur. It is to be noted that they, unlike the British and the Americans, were interested not only in China, but also in the Malay Peninsula in its own right. Nevertheless, after some time, most of their educational institutions also closed down. The reason for this was perhaps that there was an insufficient intake of students.[12]

The Roman Catholic teachers were supposed to have taught their pupils English and Chinese besides arithmetic and geography. Naturally, religious instruction would also have been part of the curriculum, but this was not reported because it was not a subject examined by the inspector.[13]

The Free Schools

According to some sources,[14] the London Missionary Society set up a Penang Free School in 1816, and a Singapore Free School in 1834. Different from the institutions established by the same organization mentioned earlier, these schools, it seems, though also imparting religious knowledge, only aimed at providing an ordinary kind of education to children. A very distinctive feature was that they were each actually a complex of schools, an English school at the secondary level, and a Chinese school, a Malay school, and a Tamil school at the elementary level.

The lower schools were supposed to be feeder schools for the higher one, that is, the better graduates from them would be promoted to the higher one for further training. The rationale for having such a system was that children should be given a grounding in their mother tongue first and then go on to acquire higher knowledge through the English language.[15] There were also free schools set up by individuals or through public donations rather than by any religious organization, for instance, the Gan Eng Seng School in Singapore set up in 1886.[16]

The British authorities had always thought that a school graduate, educated both in his mother tongue and in English, would always be more useful to society than a monolingual person. The fact was, it seems, that the government needed clerks in its various departments, as well as interpreters in the law courts, to be bridges between their own ethnic communities and their British superiors. This kind of thinking was perhaps implicit, for instance, in a speech given by Governor Sir Cecil Clementi Smith in 1893 to the Gan Eng Seng School:[17]

> The school might be devoted to the study of English, but I am glad that a knowledge of Chinese will also be gained there, which to me appears to be an essential part of the education of a Chinese boy ... The boys who grow up with a knowledge of that language and who also attach to it a knowledge of English will prove better citizens than those boys who throw off the language of the country to which they naturally belong and adopt the English language simply from a utilitarian sense of the time they are going to spend in this Settlement.

These were encouraging words. The government was actually at the time extending financial assistance to non-monolingual schools.[18]

The scheme comprising a central institution and a number of feeder schools did not, finally, perform as well as was hoped. Student intake into the feeder schools was insufficient, or teachers for them were in short supply. Eventually, they dwindled into mere vernacular classes in the central school.[19]

THE BIRTH OF MODERN CHINESE SCHOOLS

The defeat of the Manchu government at the hands of the British in the Opium War of 1839–42 was traumatic enough. Further humiliation was to follow in the coming years. In 1857 a showdown between the Manchus, on the one hand, and British and French forces, on the other, was to break out. Again the Manchus lost. Then, in 1894–95, the Manchus fought with the Japanese and were also trounced. This, of all the three wars, was perhaps the most damaging to the self-esteem of the Manchus because Japan had never been held in very high esteem. This was to force a great number of thinking men in the country to realize that there was something quite wrong with the fundamentals of the nation and that it must change in order to survive.

Perhaps this was the occasion when nationalism of a modern kind dawned upon China. Modern nationalism would mean not only the will to resist foreign pressures, but also, as the thinking men had realized, a review of the foundations on which the society had been built, and introducing reforms and changes where necessary.

Kang Yu Wei and Reforms

One such thinking man was a scholar named Kang Yu Wei who petitioned the emperor of the day, Guang Xu, to embark on an ambitious programme of modernization to rejuvenate the country. The emperor lent him a willing ear and so, in 1898, attempts were initiated for a slew of changes for the country, covering such things as establishing modern industries, remodelling the armed forces, among other initiatives. Included in the proposed reforms was the setting up of a modern system of education. Specifically, a university, including a medical school, in the capital of the country, Beijing, was to be founded. Then modern institutions of learning devoted to both Chinese and Western studies were also to be started up in the provinces. This was to be achieved by private academies, called *shu-yuan*, in the capitals of the various provinces being transformed into colleges; those in the capitals of prefectures under the provinces being changed into high schools; and, finally, those in districts under the prefectures being converted into elementary schools. An institution to teach overseas Chinese students was also to be founded for their benefit.[20]

Unfortunately, a higher authority than the emperor, the Empress Dowager, was to frown on these attempted enterprises. She put the emperor under house arrest and hunted down Kang Yu Wei and his followers, managing to arrest some of the men and executing them. Kang himself was fortunate enough to be able to escape overseas.[21]

Kang came to the Malay Peninsula. Whilst there, he pushed his ideas among the Chinese living in the country and exerted great influence among them, including in the matter of establishing modern schools for their children. A person who was a supporter of Kang had put the following on record:[22]

> When Kang Yu Wei came to the Nanyang, he began a drive for Chinese education. Dr Lim Boon Keng and Khoo Seok Wan had already formed a number of cultural societies. And Kang was invited to lecture to their members every few days. He stimulated them to think. He encouraged them to form industrial and commercial clubs, temples and societies dedicated to Confucius, and to establish schools. The T'ien Nan Shin Pao [Tian Nan Xin Bao] established by Khoo Seok Wan was strong in support of these projects.
>
> The Confucius Society [Kong Jiao Hui] was first founded in Singapore; then Kuala Lumpur followed …
>
> When Dr Lim Boon Keng and Khoo Seok Wan established the Singapore Chinese Girls' School … the constitutions of all these schools were drawn up by Kang himself. Kang also sent his followers … to teach in these schools. Then the Chinese in all the rest of the towns of Nanyang started schools too. And that there are so many Chinese schools in the Nanyang today must be attributed to the foundations that Kang had laid.
>
> In the 1906 report of the Reform Party [that is Kang's Party], it is noted that in 1905 and 1906 many Chinese schools were formed in the Nanyang, and that more than 20 teachers were sent out by the party to these schools.

Kang Yu Wei's influence was extensive indeed.

It was reported that, from Singapore, Lim Boon Keng visited the peninsula a number of times between 1894 and 1911. Whilst there he propagated the idea of establishing modern Chinese schools as well as Confucian societies. According to records, the Chung Hua Confucian set up in 1904 is believed to be the first modern Chinese school established in Penang.[23]

According to one source, the curriculum advocated by Kang Yu Wei to be adopted in the modern schools included the following subjects: the Confucian classics, self-cultivation, essay writing, calligraphy, history, geography, mathematics, science, art and craft, physical exercises, and so on. It was really a combination of Chinese and modern studies. The Chinese part would encourage the students to become loyal to the ruler in China and the modern part would turn them into useful citizens, ready to help in the reconstruction of the country.[24]

The Empress Dowager and Her Defensive Measures

Then a strange thing happened. Although the Empress Dowager had interdicted the emperor's and Kang Yu Wei's efforts to change the country, after putting them away, she herself instituted reforms in the society which were more or less of the same nature as those proposed by her victims. She did this in the hope of defusing the threat of elements hostile to her rule. She died in 1908, but those who wielded power after her in government continued with her policies. So, the regime under her and that after her established modern schools in the country. As was the case with Kang Yu Wei, the influence of this spread to the Chinese in the Malay Peninsula.[25]

It has been reported that consuls in various places were told to strive for the establishment of schools. Between 1905 and 1911, when it lost power, the Manchu government sent officials to the Nanyang every year to inspect the Chinese schools there and report back to Beijing. Such inspections were carried out according to rules set out by its *Xue Bu* [Ministry of Education]. The interest of the Manchu government in giving support to education overseas can be seen in the following record:[26]

> The Xue Bu wished to protect and maintain overseas education. The overseas Chinese were naturally patriotic towards the fatherland. They were to be trained in the principles of the Confucian classics and history, and educated in the knowledge of the world. The Chinese civilization would be made greater by this, and the economy and the livelihood of the people would be raised.

Another similar report bears out the same story:[27]

> ... the overseas Chinese were opening schools everywhere. If the Chinese Government uitilized this opportunity to encourage them, their patriotism would be greatly aroused. Chinese learning would spread far and wide, and the feeling of the scattered Chinese people [for the fatherland] would be strengthened.

In the case of schools at home, the reason for embarking upon reforms was to neutralize political opposition. In the case of schools overseas, it was also to ensure loyalty, but there was also the desire to secure material assistance from the wealthy for various enterprises.[28]

At various times during the first decade of the twentieth century, the following schools were noted to have been set up in the Malay Peninsula: the Zhong Hua in Penang,[29] the Zun Kong in Kuala Lumpur,[30] the Yu Cai in Ipoh,[31] and the Kun Cheng, a girls' school, in Kuala Lumpur.[32] The Zhong Hua in Penang was founded due to the effort of a Manchu official. The others were probably also initiated by Manchus.

These institutions were all primary schools. To give overseas children an opportunity to pursue a secondary education, the Manchu government, in 1907, founded the Jinan Xue Tang [Jinan School] in the city of Nanjing in China. The school stopped functioning, however, when the Manchus lost power in 1911.[33]

The Manchus also made a beginning with teacher training for the various primary schools in the Malay Peninsula. In 1906, an official who came from China to inspect schools initiated a half-year training class in the premises of a clan association in Penang. When this was over, it was followed by a second one.[34]

Sun Yat Sen and Revolution

Another thinking man who, like Kang Yu Wei, sensed the dangers that China was in during the last years of the nineteenth century was Sun Yat Sen. Unlike Kang, however, he did not find it useful to try to get the Manchu monarchy to reform itself. He considered it more advisable to get it overthrown and put in its place a republic.

Because of the revolutionary activities he was pursuing, Sun was on the move all the time. Like Kang, he visited the Malay Peninsula and while there, like Kang again, he pushed his political programme among the domiciled Chinese. He made headway and gathered a following.

Instruments of propaganda employed by Sun's group of revolutionaries included giving talks or lectures, and publishing the printed word. They also founded what came to be known as "reading rooms" where talks or lectures were held, and literature could be read. Of particular interest to us was the fact that many of the reading rooms established schools which became vehicles for educating young children in Sun's ideas.[35]

Table 1.2 lists these reading rooms, the places where they were located, and the schools they founded during the first two decades of the twentieth century, based on a study.[36]

Table 1.2
Reading Rooms in the Malay Peninsula (1902–19)

Year Founded	Reading Room	Place	Name of School
1902	Yi Zhi	Perak	Yu Zhi
1907	Da Cai	Perak	Dai Cai
1907	Guang Han	Perak	Xi Zhou
1910	Tong De	Singapore	Zhong Hua Girls'
1911	Yue Shu	Penang	Zhong Hua Girls'
1911	Gong Yi	Penang	Chong De
1913	Yi Zhi	Penang	Yi Hua
1913	Name unavailable	Melaka	Pei Feng
1913	Xin Hua	Perak	Xin Hua
1915	Yue Shu	Penang	Zhong Ling
1917	Tong De	Singapore	Nan Hua Girls'
1917	Tong De	Singapore	Nanyang Girls'
1918	Zhong Hua	Penang	Ri Xin
1919	Ai Qun	Johore	Pei Zhi

Source: See note 36.

These were places (the names of which are given in *hanyu pinyin*) where revolutionaries were nurtured.

The Republic Government and Overseas Chinese Schools

Sun Yat Sen and his group of revolutionaries managed eventually in 1911 to influence some of the military men in the Manchu establishment to get the Manchu emperor eased out of his throne. The monarchy thus gave way to a republic. The most authoritative man among the soldiers, by the name of Yuan Shi Kai, became the president of the new government. That was in 1912.

According to a study, like the Manchus, the Yuan government and those which succeeded his regime, for Yuan died in 1916, took an interest in the education of Chinese children living overseas. Several measures were taken to ensure that ties between home and overseas were maintained.[37]

As soon as the new administration was set up, inspectors were dispatched frequently to the Nanyang to inspect the Chinese schools there. These officials came not only from Beijing, the capital of the country, but also from the southern provinces of Fujian, Guangdong, and Guangxi, from which most of the Chinese living overseas had emigrated.[38]

In 1913, the Ministry of Education in Beijing promulgated the "Ling Shi Guan Li Hua Qiao Xue Wu Gui Cheng" [Regulations Governing the Management of Overseas Chinese Schools by Consuls]".[39] According to its stipulations, any person wishing to open a new school overseas must obtain approval to do so from a relevant consul. If approved, the new school would be registered with the Ministry of Education. The regulations also required all consuls to make known to the Chinese public any laws, regulations, and rules pertaining to education adopted by the ministry. They were also to inspect all the schools under their charge on a regular basis. In addition, they were to settle all problems arising from among the schools.

The following year, on the recommendation of the consul general in Singapore, the "Qiao Min Zi Di Hui Guo Jiu Xue Gui Cheng" [Regulations Governing the Return of Overseas Students to China to Study] was passed by the Ministry of Education. This was to help students to return to China to further their studies by joining a secondary school or a university.[40] Several years later, in 1918, the Chinese government reopened the Jinan in Nanjing to enable students returning from overseas to join a secondary school more easily.[41]

An interesting point to note now was that a new national spirit was to be inculcated in students. In 1912, the Ministry of Education issued the order that all students must undergo military training.[42] In 1918, this point was re-emphasized. Besides, students were also required to learn traditional martial arts and to study the stories of national heroes in history.[43] Textbooks used in the schools in those days were marked by three characteristics, *viz* a nationalistic fervour, an emphasis on Chinese culture, and an appreciative portrayal of scenic spots and views in China.[44] Little wonder that China's National Day was regularly celebrated every year in the Chinese schools in the Malay Peninsula from then until after World War II when local political changes put a stop to it. And both teachers and students were ever ready to render help whenever China was involved in any dispute or conflict with a foreign power.[45]

POLITICAL ACTIVITIES IN THE MODERN CHINESE SCHOOLS AND BRITISH REACTION

The political sentiments cultivated through education as one of the instruments for national rejuvenation since the end of the nineteenth century were soon to bear fruit in the form of political activities in the schools. Especially potent was the influence of Sun Yat Sen and his group which, erstwhile called the Tong Meng Hui, was now renamed the Guomindang after the founding of the republic.

When the activities were only expressions of love and support for China, but did not at the same time bring about harmful consequences on the land, the British colonial government did not see any necessity for it to interfere. But when they simultaneously disturbed the law and order, as well as hurt the economy of the colony, the British were unable to remain mere observers anymore, but stepped in to curb the exuberant nationalistic enthusiasm of the students and teachers of the Chinese schools.

The First Political Activities in Modern Chinese Schools

Below is a chronicle of political activities in modern Chinese schools.

In 1913, the Russians, through rendering military aid, attempted to lure Outer Mongolia to secede from China. When news of this reached the Malay Peninsula, the Chinese there, including the teachers and students in the schools, raised voices of protest and donated money to the Chinese government to help it go to war with the Russians. Some students even went to the extent of volunteering for military service.[46]

Yuan Shi Kai, who became the president of the new republic, was never satisfied with having attained that position. He desired and began to scheme to become the emperor of a new dynasty. The Guomindang stood in his way. The most vehement voice of opposition was from a Song Jiao Ren who fought hard for the upholding of a responsible cabinet. In 1913, Yuan got him assassinated in the railway station in Shanghai where he was to board a train to Beijing. When the Chinese school students in Singapore learnt of this, they held a memorial service to honour Song and show him their deep respect.[47]

In 1915, Yuan, in order to obtain support from the Japanese for his political scheme, signed an agreement with them which allowed the Japanese to take over the province of Shandong, extend their lease of southern Manchuria and the cities of Port Arthur and Dalian to ninety-nine years, as well as have their personnel employed as advisers in the Chinese administration to exercise control over its politics, finances, and military affairs. This was to arouse the Chinese schools in the Malay Peninsula to go on strike, make patriotic speeches against both Yuan and the Japanese, and lower their flags to half mast to register their protest. Yuan was soon to follow up on his first step by getting a Chou An Hui [Work-for-Peace Society] organized in the same year to have the existing constitution of the country abolished, and have himself declared the emperor of a new regime. The Chinese in the Malay Peninsula, including teachers and students in the schools, were greatly agitated. They sent telegrams to Beijing to demand the dissolution of the society and initiated an anti-Yuan movement.[48]

Yuan was to fail in his scheme because of opposition from one of his generals. He died in 1916, as mentioned, in frustration, and the country was plunged into chaos for years thereafter because a number of military men fought one another for power.[49] To save the country, revolutionary forces in southern China in the following year decided to set up a military government to put down the militarists and restore order. Sun Yat Sen was elected to become the commanding general to clean up the mess. The Chinese school teachers and students congratulated Sun on his appointment and gave him strong support to fight the warlords.[50]

Attitude of the Colonial Government Towards the Chinese Schools Before 1920

From the time Francis Light founded Penang until 1920, the colonial government left the Chinese a well as the Tamil schools alone. It can be said that it adopted an attitude of *laissez-faire* towards them. It extended financial assistance to English and Malay institutions, but not to the Chinese and Tamil ones. Sometimes it was the Chinese schools themselves which refused to accept assistance for fear of the interference that might follow. At other times, it was British officials themselves who did not see it fit to help.[51] The situation was borne out by the following testimony:

Governor Blundell in his report on education in the Straits Settlements in the 1850s remarked that the Chinese wished to manage their schools on their own, and refused to accept any assistance or guidance from the authorities. Because of this, there was nothing that the government could do for those institutions.[52]

The British Resident in Selangor, W.H. Treacher, in 1901 made the comment that assuming the responsibility of giving support to the mother tongue education of the children of immigrant races was not the correct policy for the government to follow. In the same year, the Chief Inspector of Schools in the Federated Malay States, J. Driver, was also noted to have rejected a suggestion from the Inspector of Schools in Perak to give money to Chinese schools. He considered it right to back up only Malay schools, but not any other vernacular institution.[53]

In addition to those reasons already mentioned for the adoption of a *laissez-faire* attitude towards Chinese schools by the British authorities, there was yet another which made them leave those schools alone. And that was the fact that these schools never gave them any trouble. Even when they got involved in the politics in China, all that they did was donate money to China or volunteer military service to help fight the Russians; hold a memorial service for a murdered politician whom they respected; send telegrams of protest home, make speeches, suspend classes for a while, lower flags to half mast to show their anger against Yuan Shi Kai; and congratulate Sun Yat Sen on his elevation. All these did not affect law and order in the land, and, therefore, caused no harm to the economic interests of the British or of any other community. Things, however, were soon to change, and the colonial government had to do something about, or interfere somehow in, the Chinese schools.

The May 4th Movement and the 1920 Registration of Schools Ordinance/Enactment

When the First World War broke out in 1914, the Japanese joined the United Kingdom and her allies to fight Germany and her friends. They soon seized the concessions given previously by the Chinese to the Germans in the Shandong Peninsula. The war ended four years later. In 1919, a peace conference was convened in Paris to discuss issues which ensued from the end of the war. China sent a delegation to attend the conference. During the proceedings, the Chinese asked for the return of Shandong to their country, as well as the abolition of the agreement which Yuan Shi Kai signed with the Japanese in 1915. The United Kingdom and France refused to entertain the requests of the Chinese because they had some secret understanding with the Japanese and, therefore took the side of the Japanese. When news of this reached China, it aroused furore among the people. On the 4th of May, the intellectuals in Beijing, including students, initiated an anti-Japanese movement. They took to the streets, marched in procession to demonstrate their anger against Japan, and voiced demands. Soon the incident was to develop into an all-nation student patriotic movement.[54]

The May 4th Movement in China instantly affected the Chinese in the Malay Peninsula. Disturbances broke out in such towns as Singapore, Penang, and Kuala Lumpur. According to one source, in Singapore and Penang, like in Beijing, there were also processions in the streets against the Japanese. There was a boycott of Japanese goods which later developed into attacks on Japanese shops and destruction of their wares. Eventually, there was a search and destruction of Japanese products everywhere, including even in Chinese business establishments, households, and brothels. There were also clashes with the Japanese and the police, and casualties resulted. All traffic on the roads ground to a halt and pedestrians disappeared. People were seriously warned to sever all relationships with their enemies. The violence ended up in full-scale riots. Finally, even Kuala Lumpur became affected with the mania and also embarked on wrecking Japanese goods. Besides workers, Chinese school teachers and students were involved in all the disturbances.[55]

In the end, the authorities had to resort to force to put a stop to all the trouble. Because Chinese school teachers and students had a big part in the upheaval, a number of them were arrested and detained. In some instances, even principals were taken into custody. Some of the detainees met with the sad fate of being banished from the country.[56]

Unlike in the past, political activism among the Chinese school population on this occasion had reason to upset the colonial authorities. The boycott and destruction of Japanese goods and riots broke law and order, and harmed the economy of the country. The politics in the Chinese schools had now gone too far. The latitude allowed them in the past must now end.[57]

As if all these were not enough, the Chinese schools refused to take part in celebrating the victory of the United Kingdom and her allies in the war. The colonial authorities were looking foward to a grand occasion. This was really pouring oil on fire.[58]

So an instrument of control had to be created to discipline the Chinese schools. These schools were to be allowed to continue, but had to be stripped off their political content. On 31 May 1920, an education bill was introduced in the Straits Settlements Legislative Council for first reading by the attorney general. The official gave a full explanation of the bill.[59] Starting first with the reasons for having it:

> As the law now stands the Government have control only over Government Schools. By this Bill they seek to gain control over all schools in the Colony ... The reasons why the Government seek to gain control over all schools are firstly, that the schools shall be properly conducted as schools; secondly, that the teachers in them shall have efficient training for teaching; and thirdly, that the teaching shall not be of such kind that is against the interests of the Government of the Colony.

Then he went on to talk about the methods by which control could be exercised:

> The first method of control was the requirement that all schools, whether old or new — that is whether they existed before the passing or after the passing of this Ordinance — shall be registered. There are penalties for non-registration, and if registration is refused, there is an appeal

from the refusal under section 15 of the Ordinance to the Governor in Council.

The second method by which this Bill are [sic] sought to be enforced is a requirement that all teachers and managers ... shall be registered, and there are penalties provided for nonregistration ...

The next heading under which control is sought is contained in section 23 of this Bill, and that relates to the regulations which the Governor in Council is enabled by that section to make for the conduct generally of schools coming within the Ordinance ...

The fourth heading is the power of the Governor to declare as an unlawful school where matters are being taught which are revolutionary or in conflict with the interests of the Government, and in that case the Governor is entitled to declare it an unlawful school.

Finally, the attorney general explained how a school could become unlawful and how such a school would be dealt with:

A school becomes an unlawful school in three ways. The first is by non-registration under the heading mentioned. The second is by a declaration of the Governor that the school is unlawfully conducted. And the third is when the school is not being conducted in accordance with regulations framed under section 20 [should be section 23] of the Ordinance.

In this last case the Director of Education who has power to inspect schools and to enter them for the purpose of seeing if they are being conducted in accordance with the regulations, may, if he finds they are not, serve notice upon the manager of the school to that effect and require him to conduct it in accordance with the regulations. If the manager of the school still refuses, the Director of Education may declare the school as unlawful. There is an appeal from the decision in section 15 of the Act. If the appeal is not successful the declaration of the Director of Education stands, and the school is thereupon unlawful. The unlawful school comes under various penalties in the Ordinance. In the first place, a teacher in an unlawful school is liable to certain pecuniary penalties, and so is the manager, and further, the Director of Education may apply to a magistrate for an order to close an unlawful school. These are the penalties which attend upon an unlawful school.

Amendments were made to the bill after debates and further amendments were made in subsequent meetings of the council. All of them, however, did not have the effect of diluting the power of the government to control the Chinese schools. On 13 October, the bill passed the third reading and became law. It was then called the Schools Registration Ordinance.[60]

A similar bill was introduced into the Federal Council in the Federated Malay States for first reading on 15 September. Content-wise, this bill was no different from the one for the Straits Settlements. Inconsequential amendments were also made to this bill on the same day. On 20 November, the council met again and the bill passed its third reading to become law. It was then named the Schools Registration Enactment.[61]

Therefore, because of the Schools Registration Ordinance in the Straits Settlements and the Schools Registration Enactment in the Federated Malay States, the Chinese schools had to behave themselves. An inspector of Chinese schools, Purcell, had the following to say when the laws were put into operation:[62]

> My job, it cannot be denied, was in essence police work. It entailed interference with the liberty of the subject to teach what he liked, to read what he liked, and to learn what he liked. Certainly, when necessary, we did not hesitate to use our powers of canceling a teacher's certificate, withholding a grant-in-aid, or closing down a school, and even, in many cases, returning a teacher to the country of his birth (regarded as the severest of all penalties).

The government really meant business.

Reaction from the Chinese Community

The first reaction from the Chinese community to the bill came from Penang. Led by a Zhong Le Chen, the Chinese schools there immediately set up an organization called the Bin Cheng Hua Qiao Xue Xiao Lian He Hui [Confederation of Overseas Chinese Schools in Penang] to deal with the situation. Zhong considered the bill harmful to Chinese education. Eventually, a petition was drawn up and given to Dr Lim Boon Keng, the Chinese representative in the Straits Settlements Legislative Council, to present to the council for its deliberation.[63] In Singapore, a Ying Shu Hua Qiao Xue Wu Wei Chi Chu [Office for Upholding Educational Matters of the Overseas Chinese in British Possessions] was also organized by the president and the principal of the Nanyang Nu Zhong (Nanyang Girls' High School), Zhuang Xi Quan and Yu Pei Gao, to air its views by distributing leaflets. It also submitted a petition to the government to request for the rescinding of control over the Chinese schools.[64]

A little later, the government had Zhuang Xi Quan arrested first, and then next day, another leader of his organization, Chen Shou Min. Finally, both men were deported back to China.[65]

After the Schools Registration Enactment was passed in the Federated Malay States, Chinese educationists in Penang appealed to the government either to postpone putting the law into operation by one year or to exempt Chinese schools from registration altogether. At the same time, they pleaded with the Chinese consul general in Singapore to request that the Chinese Foreign Ministry in Beijing intercede with the British government on their behalf. It has also been noted that an appeal was made by the whole Chinese community in the Straits Settlements as well as to the colonial office in the United Kingdom to allow the Chinese schools not to have to register at all.[66]

In the end, the Chinese decided to send a representative to China to seek personal help from the Chinese government in the matter. They would also send people to London to make appeals to the British government there. From Singapore Yu Pei Gao of the Nan Yang Nu Zhong was soon despatched to Beijing to see the Chinese Minister for Foreign Affairs. Yu's trip, however, turned out to be fruitless because the Minister said that all they could do was to make enquiries about the matter with the British government. They could not do more or protest.[67] From Penang, Zhong Le Chen and Wu Yuan He went to London to present their case. They visited the colonial office several times. Eventually, they received a refusal to their requests which came quite late. In actual fact, the British government had already approved the new legislation before they had even reached London.[68]

When finally the school laws came into operation, the teachers and managers of some schools resigned from their posts, while some others proposed going on strike, and yet others suggested closing down the schools altogether. Nonetheless, some others felt that it was better to comply with the wishes of the government and so got themselves registered. Those in the last category were the Zun Kong, the Kun Cheng, the Po Ping, the Po Rong, and the Xun Ren.[69] In Penang, a very innovative idea emerged. The suggestion was to organize a school with only fourteen students so that it did not need to be registered with the government. The school laws, after all the amendments to their original bills, required only institutions with fifteen students or more to register. This school would be called the Bin Lang Yu Di Yi Zi Zhi Xue Xiao [The Penang Island First Self-Governing School]. Thereafter, as many schools as possible on this model could be organized. Many schools on the island actually accepted the proposal and changed themselves accordingly. The scheme became so successful that it was later to lead the government to amend the school laws again to stipulate that only gatherings of fewer than ten students would be exempted from registration.[70]

According to a report by the colonial secretary of Chinese affairs, by 15 September 1921, twelve Chinese schools had registered with the government; by 5 October, the figure became twenty-eight; and by 31 October, in Penang and Perak, the number of institutions complying were fifty-five and thirty-three respectively.[71]

While the Chinese schools surrendered one by one, the colonial authorities took punitive action against those individuals who, and organizations which, continued to oppose the school laws after they had come into effect. For instance, from a total of thirty-eight persons in December 1921 alone, a Chen Xin Cheng from Penang was banished from the land, and the Xin Jia Po Hua Qiao Jiao Yu Zong Hui [General Association of Overseas Chinese Education, Singapore] was dissolved.[72] Later, there were also organizations which got in the way of the school laws and had to be punished. For instance, the Pi Li Hua Qiao JiaoYu Hui [Perak Overseas Chinese Educational Association] was proscribed because its behaviour was considered harmful to the country. Then there were also existing schools which had to close down because they refused to be registered, while others had to wind up because after registration, they found the new environment uncomfortable. Table 1.3 shows the number of schools which stopped functioning because of registration problems.[73]

Table 1.3
School Registration Statistics for 1924

Schools/Teachers/Students	Straits Settlements		Federated Malay States	
	Other Schools	Chinese Schools	Other Schools	Chinese Schools
Schools registered	272	79	272	56
Schools closed down		51		20
Teachers registered	525	384	525	280
Students	15,301		12,175	

Source: See note 73.

Grants-in-Aid for Chinese Schools

In 1923 something significant again took place. The government announced a scheme to give grants-in-aid to Chinese schools. The purpose was to get more of them to register so that they could be disciplined. The principles of the scheme were as follows:[74]

(1) It is desired to encourage and assist the education of the Chinese-speaking children through the medium of their own domestic dialect or dialects which they understand. Where a Straits born or other Chinese has no domestic Chinese vernacular, his language shall be taken as English and he shall be eligible directly for entrance to an English school.

(2) It is unnecessary to assist by grants-in-aid the teaching of English in Chinese vernacular schools.

(3) While there is no objection to the teaching of Mandarin or of English in Chinese vernacular schools these two subjects should not be considered grant-earning.

(4) It is desirable to assist by grants-in-aid the further education in their own domestic dialects of Chinese-speaking children not proceeding to English schools at the age of ten. In the case of Chinese-speaking children proceeding to English schools at the age of ten, a number of free places should be provided for those who have spent at least three years at an approved vernacular school and who are promising pupils of suitable age and the children of poor parents.

(5) The curriculum in aided Chinese vernacular schools should as far as possible be so arranged as to make it a useful preparation for an English education, with special emphasis on arithmetic and geography.

It is clear that through this scheme the government hoped that some of the brighter students in the Chinese vernacular schools could be channelled eventually into English schools to further their education. It was also stipulated by the Director of Education at that time, R.O. Winstedt, that only Chinese schools teaching in the dialects, but not those teaching in Mandarin, would be given assistance. It was thought that the former kind of institution would produce students orientated towards the local scene, but the latter would produce graduates with their eyes turned towards China.[75]

Response to the scheme from the Chinese schools was not as good as was hoped. In 1926, the Report on Education for the year stated:[76]

No application for grants were refused, but Chinese schools in the Straits Settlements have not, generally speaking, shown any desire to seek Government assistance or submit to the slight measure of control involved by the acceptance of a grant.

The attitude of the Chinese was still the same as in the nineteenth century.

Heightened Political Fervour and Stepped-Up Control by the Government

It has been noted earlier that after the death of Yuan Shi Kai, the first president of the republic, the country was plunged into chaos because a number of military men fought one another for power, and that Sun Yat Sen was entrusted with the mission of cleaning up the mess. Following this, Sun embarked on a programme of reorganizing his political party, the Guomindang, in the southern city of Guangzhou. This included admitting members of the Chinese Communist Party, which had come into being in 1921 in the wake of the May 4th Movement, into his own party as members. The aim was to improve its combative ability. He also started a military training school. He died early in 1925.

Two months later, two events were to occur which precipitated confrontation between foreign powers and the ordinary Chinese people, which stirred up intense feelings. The first incident was the killing of a Chinese worker in the employ of a Japanese factory in Shanghai by his employer. This triggered off demonstrations and strikes by students, workers, and businessmen. Foreign powers pitched their police against the Chinese, resulting in many deaths. Chinese anger spread south, and soon the residents in Guangzhou held a protest march, and when they reached a place called Shaji, they were fired upon by land as well as by the naval guns of the foreign powers. It was noted that the most ruthless among the foreigners, besides the Japanese, were the British. In mid-1925, the Guomindang appointed the commandant of Sun's military school, Jiang Jie Shi, to lead the newly trained and organized troops in the march north to Beijing, termed the Northern Expedition, to finish off self-seeking militarists. Jiang was to begin his expedition in mid-1926 and complete his work two-and-a-half years later. China was on the boil because of all these events, and the heightened political feelings and activities soon had their repercussions in the Malay Peninsula. For instance, when Sun died, the Chinese community there, including the Chinese schools, held extensive memorial services to honour him.[77]

By 1925, the school laws were, therefore, found to be inadequate. Amendments were introduced in mid-1925, and then again in the middle of the following year to plug loopholes. Finally, in July 1926 in the Straits Settlements, and in August the same year in the Federated Malay States, the old school laws were replaced altogether by new laws.

Under the original school laws, a school with fewer than sixteen pupils would not be inspected. Many schools, therefore, kept student intake to a low number, so that political propaganda could be carried on. So the first amendment in 1925 stipulated that any school, no matter how many students it had, would be inspected. Then a second amendment empowered the government to deregister a defunct school, and, under this amendment, a school would be considered defunct if it had fewer than fifteen students. The two changes were obviously aimed at the Penang scheme of schools. A third amendment required a teacher intending to be registered to provide more information about himself. And the authorities could refuse to register any applicant and punish him if he taught despite being unregistered.[78]

The 1926 amendments closed up two loopholes. One was that originally undesirable schools could not be declared unlawful if its manager hid himself and notice could not be served on him. Now the amendment said that so long as the required notice was fixed to the school premises, it would be considered served. A second weakness was that the original laws did not provide for the registration of the now unlawful school and its management committee to be cancelled, and for educational officers to enter the school and remove undesirable items such as documents containing political propaganda. The second amendment dealt with these issues.[79]

The 1926 laws which replaced the 1920 laws totally differed from the latter in the following ways. Firstly, whereas the old laws would refuse to register a school only on grounds of poor sanitation, now the school could be rejected for the reason that it could be used for carrying out political propaganda detrimental to the interests of the colony, the public, or the pupils, or be used as a meeting place for an unlawful society. Secondly, a provision not under the original laws stated that a person presenting himself to be registered as a supervisor, a member of a management committee, or a teacher, could be refused if he had been convicted by a court for an offence punishable by imprisonment, or had served in a school already declared unlawful. And in the case of a teacher, he could be disqualified if the authorities considered him likely to prejudice the interests of the colony, the public, or the pupils. Thirdly, the new laws empowered the authorities not only to enter any school and search it on suspicion that it was involved in undesirable political propaganda, but also to enter it forcibly if necessary. Any person obstructing this would be penalized. Finally, the new laws authorized the government to prohibit the use of schools for purposes seen to be undesirable. This would circumvent the argument that, when such use was made, the school might not be in session, or that it was a club or a debating society, and not a school, that was meeting on the premises.[80]

Some of the general regulations for schools made by the government under the 1920 laws were also revised in the light of the 1926 laws. Whereas, so far, those regulations provided only for banning the use of undesirable books in schools, they now also provided for the prohibition of the use of the school premises for any undesirable purposes.[81]

Intensive Political Activities in the Late 1920s and British Reaction

That the 1920 school laws came to be amended, and eventually even replaced, by new laws altogether was because trouble was on the horizon. Finally, trouble indeed arrived.

The year 1927 was the second anniversary of the death of Sun Yat Sen. In Singapore, a memorial service, attended by a huge congregation, was held in Tanjong Pagar to honour the respected Guomindang leader. Numerous students came, including those from nearly thirty Hainanese night schools. An undertaking had been given to the police that no speeches would be made and no procession held. Eventually, however, promises were broken. The procession which marched out from the venue finally, on reaching Kreta Ayer Road, clashed with the interdicting police. To make matters worse, the European driver of a trolley bus which plied that route rammed the marchers with his vehicle. An injured police inspector ran to take refuge in a nearby police station and the crowd pursued him there. This was followed by the pursuers being fired on, whereupon six students and a bystander were killed, and eleven students, according to one newspaper's report, or fourteen students, according to four newspapers' accounts, were wounded. About two weeks later, the Chinese started boycotting the services of the trolley buses and this lasted several days. Then they attacked the buses, resulting in clashes with firemen who were sent to quell them. The government stationed troops at important road junctions, and guns were even mounted. Two nights later, trouble broke out again, with the police arresting and detaining many people. By that time, however, many trolley buses had already been damaged. The police detainees were eventually released, but five Hainanese night schools were closed down. A great number of anti-British leaflets were then circulated in town.[82]

In mid-1928, a column of the Northern Expedition Army captured Jinan, the capital of Shandong province.

This aroused intense nationalistic emotions. Then, under the excuse of protecting their nationals in the province, the Japanese bombed Jinan, killing thousands of people, both civilians and soldiers. The Chinese troops were in no position to take them on and had to retreat.

The event agitated the Chinese everywhere, including the Malay Peninsula. Under Singapore's lead, *chou zhen hui* (relief fund committees) were set up throughout the land to collect donations for the victims and the troops. The Chinese schools were extensively and deeply involved in this. Besides doing various things to help raise funds, they contributed money of their own. A lively boycott of Japanese goods was launched which went so well that the colonial government felt that it might precipitate an open conflict between the two communities in the country. Consequently, it ordered all the *chou zhen hui* closed.[83]

On the third anniversary of the death of Sun Yat Sen, according to one source, communists, who were also members of the Guomindang, threw bombs at police stations, distributed inflammatory leaflets everywhere in the peninsula, spreading the story that European police officers were being killed by Chinese, and also sticking up posters everywhere which were equally seditious in nature. It was noted at the same time that because they were found to be in possession of communist documents and propaganda materials, many Chinese schools were closed down and many students taken into police custody. Further information regarding the Chinese schools stated that in that whole year, thirteen Hainanese night schools were shut down in the Straits Settlements, two such schools were deregistered and another four were refused registration in the Federated Malay States.[84]

Guomindang Rule in China, Pressure from the Japanese, and Developments in the Malay Peninsula

Midway through the Northern Expedition, Jiang Jie Shi set up a government in the city of Nanjing. This was to rival the one already set up earlier in the city of Wuhan, which Jiang considered to be too much under the influence of his party's own allies, the communists. He did not like their ideology. He followed this act up with purging the communists within his own establishment in Nanjing, hunting them down, and trying to annihilate them altogether. He had his government completely dominated by the Guomindang. Both the Wuhan and the Nanjing set-ups were, of course, pitted against the regime in Beijing.[85]

The new government had ambitious ideas for rejuvenating a weak China. One of the new enterprises was to launch a new kind of education for the country. Education was to be "party-ized". What that meant was infusing education with the ideology of the Guomindang. And the ideology of the Guomindang was the philosophy of Sun Yat Sen, which was called the Three People's Principles [the San Min Zhu Yi]. At the time when Sun reorganized the Guomindang and established a military school in Guangzhou to prepare for the Northern Expedition, he expounded these Three People's Principles systematically in a series of lectures. The first principle was the Principle of Nationalism [Min Zu Zhu Yi], the second the Principle of People's Sovereignty [Min Quan Zhu Yi], and the third was the Principle of People's Livelihood [Min Sheng Zhu Yi]. What applied to education in China applied also to Chinese schools in the Malay Peninsula. New curricula and new textbooks, based on the new requirements, therefore, came to be designed and compiled for the overseas schools. This was to orientate them more closely to China, so that students would become loyal and active supporters of the Guomindang. The Chinese schools in the Malay Peninsula became as a consequence even more deeply politicized than before.[86]

The split between Jiang Jie Shi and the communists was to tell on the latter heavily. In the Malay Peninsula, they became dormant in the Chinese schools for a while. Soon, however, in 1930, they got themselves reorganized into the Malayan Communist Party, and subsequently became a force again in those schools and resumed their strident activities. Because of this, just like they were in the hands of the Guomindang, these schools became moulded into highly effective political weapons.[87]

The governor of the Straits Settlements and high commissioner to the Federated Malay States from 1929 to 1934 was Sir Cecil Clementi. Sir Cecil, besides not being fond of the communists, had a distinct dislike for the Guomindang. To him, the Guomindang was cultivating anti-British sentiments among the students in the Chinese schools as well as diverting their loyalty from the Malay Peninsula to China. So he had no interest in giving much latitude to those schools.[88]

One of the first things Sir Cecil did on assuming office in Singapore was to ban the Guomindang. This drove the party underground, which for a while disrupted its activities in the Chinese schools. Textbooks used in the Chinese schools before the Northern Expedition did not carry contents objectionable to the colonial authorities. During the Manchu days, students were taught merely to be loyal to the emperor, filial to parents and ancestors, and self-cultivation. When the Manchu Dynasty gave way to the republic, ideas of democracy and liberty were introduced. However, the Northern Expedition was to change the textbooks for the schools into something quite repugnant. It was reported that in 1925, when the Northern Expedition was slated to start, anti-foreign, including, of course, anti-British, sentiments and other objectionable items were discovered. Nevertheless, it was not until 1928 that subversive books first came to be proscribed. That was the year the Northern Expedition was completed and Jiang Jie Shi seized total power. So, Sir Cecil not only continued with the practice of banning school textbooks, but even stepped up the practice. Then in 1932, according to one source, or 1933, according to another, he announced unequivocally that the government would promote only Malay education. Future applications for grants-in-aid from the Chinese schools would not be entertained, although those that were being assisted at the time would continue to be assisted.[89]

The Japanese, since the Meiji Restoration, had always entertained ideas of overseas expansion. We have seen that they fought a war with the Manchu Dynasty of China and were victorious. We have also noted how they cooperated with Yuan Shi Kai so that Yuan could further his political ambitions, and they, through him, could harvest great gains in China. We have also seen that, during the First World War, they seized the German concessions in the Shandong Peninsula and refused to return them to China. During the Northern Expedition, when a column of Jiang Jie Shi's army reached Jinan in Shandong, they were bombed by the Japanese and had to retreat. Then, in 1931, they made a very bold move in Manchuria. They seized Shenyang and a number of other towns, and proceeded to set up the dethroned last emperor of the Manchu Dynasty of China, Pu Yi, as the monarch of a new state in Manchuria, named Manzhouguo. Of course, Pu Yi was only to be a puppet in their hands.[90]

The event created a furor among patriotic Chinese in China. The Chinese community and the Chinese schools in the Malay Peninsula, as usual, were also aroused. They went about collecting aid for the fatherland. But they did not seem to have been able to go very far because Sir Cecil Clementi watched them very closely and fettered their activities.[91]

In the face of Japanese aggression and the apparent possibility that they would go further, a strange thing happened in the politics of China. The Guomindang suspended its campaign of attempting to destroy the Chinese Communist Party and its forces utterly, and settled its dispute with it instead. This came about because the generals sent by Jiang Jie Shi to north-western China to annihilate the communists suddenly changed their political attitude and forced Jiang, when he visited them on one occasion, to stop fighting the communists and instead formed an alliance with them to take on the Japanese. Jiang had to oblige. Thereafter, the Guomindang and the Chinese Communist

Party were allies again, and the rapprochement had its effects in the Malay Peninsula.[92]

By this time, besides getting intensely fired up by the political developments in China, the Chinese schools had multiplied to a great number. Many of them could not be controlled by the government because they kept their enrolments low, to fewer than fifteen pupils in each institution, so that they could escape having to observe the school laws. The government felt that it had to plug this loophole. So, in 1937, amendments were again introduced to those laws. Firstly, whereas as the laws then stood, only schools of fifteen students or more needed to be registered with the educational authorities, now only those with fewer than ten students would be exempted from registration. Secondly, any school opening anew would have to deposit a sum of money or enter into a bond of such a sum with the government before it would be registered. And registration could also be denied to any new applicant if it was considered unnecessary or prejudicial to the interests of the colony or the public. And, finally, the director of education was now empowered not only to refuse to register a teacher — which had already been provided for in the original laws — but also any supervisor or management committee member on grounds that registration would be harmful to the interests of the colony, the public, or to the students themselves. The director could also refuse registration if any of them had worked in a school already deregistered for having failed to comply with the general regulations.[93]

The Japanese finally launched a full-scale invasion of China in 1937 and started a war with the Chinese which ended in 1945. The Chinese community in the Malay Peninsula, including the Chinese schools, were aroused to pitch in their full strength to help their kith and kin in China fight the Japanese. They collected money as well as other forms of aid to send back to China, and also engaged in various activities to shore up the patriotic struggle. Members of both the local Guomindang and the communists lent their hands to these efforts, very often in disguise. From the beginning until 1941, when the Japanese attacked the Americans by bombing Pearl Harbor, unleashing an all-out invasion of Southeast Asia where the British possessions of the Malay Peninsula and northern Borneo were situated, the colonial authorities did not interfere with the patriotic activities of the Chinese in the hope that the war in China would hold up Japanese plans to attempt to conquer Southeast Asia.[94]

To raise funds and to collect other forms of aid, *chou zhen hui* (relief fund committees) sprang up everywhere in the peninsula among the Chinese.

Such committees also appeared in the Chinese schools. All these organizations eventually became united under one umbrella organization called the Nan Yang Hua Qiao Chou Zhen Zu Guo Nan Min Zong Hui [Nanyang Overseas Chinese General Association for the Relief of Refugees in the Fatherland], headed by Chen Jia Geng. There were other organizations besides these which were immersed in the war effort. There were, for instance, an Overseas Chinese Anti-Enemy Back-up Society and a Students' Anti-Enemy Back-up Society. Besides raising funds and collecting other forms of aid, a boycott of Japanese goods was mounted, and a great deal of propaganda was carried out. And young persons, both male and female, were noted to have returned to China to train in military schools to become officers and join in the fight.[95]

While the colonial authorities gave the Chinese plenty of room to help China fight the Japanese, they, however, prohibited them from mounting processions and demonstrations against their enemies, or starting a boycott of or destroying their goods, as these would upset law and order and harm the economy of the land. In the heat of the conflagration, however, many Chinese were unable to contain themselves and very soon violated the special restrictions. The government responded by having them warned or punished.[96]

In 1939, the government developed an even dimmer view of Chinese activities which could disturb the peace of the land and affect the economy. This was because now Germany had started a war with the United Kingdom in Europe. Being tied down by the Germans in the west, the British did not wish to tangle with the Japanese in the east as well. While the European war was only looming, the colonial authorities ordered all the *chou zhen hui* to be registered so that they could be controlled, a measure which they did not take in the past. And after the war started, they told all the Chinese schools to sever their connections with the *chou zhen hui*. This dealt a severe blow to the fund-raising effort. However, eventually, when in 1941 the Japanese launched their invasion of Southeast Asia, the government not only returned the freedom to the Chinese community to deepen their patriotic efforts, but also enlisted their help to fight the incoming Japanese.[97]

It is noteworthy that when war at last broke out between Germany and the United Kingdom, the wife of Sir Shenton Thomas, then governor of the Straits Settlements and high commissioner to the Federated Malay States, launched a patriotic fund to garner support for the British empire. The Chinese responded generously to Lady Thomas' appeal. Organizations were set up to collect donations. The Chinese schools helped in this effort to collect money besides contributing funds of their own, just like they did for China's struggle against the Japanese.[98]

THE CHINESE SCHOOLS ON THE EVE OF THE PACIFIC WAR

It is now perhaps time to give a picture of the situation the modern Chinese schools founded by the Chinese themselves had reached from the early days until the outbreak of the Pacific War. No mention is given to those institutions which came before the modern ones because these dwindled into insignificance next to their up-to-date rivals.

Firstly, we note the fact that their numbers, and the number of students learning and teachers teaching in them, kept increasing. This was in spite of the ill fortune that befell them after 1920, when the colonial government kept throwing rings around them. Nevertheless, the government still gave them a free hand to develop as long as they did not participate in politics harmful to the interests of the peninsula. The deciding factor that kept pushing their numbers up was that more and more Chinese emigrated to the Malay Peninsula. This continuous increase in immigration was already shown in Table 1.1. With the increasing number of adults came an increasing number of children, who either arrived along with their parents from China, or were born locally. This ever increasing number of children led to an ever rising number of schools for their education. Table 1.4 shows the annual increases in the number of Chinese schools in the country from 1921 to 1938, together with parallel increases in the number of students learning, and teachers teaching, in them. The years from 1930 to 1932 were exceptions, however, when there were actually decreases because of the effects of the Great Depression.[99]

Secondly, as was to be expected, all the schools, when they started, provided only a very basic level of education. Then some of them, as time went by, offered higher and higher classes and kept improving. The classes available in Chinese schools in the 1920s and 1930s were kindergarten, lower primary, higher primary, junior middle, and, finally, senior middle. Table 1.5 is a sample of some of the schools, illustrating their progress over the years.[100]

Thirdly, there was the question of curricula. The thing to note about this is that they kept being changed over time to fulfil new requirements, particularly when there was a change in government or a change in the policy orientation of the same government in China. For instance, when the Manchu regime gave way to the republic, there was a change in curriculum. The new

Table 1.4
**Annual Increase in the Number of Chinese Schools,
Students and Teachers in the Straits Settlements and
the Federated Malay States, 1921–38**

Year	Schools	Students	Teachers
1921	252	—	589
1922	391	—	980
1923	537	—	1,362
1924	564	27,476	1,257
1925	643	33,662	1,390
1926	657	36,380	1,493
1927	665	40,760	1,637
1928	696	43,961	1,806
1929	711	46,911	1,900
1930	716	46,367	1,980
1931	657	39,662	1,867
1932	669	41,858	1,929
1933	731	47,123	2,021
1934	766	54,618	2,371
1935	824	62,014	2,730
1936	860	70,483	3,058
1937	933	79,993	3,415
1938	1,015	91,534	3,985

Source: See note 99.

authority emphasized military training, traditional martial arts, and being familiar with the lives of national heroes. Subjects of a modern nature were also introduced, of course. And when the republic, dominated by militarists, was replaced by the Guomindang administration, there was yet another modification. As was noted earlier, soon after Jiang Jie Shi seized power, it was decided that education must spread the teachings of San Min Zhu Yi, and there were also other new subjects introduced to the students. During the republican days, Yuan Shi Kai at first allowed students to stop studying the traditional Confucian classics, but later, when he began to implement the idea of crowning himself the new emperor of China, he restored the learning of those books.[101] All these events naturally necessitated revisions of the curricula for schools. The Chinese schools in the Malay Peninsula followed everything the schools in China did. They modified and changed frequently to follow the ever changing trends and there was not much stability.

Table 1.5
Standards in Various Chinese Schools in the 1920s and 1930s, and the Years when They Were First Started

School	Kindergarten	Years when first started			
		Lower Primary	Higher Primary	Junior Middle	Senior Middle
Zhong Hua, Muar		1912	1912	1924	
Pei Feng, Melaka		1913	1915	1925	
Zhong Hua, Seremban		1913	1917	1934	
Kun Cheng, Kuala Lumpur		1908	Unavailable	1925	1940
Zun Kong, Kuala Lumpur		1906	1914	1924	1935
Zhong Hua, Kuala Lumpur		1919	Unavailable	1939	
Yu Cai, Ipoh		1912	1919(?)	1924	1940
Hua Lian, Taiping		1911	Unavailable	1937	
Xie He, Penang	1928	1929	1932	1939	
Zhong Ling, Penang		1917	1917	1923	1931

Source: See note 100.

Tables 1.6–1.8 show how the Fujian Association in Singapore had two separate curricula for its lower primary and higher primary in 1929, and then, just two years later, modified these two into just one single curriculum for its lower and higher primary combined.[102]

Table 1.6
1929 Curriculum for Lower Primary, Fujian Association, Singapore

Subject \ Standard (Hrs/Wk)	1	2	3	4
Lower Primary				
National Language	9	9	9	9
Arithmetic	4	4	5	5
General Knowledge	4	4	5	5
Art & Craft	3	3	2	2
Physical Exercise & Music	5	5	4	4
Foreign Language			6	6
Total	25	25	31	31

Source: See note 102.

Table 1.7
1929 Curriculum for Higher Primary, Fujian Association, Singapore

Subject \ Standard (Hrs/Wk)	1	2
Higher Primary		
National Language	6	6
Arithmetic	5	5
Hygiene	2	2
Civics	1	1
History	2	2
Geography	2	2
Nature	2	2
Craft	1	1
Art	1	1
Music	1	1
Physical Exercise	2	2
Foreign Language	8	8
Commerce	2	2
Book-Keeping	1	1
Total	36	36

Source: See note 102.

Fourthly, there was the issue of school textbooks. It was apparent that with the changes in curricula, textbooks, at least sometimes, had to be written anew to conform with such changes. So new textbooks came to be written again and again over time. Another point to note about school textbooks was the impact the May 4th Movement had on their compilation. That movement was not only a demonstration against the Japanese, but also a call to discard the old culture of the country in exchange for a new one. A part of this cultural change was that, from then onwards, the nation was no longer to write in *wen-yan* (classical vocabulary) in all communications,

Table 1.8
1931 Curriculum for Lower and Higher Primary Combined, Fujian Association, Singapore

Subject \ Standard (Min/Wk, Percentage)	1 & 2		3 & 4		5 & 6	
National Language	400	36	400	30	310	19
Arithmetic	180	16	180	14	220	14
Hygiene	180 (General Knowledge)	16	180	14	40	3
Civics					40	3
History					90	6
Geography					90	6
Nature					100	6
Craft	90	8	50	4	50	3
Art	50	4	50	4	50	3
Music	80	8	90	7	40	3
Physical Exercise	140	12	90	7	90	6
Foreign Language			270	20	300	19
Commerce					90	6
Book-keeping					50	3
Total	1,120	100	1,310	100	1,560	100

Source: See note 102.

but to write in *bai-hua* (colloquial language). Another point was the introduction of punctuation marks in all written materials. All these were to affect the way school textbooks were to be compiled. One other item required by the cultural change was that, from then onwards, all schools were no longer to teach students using dialect, but through *guo-yu* (national language). It was perhaps also noteworthy that most of the post-Republic books, including those issued under Guominadang rule, were mostly published by two publishers, namely the Commercial Press and the Zhong Hua Book Company.[103] As the colonial government very often found textbooks coming from China obnoxious, they thought of plans to have textbooks compiled locally so they would not be so China-orientated, but this never came to pass.[104]

Finally, there was the question of teacher supply. We have seen earlier in this book that, when Kang Yu Wei began modern Chinese schools in the Malay Peninsula, he sent his students to teach in those schools. From then onwards, especially during the earlier days, Chinese schools of whatever political hue came to be staffed by intellectuals from China. Besides the textbooks that they used to teach their students, these intellectuals were clearly the influence that moulded the political attitude of their wards most directly. As they were born, bred and educated in China, they were, naturally, China-orientated. They, therefore, turned the eyes of young children to look towards China too. This, as explained earlier, made the colonial authorities very unhappy. One of the amendments to the 1920 school laws required that teachers be locally born.[105] Because of the undesirability of teachers imported from China, the possibility of the government training Chinese locally born to be teachers to replace them was actually mooted under Sir Cecil Clementi. However, the plan was never realized in the Straits Settlements, although it was carried out in the Federated Malay States.[106] Parallel to the issue of the unwise practice of permitting teachers originating from China to teach in the Chinese schools was the problem of a shortage of teachers, even with them coming. This was because the number of Chinese schools kept increasing. The government eventually adopted a policy of giving subsidies to those Chinese schools which were ready to train locally born Chinese for their own use, or for the use of fellow schools.[107]

From as early as 1906 until 1936, the following institutions were noted to have run normal classes at various times over the years. In Penang, there were the Ping Zhang Association, the Fu Jian Nu Xiao, the Fu You Nu Xue, and the Bin Hua Nu Xiao; in Singapore, there were the Nan Yang Nu Zhong, the Yang Zheng, the Jing Fang Nu Xiao, and the Zhong Hua Nu Xue; in Kuala Lumpur, the Zun Kong and the Kun Cheng; in Muar, the Hua Nan Nu Xiao (later renamed the Zhong Hua); and in Sitiawan, the Nan Hua. These classes could have been at a junior or senior level, and their duration could have been anything from half a year to four years. They were supported by the colonial government.[108]

The duration of these classes varied greatly because they were ad hoc in nature. In fact, their curricula varied as much as their names. The result of it all was that the standard of achievement of their student teachers was not uniform throughout.[109]

The curricula for such normal classes were, on the whole, the same as those for ordinary middle schools. What they had, which the ordinary middle schools did not have, were the subjects of pedagogy and letter writing.[110]

THE TOTAL EDUCATIONAL SCENE IN THE MALAY PENINSULA ON THE EVE OF THE PACIFIC WAR

As we will have to refer to the total educational scene in the Malay Peninsula in subsequent discussion, it is perhaps advisable to say a few brief words about it before concluding this chapter. By the total educational scene, we meant that besides Chinese schools, there were also English, Malay and Tamil schools.

On the eve of the Pacific War, some Chinese schools had already established senior middle classes. Graduates of these classes could further their education by going to China to join colleges or universities. The English schools, because of governmental support, had as early as in 1891 — long before their counterparts started the last year of their senior middle classes — initiated the comparable Standard Nine. Students of this level could sit for the Senior Cambridge Local Examination. Those who passed this could join an institute to train to become teachers, technicians, medical practioners, or agriculturists, while others could join a Queen's Scholarship class to study for one year after which they could enrol in a local or a foreign tertiary institution. There were also openings for students who failed to reach Standard Nine, but passed only Standard Five or Six, in trade schools.[111]

The Malay schools were, however, not as advanced as the Chinese and English schools. They offered only primary level classes and not secondary classes. However, students who passed only Primary Four could join special Malay classes after which they could enrol in an English school for Standard Four. Those who passed Primary Six were given opportunities for further education by going on to a trade school, an agricultural college, or a teachers' training college.[112]

The Tamil schools, like the Malay schools, had only primary, but not secondary, classes. Students who graduated from these institutions usually start working immediately.[113]

Figure 1.1 portrays the total educational scene in the country, including institutions of all the four different language media, just before 1941.[114]

Figure 1.1
The Malayan School System in the 1930s

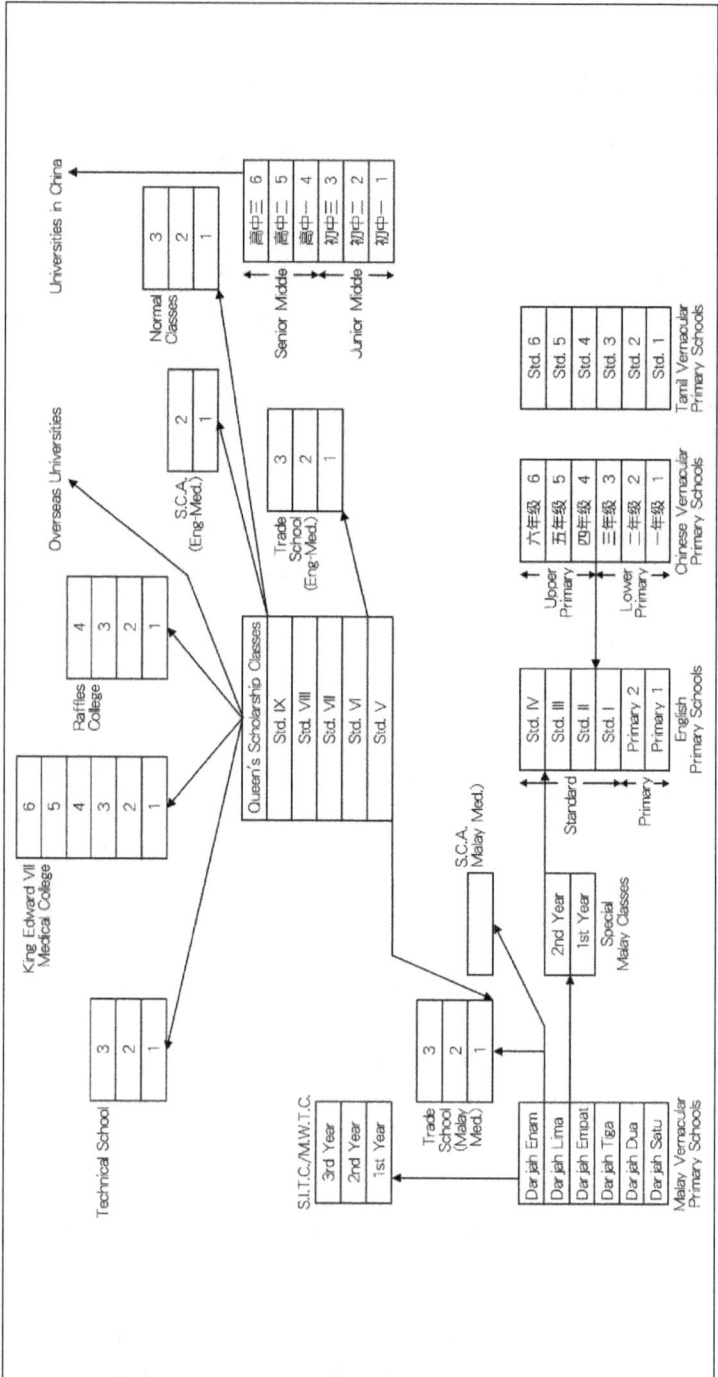

Universities in China

Normal Classes
| 3 |
| 2 |
| 1 |

Senior Middle
高中三	6
高中二	5
高中一	4

Junior Middle
初中三	3
初中二	2
初中一	1

Overseas Universities

S.C.A. (Eng.-Med.)
| 2 |
| 1 |

Trade School (Eng.-Med.)
| 3 |
| 2 |
| 1 |

King Edward VII Medical College
| 6 |
| 5 |
| 4 |
| 3 |
| 2 |
| 1 |

Raffles College
| 4 |
| 3 |
| 2 |
| 1 |

Queen's Scholarship Classes
| Std. IX |
| Std. VIII |
| Std. VII |
| Std. VI |
| Std. V |

Technical School
| 3 |
| 2 |
| 1 |

S.C.A. (Malay Med.)

S.I.T.C./M.W.T.C.
| 3rd Year |
| 2nd Year |
| 1st Year |

Trade School (Malay Med.)
| 3 |
| 2 |
| 1 |

Special Malay Classes
| 2nd Year |
| 1st Year |

Malay Vernacular Primary Schools
| Darjah Enam |
| Darjah Lima |
| Darjah Empat |
| Darjah Tiga |
| Darjah Dua |
| Darjah Satu |

English Primary Schools
Standard
| Std. IV |
| Std. III |
| Std. II |
| Std. I |
Primary
| Primary 2 |
| Primary 1 |

Chinese Vernacular Primary Schools
Upper Primary
六年級	6
五年級	5
四年級	4
Lower Primary
三年級	3
二年級	2
一年級	1

Tamil Vernacular Primary Schools
| Std. 6 |
| Std. 5 |
| Std. 4 |
| Std. 3 |
| Std. 2 |
| Std. 1 |

Key: S.C.A. – Serdang College of Agriculture   S.I.T.C. – Sultan Idris Training College   M.W.T.C. – Malay Women's Training College
Source: Adapted from Francis Wong Hoy Kee & Ee Tiang Hong, *Education in Malaysia*, Kuala Lumpur, 1975, pp. 34–35.

The outbreak of the Pacific War and the subsequent occupation of the Malay Peninsula by Japanese forces closed an era in the history of Chinese schools in the country.

To summarize, the first Chinese schools established in the country for the education of Chinese children were the old-style schools which taught the traditional Confucian curriculum. In those early days, Christian missions also founded schools for Chinese students in order to nurture church workers. One of the missions started, along with private sources, schools which imparted an ordinary education.

The first modern Chinese schools were established due to the influence of Kang Yu Wei, the reformer, the Manchu court and Sun Yat Sen, the revolutionary. Such schools were instruments for the modernization of China and were politicized.

The May 4th Movement in China of 1919 precipitated an anti-Japanese movement among the Chinese schools in the peninsula which hurt the economy of the country. Prior to this, the colonial government had adopted a *laissez-faire* attitude towards Chinese schools as they were peaceful. However, there was now a new situation. So, in 1920, it adopted a School Registration Ordinance and an Enactment in the Straits Settlements and the Federated Malay States respectively to control them. It also devised a grants-in-aid scheme to persuade them to accept control.

The preparation for, and the execution of, the Northern Expedition in China in the 1920s heightened political fervour and activities among the Chinese schools in the peninsula. School laws were amended and then replaced with new legislation altogether for tighter control over them.

The Guomindang, which came to rule China after the Northern Expedition, sought to "party-ize" education, which caused Chinese schools in the peninsula to become more highly politicized than ever. Reacting, the colonial government banned the local branch of the Guomindang, censored Chinese school textbooks and further amended the school laws. The colonial government also took punitive action against the communists, who also had an influence on the Chinese schools.

In 1937, the Japanese launched a full-scale invasion of China. The war aroused the local Chinese schools to initiate a campaign to raise funds and other forms of aid for China to help the government there fight the Japanese. The freedom allowed by the colonial government for such activities varied according to changes in Britain's relationships with Japan and Germany.

In spite of the fetters put on them by the colonial authorities, Chinese schools during the pre-Pacific War days kept multiplying, and upgrading themselves from offering primary classes to providing secondary level education.

Notes

1   Ooi Jin Bee, *Land, People and Economy of Malaya* (Oxford, 1963), p. 113.
2   Zheng Liang Shu, *Ma Lai Xi Ya Hua Wen Jiao Yu Fa Zan Shi*, vol. 1 (Kuala Lumpur, 1998), pp. 1–6 and 31–33. Mok Soon Sang, *Ma Lai Xi Ya Jiao Yu Shi, 1400–1999* (Kuala Lumpur, 2000), pp. 10–11 and 13; UCSCA, *Hua Guang Yong Yao* (Kuala Lumpur, 1993), p. 2.
3   Mok Soon Sang, op. cit., p. 13.
4   The Straits Settlements, *Straits Settlements Annual Report, 1884*, pp. C176–78.
5   Tan Liok Ee, *The Politics of Chinese Education in Malaya, 1945–1961* (Oxford, 1997) (hereafter Tan Liok Ee, op. cit. 1) p. 13.
6   Lee Ting Hui, *Chinese Schools in British Malaya: Policies and Politics* (Singapore, 2006), p. 2.
7   Tan Liok Ee, "Da Ma Ban Dao Hua Wen Jiao Yu de Fa Zan", in UCSTA, *Jiao Zong 33 Nian* (Kuala Lumpur, 1987) (hereafter Tan Liok Ee, op. cit. 2), pp. 741–54.
8   Mok Soon Sang, op. cit., p. 14. Lee Ting Hui, op. cit., pp. 3–5.
9   Lee Ting Hui, op. cit., p. 4.
10 Lee Ting Hui, op. cit., p. 5.
11 Ibid.
12 Ibid.
13 Ibid.
14 Mok Soon Sang, op. cit., pp. 14–15. Lee Ting Hui, op. cit., pp. 6–7.
15 Lee Ting Hui, op. cit., p. 6.
16 Lee Ting Hui, op. cit., p. 7. Mok Soon Sang, op. cit., p. 15.
17 Lee Ting Hui, op. cit., p. 6.
18 Ibid.
19 Lee Ting Hui, op. cit., pp. 6–7.
20 Immanuel C.Y. Hsu, *The Rise of Modern China* (Kuala Lumpur, 1975), p. 456.
21 Immanuel Hsu, op. cit., p. 462.
22 Lee Ting Hui, op. cit., p. 17. Nanyang refers to the seas south of China, the name given to the region where Malaysia and Singapore are situated.
23 Zheng Liang Shu, op. cit., vol. 1, pp. 96–97.
24 Zheng Liang Shu, op. cit., vol. 1, p. 92.
25 Lee Ting Hui, op. cit., p. 8.
26 Lee Ting Hui, op. cit., p. 12.

27   Ibid.
28   Ibid.
29   Zheng Liang Shu, op. cit., vol. 1, pp. 148–49; Lee Ting Hui, op. cit. p. 11.
30   UCSCA, op. cit., p. 2.
31   Ibid.
32   Ibid.
33   Lee Ting Hui, op. cit., p. 16. Zheng Liang Shu, op. cit., vol. 1, p. 282.
34   Zheng Liang Shu, op. cit., vol. 1, p. 110–12.
35   Zheng Liang Shu, op. cit., vol. 1, p. 130.
36   Zheng Liang Shu, op. cit, vol. 1, pp. 141–44.
37   Zheng Liang Shu, op. cit., vol. 1, pp. 262–63.
38   Ibid.
39   Zheng Liang Shu, op. cit., vol. 1, pp. 274–75.
40   Zheng Liang Shu, op. cit., vol. 1, pp. 275–76.
41   Zheng Liang Shu, op. cit., vol. 1, p. 279.
42   Zheng Liang Shu, op. cit., vol. 1, p. 292.
43   Lee Ting Hui, op. cit., p. 38.
44   Zheng Liang Shu, op. cit., vol. 1, pp. 352–70.
45   Personal experiences of the authors.
46   Lee Ting Hui, op. cit., p. 33.
47   Lee Ting Hui, op. cit., p. 34.
48   Ibid.
49   Li Yun Han, *Zhong Guo Jin Dai Shi* (Taiwan, 2005), pp. 255–71.
50   Lee Ting Hui, op. cit., p. 34.
51   Lee Ting Hui, op. cit., pp. 2–3.
52   D.D. Chelliah, *A History of Educational Policy of the Straits Settlements, 1800–1925* (Kuala Lumpur, 1947), p. 80.
53   Tan Liok Ee, op. cit. 1, p. 18; Zheng Liang Shu, op. cit., vol. 2, pp. 3–4.
54   Li Yun Han, op. cit., p. 272.
55   Zheng Liang Shu, op. cit., vol. 2, pp. 15–17; Lee Ting Hui, op. cit., pp. 42–43.
56   Zheng Liang Shu, op. cit., vol. 2, p. 17.
57   Lee Ting Hui, op. cit., p. 46.
58   Zheng Liang Shu, op. cit., vol. 2, p. 30; Lee Ting Hui, op. cit., pp. 45–46.
59   Lee Ting Hui, op. cit., pp. 46–47.
60   Lee Ting Hui, op. cit., p. 56; Zheng Liang Shu, op. cit., vol. 2, p. 124.
61   Ibid.
62   Tan Liok Ee, op. cit. 1, p. 21.
63   Zheng Liang Shu, op. cit., vol. 2, p. 56; Lee Ting Hui, op. cit., p. 48.
64   Zheng Liang Shu, op. cit., vol. 2, p. 59; Lee Ting Hui, op. cit., pp. 48 and 51.
65   Zheng Liang Shu, op. cit., vol. 2, pp. 125 and 128–29; Lee Ting Hui, op. cit., pp. 51 and 56.

66 Zheng Liang Shu, op. cit., vol. 2, p. 130; Lee Ting Hui, op. cit., p. 58.
67 Zheng Liang Shu, op. cit., vol. 2, p. 132; Lee Ting Hui, op. cit., pp. 57–58. The name of the organization dispatching the representative is the not the same in the two sources.
68 Zheng Liang Shu, op. cit., vol. 2, pp. 150–53; Lee Ting Hui, op. cit., p. 58.
69 Zheng Liang Shu, op. cit., vol. 2, pp. 148–49; Lee Ting Hui, op. cit., p. 58.
70 Lee Ting Hui, op. cit., p. 60.
71 Zheng Liang Shu, op. cit., vol. 2, pp. 154–55.
72 Zheng Liang Shu, op. cit., vol. 2, p. 160; Lee Ting Hui, op. cit., p. 60.
73 Zheng Liang Shu, op. cit., vol. 2, pp. 181–82.
74 Lee Ting Hui, op. cit., p. 60.
75 Kua Kia Soong, *A Protean Saga: The Chinese Schools of Malaysia* (Kuala Lumpur, 1985), p. 34.
76 Lee Ting Hui, op. cit., p. 61.
77 Zheng Liang Shu, op. cit., vol. 2, pp. 182–83; Li Yun Han, op. cit., pp. 345–46; Lee Ting Hui, op. cit., p. 71.
78 Zheng Liang Shu, op. cit., vol. 2, pp. 227–29; Lee Ting Hui, op. cit., p. 72.
79 Lee Ting Hui, op. cit., pp. 74–75; Zheng Liang Shu, op. cit., vol. 2, pp. 231– 32.
80 Lee Ting Hui, op. cit., pp. 76–78; Zheng Liang Shu, op. cit., vol. 2, pp. 232–33.
81 Lee Ting Hui, op. cit., p. 78.
82 Zheng Liang Shu, op. cit., vol. 2, pp. 185–89; Lee Ting Hui, op. cit., pp. 79–80.
83 Zheng Liang Shu, op. cit., vol. 2, pp. 190–93; Lee Ting Hui, op. cit., p. 83.
84 Zheng Liang Shu, op. cit., vol. 2, pp. 193–96.
85 Li Yun Han, op. cit., pp. 348–51.
86 Zheng Liang Shu, op. cit., vol. 2, pp. 197–202; Lee Ting Hui, op. cit., pp. 85–86.
87 Lee Ting Hui, op. cit., pp. 103, 107–08 and 159.
88 Lee Ting Hui, op. cit., pp. 105 and 122.
89 Lee Ting Hui, op. cit., pp. 105–07 and 159; Kua Kia Soong, op. cit., pp. 39–40.
90 Li Yun Han, op. cit., pp. 394–96; Lee Ting Hui, op. cit., p. 116.
91 Lee Ting Hui, op. cit., pp. 116–18.
92 Li Yun Han, op. cit., p. 388.
93 Zheng Liang Shu, op. cit., vol. 2, p. 239; Lee Ting Hui, op. cit., pp. 133–34.
94 Lee Ting Hui, op. cit., pp. 154–55.
95 Ibid.
96 Lee Ting Hui, op. cit., pp. 144–48.
97 Lee Ting Hui, op. cit., pp. 148–49.
98 Lee Ting Hui, op. cit., p. 148.

[99] Mok Soon Sang, op. cit., p. 19; UCSCA, op. cit., p. 3.

[100] Zheng Liang Shu, op. cit., vol. 2, p. 288; Mok Soon Sang, op. cit., p. 18.

[101] Lee Ting Hui, op. cit., pp. 35–36.

[102] Mok Soon Sang, op. cit., pp. 21–22.

[103] Zheng Liang Shu, op. cit., vol. 1, pp. 348–52.

[104] Lee Ting Hui, op. cit., pp. 106–07.

[105] Mok Soon Sang, op. cit., p. 36.

[106] Lee Ting Hui, op. cit., p. 106.

[107] Ibid., Zheng Liang Shu, op. cit., vol. 1, p. 334.

[108] Zheng Liang Shu, op. cit., vol. 1, pp. 327–30.

[109] Zheng Liang Shu, op. cit., vol. 1, pp. 329–30.

[110] Zheng Liang Shu, op. cit., vol. 1, pp. 279–82.

[111] Wong Hoy Kee, Francis, and Ee Tiang Hong, op. cit., pp. 34–35, Figure 1.1; Mok Soon Sang, op. cit., pp. 38–40.

[112] Ibid.

[113] Ibid.

[114] Mok Soon Sang, *Pendidikan di Malaysia*, Terbitan Ke-13 (Kuala Lumpur, 2000), p. 27.

2

FROM THE JAPANESE OCCUPATION TO SELF-GOVERNMENT

The Japanese took over the Malay Peninsula from the British between the end of 1941 and the beginning of 1942. Thereafter, they ruled the land until 1945 when they lost the Pacific War and had to return it to the British. While there, as to be expected, they tried to promote education through their own language at the expense of all other languages.

Before the war, the British had ruled the Straits Settlements directly, and the Federated as well as the Unfederated Malay States indirectly, through their sultans. On recovering the peninsula, they tried immediately to alter this system. They made an attempt to do away with the sultans, join their states into one unit with Penang and Malacca, and rule the whole country directly. As before, they continued to govern Singapore separately. They also treated the immigrant races, the Chinese and Indians, on par with the Malays and granted them citizenship on easy terms. All these would promote the development of a Malayan nation. However, the scheme ran into very strong opposition from both the conservative and radical Malays. Later, the British also came up against a rebellion led by the Chinese communists who aimed to take total power from them. From then on, they made compromises to the conservative Malays step by step. First, while amalgamating the Federated and Unfederated Malay States, together with Penang and Malacca, into one unit, they reverted to the traditional practice of ruling the new set-up indirectly. Not so long after that, they conceded to them self-government.

Along with all the changes in the power configuration of the country came changes in the field of education. The British at first tried to make their language the premier medium of instruction in schools, while giving the Chinese, Malay, and Tamil languages equal status. In this, they met with vigorous protest from the conservative Malays. They then used the strategy of allowing the Malay language to take a place just next to the English language, and phasing out the Chinese and Tamil languages. This move was strenuously criticized by the Chinese and Tamil communities, whom they ignored. Eventually, just before they granted self-government to the country, they attempted to launch a scheme to phase out not just Chinese and Tamil languages, but also the Malay language as well. In this, they were met with resistance from the Malays. However, before self-government came, the Malays and Chinese of the conservative kind, to whom power would be devolved, reached an understanding whereby the Chinese language was allowed to be continued to be used.

THE CHINESE SCHOOLS DURING THE JAPANESE OCCUPATION

Besides the British, the Japanese were the most hostile towards the Chinese. This was because Japan was at war with China, and the Chinese in the Malay Peninsula gave support to their home country against them. Once the Japanese were in the peninsula, they rounded up the Chinese and purged them of anti-Japanese elements. Thousands of Chinese were detained and killed, or were never heard of again. Among the victims were many Chinese school teachers and students.[1] At the same time, they closed down all the Chinese schools. Some school buildings were used as administrative centers or as army camps. A few of the sports fields or gardens were turned into farmland to grow food. In the process, quite a number of these school infrastructure was seriously damaged. This situation was to last till the immediate months after the return of the British at the end of the Pacific War.[2]

A little later, the Japanese ordered schools of all language streams to be re-registered with them. Out of a total of 370 Chinese schools in Singapore from pre-war days, only 21 were reopened, along with 36 English, 22 Malay and 8 Tamil schools. Figures for Peninsular Malaya, unfortunately, were unavailable.[3] After re-registering, they were all transformed into institutions which had to use the Japanese language as the medium of instruction. Chinese, English, Malay, and Tamil languages were allowed to be taught only as separate subjects, and the time allotted to their teaching was reduced, compared with pre-war days.[4]

Mathematics, geography, history, civics, and general knowledge were all forbidden to be taught. And about 200,000 textbooks, except dictionaries and geography readers, were consigned to the flames. The dictionaries and geography readers were retained because the Japanese needed them for their own reference.[5]

The structure of pre-war Chinese schools were six years of primary, three years of junior middle, and three years of senior middle classes. Now they had to follow the Japanese system of seven years of primary and four years of secondary education.[6] Their names also had to be all changed. Formerly, they had all kinds of designations, usually with ennobling connotations, but now they could only be named after the names of the streets or roads where they were located.[7] The word "school" also had to be converted into the Japanese equivalent *katakana*, a script used to write foreign or onomatopoeic words.[8]

The Japanese aimed to "japanize" all the conquered peoples.

FROM MALAYAN UNION TO FEDERATION OF MALAYA

The British returned to the peninsula in September 1945. A month afterwards, an envoy from London, Sir Harold MacMichael, appeared with treaties to establish a Malayan Union in place of the former administrative system. The proposed union would, firstly, transfer the sovereignty of the sultans to the British Crown; secondly, absorb the autonomy of the individual Malay states unto itself; and, thirdly, allow non-Malays in the country to enjoy the same privileges previously reserved only for Malays, including obtaining citizenship. The sultans all signed the treaties.[9]

During the pre-war years, the governor of the Straits Settlements was simultaneously the high commissioner to the Malay States. Under the Malayan Union scheme, he retained his jurisdiction over Singapore only as the mainland would have its own governor.[10]

The reasons for setting up the Malayan Union were, according to one source, "[to] ensure administrative efficiency and military security and eventually weld the population together in a sense of Malayan nationhood".[11] Other considerations were that, on the one hand, the Malays had collaborated with the Japanese during the Pacific War; on the other, the Chinese had helped the British fight the Japanese as guerillas.[12]

The scheme of the Malayan Union was released to the public in January 1946. At once it raised a storm of protests from both the conservative and radical Malays. The conservative group convened a congress of a great number of Malay organizations from all over the country to establish a new organization of national unity, the United Malay National Organization (UMNO), to spearhead the opposition. It was led by a Dato Onn Jafaar. The union was inaugurated on 1 April 1946. UMNO was able to persuade the sultans not to participate in the occasion.[13]

The radical group centred around a Malay Nationalist Party (MNP). This group advocated that a union should include not only the Malay states in the peninsula, but also Singapore and Indonesia as well. It also stood for the interests of the ordinary Malays, at the same time defining a Malay as someone who had assimilated into the Malay culture, regardless of the person's ethnic origin.[14]

The opposition caught the British by surprise. They were unaware that the Malays had become so nationalistically conscious. They retreated. The British initiated negotiations with UMNO to devise a new political arrangement for the country, but ignored the MNP because compromising with it would incur greater harm to British interests.[15]

The agreement reached with UMNO was a Federation of Malaya, including all the Malay states and the settlements on the mainland, but excluding Singapore which would remain a crown colony. In the new scheme, the sultans would retain their status, their states would not have to lose their individuality, the Malay race could keep their special privileges, and the non-Malays in the country would be able to acquire citizenship but on stricter terms. The government of the country, like in pre-war days, would be headed by a British High Commissioner, but separate from the governor for Singapore, who would be assisted by a Legislative and an Executive Council whose members would be appointed by him. Of special relevance to our discussion were the provisions that the high commissioner was empowered to control the external affairs, defence and internal security of the country to ensure that the British would not be displaced, and that decisions regarding immigration and the conferment of citizenship should not be made except with the concurrence of the sultans to protect the interests of the Malays.[16]

The new federation was established on 1 February 1948.[17] Henceforth, in all their political moves in the peninsula, the British had to consider the opinion of the Malays first, as represented by UMNO, before that of any other community.

The attempt to replace indirect rule in the Malay states with direct rule had not succeeded.

The Rehabilitation and Growth of Chinese Schools

With the departure of the Japanese and the return of the British at the end of the Pacific War, Chinese schools, like those of other language media, had to be rehabilitated. This was successfully achieved, and these schools continued the pre-war general trend of expansion.

Many problems faced the rehabilitation exercise. One was the failure to recover school buildings because for a period of months British troops, like their Japanese counterparts, occupied these buildings for their own use. Next was the damage done to those buildings and their equipment, primarily during the Japanese Occupation. Thirdly, the schools used to be run by management committees, but now there was no one to take charge of them. Fourthly, the classrooms were excessively crammed with students. This came about because students from the pre-war days, who were overaged, and new students from the post-war years, who were of the correct ages, had to be accepted into the same classes. And, finally, there was a shortage of teachers. This happened because the number of students compared with pre-war days had increased. Then, when peace was restored after the war, both the Guomindang and the communists resumed their activities in the schools. Some of the teachers had collaborated with the Japanese when the latter were around. The Guomindang refused to register these people so they were unable to teach. Under this ruling, even those who had not worked with the Japanese, but who were now taking the side of the communists, were accused of being traitors and barred from teaching. However, all these problems were eventually overcome and, by about the end of 1947, the schools were all rehabilitated.[18]

The rehabilitation exercise was carried out at a time when talk about the Malayan Union scheme was very much in the air. Under this scheme, the British authorities, as noted, had given the Chinese community a better deal in the country. Some Chinese schools had been receiving grants-in-aid from the government in the pre-war days. Now such financial assistance for them was resumed. On top of that, new schools were added to the list. The authorities also forked out money for the repair of school buildings, purchase of new equipment, and so on.[19]

As the Chinese schools in those days were still a branch of the educational system in China, the Guomindang government also stepped in quickly to help in the rehabilitation programme. The consul-general in Singapore, leading consuls in the various towns on the mainland, led Chinese school principals and wealthy Chinese in the effort. Officials from the Ministry of Education in China were also dispatched to attend meetings and make contributions.

Table 2.1
Numbers of Chinese Primary and Secondary Schools, Pupils and Teachers in the Malay Peninsula, 1946–55.

Year	No. of Schools		No. of Pupils		No. of Teachers	
	Pr.	Sec.	Pr.	Sec.	Pr.	Sec.
1946	1,004	15	158,037	4,508	4,064	194
1947	1,379	22	190,349	3,194	5,179	201
1948	1,362	21	185,670	3,474	5,328	220
1949	1,336	27	198,126	4,450	5,348	265
1950	1,317	32	210,336	6,159	5,865	380
1951	1,168	38	198,840	7,503	5,942	426
1952	1,199	40	227,803	11,378	5,565	462
1953	1,211	46	236,041	14,840	6,282	455
1954	1,231	53	232,818	18,306	6,458	503
1955	1,265	55	255,158	23,397	6,642	964

Source: See note 21.
Note: The numbers given for secondary schools included institutions which were full secondary schools as well as those in which only secondary classes were conducted.

Millions of dollars were released as well. However, when the money passed through the Overseas Chinese Commission for distribution, it was embezzled by corrupt officials.[20]

After the schools were rehabilitated, there was, generally speaking, an augmentation of their numbers. Table 2.1 shows this phenomenon in the Malay Peninsula.[21] In Singapore, the picture was as shown in Table 2.2:[22]

Table 2.2
Numbers of Chinese Schools, Students and Teachers in Singapore, 1946–49

Year	Schools	Students	Teachers
1946	284	46,312	1,089
1947	306	53,478	1,804
1948	318	65,371	1,722
1949	349	73,500	1,980

Source: See note 22.
Note 1: The source does not show a distinction between primary and secondary schools.
Note 2: The source does not have figures up to 1955.

The general upward trend of the figures in the tables was probably due to an increase in the number of children in the country.

English to be the Premier Language and the Vernaculars to be Equals amongst Themselves

The Cheeseman Plan

Soon after the British had returned to the Malay Peninsula after the war, they appointed a committee to review the education system in the country and make recommendations for its reform. In tune with the spirit of the Malayan Union, the objective was to cultivate a sense of nationhood among its diverse population. The committee was headed by the then director of education in the Malayan Union, H.R. Cheeseman.[23]

Cheeseman submitted a plan to the Malayan Union Advisory Council, the governmental body of the Union. This was accepted in December 1946.[24] What Cheeseman recommended, in summary, were as follows:

(1) There should be two kinds of schools in the country. One kind would use English as its medium of instruction, and the other would use the mother tongue.
(2) English schools would teach the mother tongue as a subject.
(3) The non-English schools must teach English as a compulsory subject.
(4) Primary education for any kind of school should be free.
(5) Comprehensive vocational education should be started.

There was no reaction to Cheeseman's plan from the Chinese community, but it was opposed vehemently by UMNO. The party's secretary-general wrote to the governor of the union to let him know that, at a time when negotiations were underway to devise a new political arrangement to replace the union, discussion of a new educational policy was not right. UMNO could not accept the treatment of all four language streams of primary education on an equal basis. Any future educational policy must conform to the terms, aims, and ideals of the projected new constitution.[25]

Because of the protest from UMNO and the fact that the government was busy reconstructing the country after the war, the plan was eventually put aside.[26]

The Ten-Year Education Plan in Singapore

In tune with the spirit of the Malayan Union scheme and at the same time as the Cheeseman Plan was approved in Peninsular Malaya, the director of education in Singapore, J.B. Neilson, proposed a Ten-Year Education Plan for the island. The plan was accepted by the governor's Advisory Council in August 1947 and implemented in 1948.[27]

The provisions of the plan, in essence, were:[28]

(1)   Primary schools of all language streams could continue to use their separate languages as their different medium of instruction.

(2)   The curricula of primary schools of all language streams should be standardized.

(3)   Chinese, Malay, and Tamil primary schools should teach English as a subject.

(4)   After the third year, outstanding students from the Chinese, Malay, and Tamil primary schools should be channelled into special classes in the English primary schools for special training in the English language so that they could enrol in those English primary schools at the appropriate level.

(5)   Education at the primary level should be free.

(6)   Secondary schools should use only English as the medium of instruction. The Chinese, Malay, and Tamil languages were to be taught as separate subjects.

For point five, when the Ten-Year Education Plan was implemented in the latter part of 1948, five per cent of the students in the Chinese and Tamil primary schools, which were already receiving grants-in-aid from the government, were allowed total remission of fees. The following year, all students in primary schools of all language streams were granted exemption.[29]

There was severe criticism of the plan from some Chinese community leaders and eight leading Chinese secondary schools. Led by Chen Jia Geng, the primary leader of all the *chou zhen hui* [relief fund] movements to help China in pre-war days, they expressed the feeling that, by giving some money to the Chinese schools, the government was aiming to exercise greater control over them. If the assistance was accepted, thereafter, power over the employment of teachers, as well as the choice of materials for teaching, would all be in the government's hands. Pupils raised in such circumstances would be slaves to the government.[30]

Unlike in the case of the Cheeseman Plan, there was no opposition from the Malay community in Singapore to the Ten-Year Education Plan which accorded equal status to the other languages as Malay. The reason for this is unfathomable.

Regardless of what leaders of the Chinese community and leading Chinese secondary schools thought, many Chinese primary schools went ahead with accepting financial assistance from the government. The factor of poverty was telling. It was reported that by June 1949, 205 Chinese primary schools were receiving aid, and, out of this number, 151 were previously not receipents. By early 1950, this number had increased to 245, and, out of this new number, 181 were previously entirely on their own. In the years that followed, the total number of schools accepting governmental help increased.[31]

Malayanization

As political development in the country evolved, particularly with the rise of Malay nationalism, a sentiment arose that the China orientation of the Chinese schools was unacceptable. In the few years immediately after the end of the Pacific War, the Guomindang re-established its ties with those schools. As noted, it made an effort to help in the rehabilitation of those schools. In addition, the Malayan Communist Party also resumed their activities there, and, in 1948, merely several months after the establishment of the Federation of Malaya, it rose in rebellion to try to seize power. And in the following year, the Chinese Communist Party secured ultimate victory over the Guomindang in China in a civil war. The Malayan Communist Party had always had links with the Chinese Communist Party. This scenario was to cause further unease in the ruling circles in the peninsula. Therefore, talks about Malayanizing the Chinese schools, that is, reorientating them from China to Malaya, began to surface.

At some point during the communist revolt, a Chinese newspaper published a report which touched upon the tenseness of the situation at the time. According to the writer, from the outbreak of the communist uprising, the Chinese schools were plunged into difficulties that could not be imagined. Because a number of Chinese school students were involved in the revolt, the schools from which they came were made sacrificial lambs for their mischief. All at once, it seemed that all Chinese schools had unsteady inclinations, every Chinese school student was a criminal with leftist thinking, and every Chinese school textbook had seditious contents.[32]

The subject of Malayanization stimulated a great deal of discussion. But what would the term actually involve. The person who defined it was no less than a very senior official in the government at the time who stated to the press that Malayanization would mean that English and Malay would be regarded as the premier medium of instruction in schools and that other languages could be studied only as optional subjects. The practice then of allowing non-English schools to use their own languages to teach their students would be discontinued. Chinese schools from then on would have to make a clear distinction between China and Malaya, and choose their object of loyalty accordingly.[33] The official's statement caused great alarm in the Chinese community.

English and Malay to the Fore

A Supplementary Plan to the Ten-Year Education Plan in Singapore

In 1949, the government announced a supplementary plan to the Ten-Year Education Plan implemented in Singapore.[34] This supplementary plan deviated from the spirit of the original plan and sought to enhance the leading position of English further and elevate Malay from an equal status with Chinese and Tamil to a higher position, just behind English. The supplementary plan proposed that, between 1950 and 1960, the 72,000 students then in the Chinese schools should gradually be reduced to 25,000, and the 42,000 then in the government English and Malay schools should gradually be increased to 128,400. The Ten-Year Education Plan had envisaged building five new English schools every year during the period. Now the supplementary plan suggested setting up another eighteen. The authorities believed that parents, who at the time sent their children to schools not using English as the medium of instruction, would, if given the freedom, choose to put them in those which used English instead. The number of students rechannelled would be impressive. Eventually, therefore, education through the Chinese language was to shrink and education through English was to expand.[35]

The First Report of the Central Advisory Committee on Education

After the establishment of the Federation of Malaya, in September the next year, the government appointed a Central Advisory Committee on Education to review the educational system in the country. Recommendations for changes and reforms were made since the Cheeseman Plan. It was headed by M.R. Holgate who had replaced Cheeseman as the director of education. Holgate submitted his report, the First Report of the Central Advisory Committee on Education, or the Holgate Report as was commonly known, to the Federal Legislative Council in mid-1950.[36]

Holgate's recommendations were as follows:[37]

Paras. 1-5. That the ultimate desirable objective be free (and compulsory) primary education in the medium of English.

Paras. 6-7. That the educational system should move towards the provision of free primary education (a six-years' course) for all children in

(a) schools in which the medium of instruction is English, with Malay as an obligatory subject;
(b) schools in which the medium of instruction is Malay, with English as an obligatory subject.

Both types of schools should provide facilities for the learning of Chinese and Indian (Tamil) by pupils whose parents so desire.

Para. 8. That:

(a) increased facilities be provided, as early as possible, for the transfer from vernacular to primary English schools of pupils of any race who reach the prescribed standard. No fresh grants should be paid for newly-established post-primary vernacular classes;
(b) the Government "Normal", or Middle, schools contemplated in the Development Plan should be established as soon as possible, and on their establishment the present grants given to post-primary Chinese Middle classes should cease;
(c) no grants should be paid in respect of classes in new Indian and Chinese vernacular schools above the 2nd year unless English is taught or above the 3rd year unless Malay and English are taught to approved syllabuses by teachers of approved qualifications;
(d) the cost of teaching Malay and English in aided vernacular schools should be borne by the Government as additional grants to those now given.

Para. 9. That the implementation of the "free primary education" policy in respect of English schools should in the meantime be deferred.

Holgate also recommended that, at the secondary level, all teaching must be in English.

Strangely enough, the report was not attacked by the Chinese community, though by its recommendations their primary schools would be the greatest losers. However, it was vociferously assaulted by Dato Onn from UMNO in the Legislative Council. Onn declared that what the report recommended would do untold harm to the Malays and their language. He stated that the country should have schools of only one language and that language was Malay. Even English was a foreign language just like Chinese and Tamil. The Malays accepted English only because they needed it. Government money should be spent only on Malay and English schools and on no others.[38]

Because of Dato Onn's objections, the Holgate Report was shelved, pending the findings of another committee which would soon be appointed.[39]

Registration of Schools, 1950

The communist uprising was to bring great suffering to the Chinese schools. On the heels of the revolt, the government proclaimed a state of emergency in the country. All radical organizations, including the MNP, were banned or dissolved. The government detained, punished, or deported many suspected Chinese to control the situation. In the whole peninsula, a total of 212 Chinese schools were closed down. The number of students and teachers also fell as a consequence, the former by 11,496, and the latter by 292. Of the students and teachers affected, 92 were detained, 101 disappeared without a trace, and 16 were killed.[40]

To meet the communist challenge in the Chinese schools head on, the government revised the pre-war school registration ordinance and enactment to seek wider and stronger control over them. Thus, in early 1950, a new Registration of Schools Law was adopted.[41]

Crucially, the greater powers sought by the government could, for instance, be seen in two areas. In the past, only the normal kind of schools with at least ten students and located at a particular address would come under the purview of the laws. Now, the net was cast wider to include even correspondence schools, regardless of what enrolments they had or where they conducted their businesses. Also, in the past, if a person applying to be the supervisor of, or a teacher in, a school was unqualified, he would be refused registration. Now if such a person were to do so, and if his name appeared in a school which was also applying for registration, that school would not be registered either.[42]

Soon after the passing of the Registration of Schools Law, noteworthy incidents occurred in several Chinese schools.[43] Early in May 1950, the government announced that an Education Week would be convened to promote, through various activities, a local consciousness, especially an anti-communist consciousness, among school students. Following this, anti-British propaganda materials were discovered in the Overseas Chinese

High School and several other Chinese schools in Singapore. The materials called on teachers and students not to take part in the event on pain of being severely punished in case of disobedience. The materials were issued in the names of the communist armed forces and an Anti-British League.

The authorities responded to the challenge by having the Overseas Chinese High School as well as the Nanyang Girls' High School besieged and searched. Communist documents and propaganda handbills as well as proscribed books and periodicals were uncovered. In the former, a teacher and nineteen students were arrested and taken away.

The two schools were then served notice to explain why, according to the provisions of the Registration of Schools Law, they should not be closed. This was followed by several months of negotiations between the school committees and the government. Eventually, the schools were allowed to continue, but they had to accept conditions that would have them sanitized.

In June, the authorities also raided and searched the Xing Zhong Primary and Secondary Schools in Sungei Siput, and the Zhong Hua and Xing Hua schools in Klang. Communist literature and documents were uncovered. At the Xing Zhong schools, nine teachers and two students were detained, and at Zhong Hua and Xing Hua, one teacher and nine students, and two teachers and five students were arrested, respectively. For reasons unknown, the Xing Zhong school was not ordered closed. The latter two were closed, but were later given permission to reopen only when they accepted conditions imposed upon them.[44]

The Chinese Schools to Give Way Further

A Six-Year Education Plan in the Federation of Malaya

In July 1950, the Federation of Malaya adopted a Six-Year Education Plan to develop education in the country. It listed three areas for development, namely, teacher training, primary education, and secondary education.[45]

For teacher training, the plan budgeted in part, as shown in Table 2.3, different funds for the different language streams between the years 1950 and 1955.[46] Of the different language streams, the Malay stream was given the largest amount, the English stream, second, the Chinese stream, third, and the Tamil stream, fourth. That different proportions were allocated to the different language streams was significant.

As seen in the previous chapter, during the days before the Pacific War, the government had undertaken the training of teachers for the Chinese

Table 2.3
Funds Allocated to Different Streams of Teacher Training, 1950–55

	1950	1951	1952	1953	1954	1955	Total
English Teacher Training	—	0.7	1.15	0.02	—	—	1.87
Malay Male Teacher Training	—	0.75	0.41	0.02	—	—	1.18
Expansion For Malay Female Teacher Training Classes	—	0.229	0.015	0.005	—	0.011	0.26
Opening Malay Teacher Training Classes	—	—	0.83	0.5	0.02	0.01	1.36
Tamil Teacher Training	—	0.01	0.005	0.02	—	—	0.035
Chinese Teacher Training	—	0.62	0.02	0.225	—	—	0.865

Figures are in million dollars.

Source: See note 46.

schools in the Malay States, but not in the Straits Settlements. After the war, this practice was continued. The Six-Year Plan envisaged carrying on with this practice, but it had to take an inferior position behind Malay and English teacher training.[47]

Before the war, the government undertook the training of teachers for the Chinese schools because the teachers imported from China made their students China-oriented, and there was also a shortage of teachers due to the fact that Chinese schools multiplied very rapidly in numbers. After the war, with the Chinese Communist Party taking over power in China in 1949, the importation of teachers became an even more dangerous proposition. In fact, the government had to ban the immigration of Chinese from China altogether. This resulted in an even shorter supply of teachers for the Chinese schools. So, there was little choice for the government, but to continue with the practice of training teachers for these schools.

In the plan to develop primary education, the promotion of English schools, Malay schools, commercial schools, and the construction of dormitories were envisaged. And in that for secondary education, what was to be undertaken was the expansion of Malay colleges and Malay girls' schools, the building of new industrial schools, and the inauguration of university preparatory classes. In all these plans, the Chinese schools had no place. They were not to join the mainstream education.[48]

The Six-Year Education Plan also made allocations of finance for all the six years of primary education to the four different streams for them to cover their expenditures for expansion, including teacher training, and their recurrent spending. Table 2.4 gives the breakdown of the spending by the different language streams.[49]

Table 2.4
Capital and Recurrent Expenditure of the Four Language Streams of Education

Schools	Capital Expenditure	Recurrent Expenditure	Percentage
English	20.470	5.743	58.3
Malay	13.645	4.28	39.2
Chinese	0.865	0.194	2.3
Tamil	0.035	0.074	0.2

Figures are in million dollars.

Source: See note 49.

In March 1950, the school population in the different kinds of schools were:[50]

Table 2.5
School Populations in the Different Kinds of Schools in 1950

Schools	Number of Students	Percentage of Total
English	103,570	14.2
Malay	276,718	43
Chinese	221,660	36.4
Tamil	41,471	6.4

Source: See note 50.

The Chinese school population numbered 36.4 per cent of the total school population in the country, but was given only 2.3 per cent of the financial resources to be distributed to schools of all streams.

The Chinese community was not satisfied with what they were given. A political party which represented their interests, the Malayan Chinese Association (hereafter the MCA), took up their case with the education authorities. The reply given was that the number of Chinese schools in the country was vast. To increase financial assistance to them would incur too great an amount of expenditure.[51]

At that time, not every Chinese school in the country was receiving aid. For instance, in the states of Selangor and Perak, there were 206 and 283 Chinese schools respectively, and out of these only 146 in each state were given assistance. Besides, money was given only to students who were born locally and one of whose parents was a Malayan citizen. On top of these, only 3 per cent of all students in a school could apply for grants.[52]

The MCA was a political party formed by conservative Chinese on 27 February 1949. It was led by Tan Cheng Lock, a local born from Malacca whose ancestors had long resided in Malaya. The Malayan Communist Party had risen in revolt in June 1948 and the MCA was established as a counter to this party to win the allegiance of the Chinese community.[53]

Chinese Schools in the Federation to Teach Malay

As part of Malayanization, in December 1949, the Legislative Council in the Federation of Malaya passed a motion which stipulated that all government and government-aided primary schools must teach the Malay and English languages as part of their syllabuses. This was to begin from the final school term in 1950. Aided primary schools would include those Chinese primary schools which were then enjoying grants-in-aid from the government.[54]

The Chinese community was not unwilling to accept the decree as they were domiciled in the peninsula. Their primary schools were already teaching English as a subject besides using Chinese as the medium of instruction. But, they asked, would learning a third language overburden the capacity of the very young students? Also, as Chinese primary schools had to teach Malay besides already teaching English, why were English primary schools barred from teaching their students Chinese? At that time, the educational authorities had ordered that Chinese could not be taught in English primary schools unless approved by the principals. So, to be fair, English and Malay primary schools should hold Chinese and Tamil classes for their Chinese and Tamil students, they argued.

Regardless of the concerns of the Chinese community, the decree of the Legislative Council took effect in the end. However, because the government had not made full preparations to implement its own scheme, the Chinese primary schools ended up having to start teaching Malay only from

Primary Four onwards, and the English primary schools from Primary Three onwards. Three periods a week were assigned to the subject.

Chinese Schools to Follow English Schools in Arranging their School Terms

Chinese schools in the Malay Peninsula had all along followed a two-term school year. The first term was from July to December, and the second, from January to June. The English schools, on the other hand, had a three-term school year. The first term was from January to April, the second, from April to August, and the third, from September to December. It was at the beginning of their respective first terms that the two different kinds of schools recruited new students.[55]

In August 1949, in the Federation of Malaya, and in the following month in the same year in Singapore, the educational authorities announced that Chinese schools must in the future recruit new intakes only in spring and not in autumn. Any disobedience would result in grants-in-aid and remission of fees being withdrawn. Later, the educational authorities also launched a scheme whereby Chinese schools would follow the English schools in having a three-term school year instead of a two-term year.

The Chinese community was not happy with the order. They argued with the authorities about the disadvantages the plan would bring to their schools, while the authorities tried to point out to them the benefits that the proposal would accrue to their schools and to schools of other language streams. The debate went back and forth. The Chinese community suspected the authorities of having ulterior motives.

Finally, towards the end of the year, the government in both territories announced that the new proposal, regardless of the concerns of the Chinese community, would take effect from 1951.

Further Steps by the Government and Chinese Reaction

The Barnes Report and the Formation of the United Chinese School Teachers' Association

Following Dato Onn's opposition to the First Report of the Central Advisory Council on Education and the suspension of that report mentioned earlier, in 1950, the Central Advisory Committee on Education appointed another committee to review the status of Malay education in the country with a view to making recommendations for its improvement. The committee was headed by a British academic, L.J. Barnes. The report submitted by this committee did not limit itself to its terms of reference, but deviated to making recommendations for all streams of education. It was released to the public in June 1951.[56]

The recommendations and suggestions of the report contained, in essence, as these impacted on Chinese education, the following terms:[57]

(1) Primary schooling should instil a common Malayan national consciousness among students. It should be reorganized on a new interracial basis.

(2) Such proposed interracial primary schools should be called National Schools.

(3) Such schools would teach in both English and Malay and would produce pupils who would be bilingual by the end of the course, the best of whom would proceed direct to an English-medium post-primary school.

(4) In principle, the present system of separate vernacular schools for the several racial communities should end. They should be replaced by a single type of primary school common to all. This objective, however, could be achieved only gradually. The vernacular schools would continue for some years concurrently with the development of the National Schools. But, in the allocation of public resources to primary education, priority should be given to National Schools.

(5) The proposed scheme would be seriously weakened if any large proportion of the Chinese, Indian, and other non-Malay communities were to choose to provide their own primary classes independently of the National Schools. Therefore, it would be sought to make it as easy as possible for all non-Malays to associate themselves with the scheme. The National Schools would give, in terms of staff, premises, and equipment, the best primary education available in Malaya. They would charge no fees. They would teach English to all from Standard One onwards, and they would form the broad highway of admission to all post-primary levels of education.

According to these recommendations, there would in future only be English-Malay primary schools in the country which would be regarded as National Schools. Chinese and Tamil primary schools would be phased out.

The report raised a storm of protest from the Chinese community. Especially agitated were Chinese school teachers. Their organizations in the various states and settlements in the federation banded together and established a Hua Xiao Jiao Shi Hui Zong Hui [United Chinese School Teachers' Association, hereafter UCSTA] to defend the interests of Chinese education. The UCSTA embraced three declared aims, *viz* the reform of Chinese education, the propagation of Chinese culture and the advancement of the welfare of Chinese school teachers, thus setting off a Chinese education movement. It was inaugurated on 25 December 1951 and was to play a leading role in the development of Chinese education in the years ahead. One of the leading lights of this newly formed organization was a teacher from the Zun Kong School in Kuala Lumpur, Lim Lian Geok. In 1953, Lim got elected to be the president of the organization after two previous presidents, and became the life and soul of the UCSTA.[58]

The Fenn-Wu Report

Because of the protest of the Chinese community against the Barnes Report, the British High Commissioner appointed a committee to study the situation of the Chinese schools and make recommendations. The committee consisted of only two members, W.P. Fenn, an educationist from the United States of America, and T.Y. Wu, an official from the United Nations. Fenn and Wu came up with a report which, in recommendations, differed vastly from those of the Barnes Report.[59]

Summarized below is the essence of what Fenn and Wu recommended:

(1)   The Chinese were ready to learn not only Chinese, but also English and Malay. They should be encouraged in this inclination.

(2)   Any attempt to force unwilling fusion among the different races would only lead to further cleavage.

(3)   It was true that the Chinese schools suffered from a China-consciousness, inadequately trained and inadequately paid teachers, as well as poor equipment.

(4)   To resolve the problem of Chinese schools having a China conscious-ness, a Committee for Revision and Preparation of Textbooks for Use in Chinese Schools should be set up to produce Chinese school textbooks with a Malayan background, to replace those produced in China, so as to promote a Malayan consciousness among Chinese school students.

(5) To resolve the problem of inadequately trained teachers, a National Institute should be established to which selected Chinese educators should be sent for training. These educators, when trained, would staff refresher institutes and teacher training institutes. Eight Chinese educators should also be sent abroad annually for training, and immigration laws should be made flexible enough to allow a limited number of Chinese scholars to enter the country to lecture. In the long term, a teacher training institution should also be established. Initially, this institution would concentrate on preparing teachers for Chinese schools, but ultimately it would become a non-communal school for all races.

(6) To resolve the problem of inadequately paid teachers, qualified teachers in Chinese primary schools should be supported by the government to such an extent that the schools would them-selves be able to provide equally satisfactory terms of service for all others.

(7) As for poor equipment, the government should increase its subsidies to Chinese schools by 100 per cent in 1952 and by another 100 per cent in the following year.

(8) An ad hoc committee should also be formed to deal with problems found commonly in Chinese schools, and to cooperate constructively with the government.

(9) The present instruction in the Chinese, English, and Malay languages was not satisfactory. Programmes to improve such must be devised. In the cases of Chinese and English, two teams of experts should be engaged to develop better textbooks as well as to introduce modern teaching methods.

The Fenn-Wu Report, when released, was met with both praise and contempt from the Chinese community. There were some who were happy because it defended Chinese education, but there were also some who felt that the Report did not go far enough in that defence.[60]

Second Report of the Central Advisory Committee on Education

Because of the great divergence in views of the Barnes and the Fenn-Wu Reports, the government thought it wise not to present them to the Federal Legislative Council for deliberation in order to avoid disputes that might arise. Instead, it sent the two reports to the Central Advisory Committee on Education for it to assess and make recommendations accordingly. A new committee was constituted for the purpose under L.D. Whitfield who was the then acting director of education. Whitfield completed his mission and submitted what came to be known as the Second Report of the Central Advisory Committee on Education in September 1951.[61]

The Second Report of the Central Advisory Committee on Education sided with Barnes, and gave consideration to Fenn and Wu only marginally, and only in those areas where the latter took the same stand as the former. The gist of its opinions were:[62]

(1) Education through the Malay language should be elevated, and the Malay race should find its proper place among the other races in the country.

(2) National Schools should be of two kinds. They should use either English or Malay as their medium of instruction.

(3) Students in Chinese and Tamil primary schools should, for the first two years, be taught in their respective mother tongues, and learnt English as a subject. From the third year onwards, they should also learnt Malay as another subject.

(4) As for teacher training, candidates for admission should have passed the one-year post-Standard Nine class and have acquired a pass in the Malay language. Those with an additional pass in the Chinese or Tamil languages would be particularly welcome.

This in practice would mean that in future most teachers would had come from the National Schools. Teaching staff for the Chinese or Tamil primary schools would be those who had acquired a pass in the Chinese or Tamil language.

(5) Chinese and Tamil primary schools would fade away in the future. If the right methods and measures to bring this about were taken, the transition would be speeded up and would be welcomed by parents. These schools should be gradually transformed into National Schools.

(6) During the period of transition, the government should continue to extend financial assistance to Chinese and Tamil primary schools. Even when a sufficient number of National Schools had been set up, any racial group which wished to set up private non-National Schools should be allowed to do so.

The report also agreed that aid given to the Chinese schools should be increased by 100 per cent in 1951, and by another 100 per cent in 1952. It agreed as well with the suggestion that Chinese school teachers should be better paid.

(7) The contents of textbooks used in schools of all language streams should be the same.

It seemed that all these recommendations amounted to giving education through English the first place, Malay the second place, and Chinese or Tamil the third place.

As expected, because this Second Report of the Central Advisory Committee on Education was biased towards the Barnes Report, and unfavourable to the Fenn-Wu Report, it was severely criticized by the Chinese community.[63]

On the heels of Whitfield submitting his report, the government appointed a special committee to draft legislation to give effect to Whitfield's conclusions or such other conclusions that might be reached by the committee itself. This special committee was led by the then attorney-general M.J. Hogan.[64]

Hogan did not complete his work until October 1952. Meanwhile two events intervened to which we need to turn our attention first.

Chinese Primary School Textbooks Malayanized

The first event was that the government took steps to have textbooks used in Chinese primary schools malayanized. This was in line with the recommendations of the Fenn-Wu Report and the Second Report of the Central Advisory Committee on Education. In this effort, the Federation of Malaya and Singapore worked together. Several committees were set up for the purpose, and notable Chinese book publishers were mobilized to form a new company to publish the new textbooks.[65]

The syllabuses for the various school subjects were soon released. Hygiene and science and similar subjects did not arouse any dispute, but civics, history, and geography were sensitive. When finalized, the emphasis given in the latter three subjects to Malaya and Southeast Asia, China, the world at large, and "neutral" respectively for the six primary school years was as shown in Table 2.6.[66]

The proportion for China was limited.

The Chinese community accepted the need to malayanize textbooks used in their primary schools. In fact, several of the leaders of the UCSTA

Table 2.6
Emphasis Given to Different Regions for Civics, History, and Geography

Civics

Malaya & SEA	China	The World	"Neutral"
5 topics	0	3 topics	1 topic

History

Malaya & SEA	China	The World	
14 topics	3 topics	5 topics	

Geography

Malaya & SEA	China	The World	"Neutral"
5 topics	3 topics	3 topics	1 topic

Source: See note 66.

joined in the compilation effort. The only concern was that content relating to China would be thrown out in unlimited measure, but that was settled in the end.[67]

A New Salary Scheme for Chinese Primary School Teachers

Textbooks conditioned the minds of school students. So were the teachers. China-orientated teachers would mould their students to become China-orientated too. Hitherto, the appointment, transfer, promotion, and dismissal of teachers were in the hands of the management committees of the schools. That was because their salaries were paid by such committees. The government now saw it necessary to take away such powers from the committees and entrust this to itself. This would ensure that only acceptable teachers would be employed in the schools. So in mid-1952, the government announced that it would shoulder the responsibility of paying Chinese primary school teachers with a salary aid scheme which would be better than what such teachers were then getting from the school committees.[68]

The proposition was also a response to the Fenn-Wu Report and the Second Report of the Central Advisory Committee on Education, which had recommended that Chinese primary school teachers should be given improved service conditions.

Initially, the announcement was received positively by the Chinese community. But after a while, suspicion and fear crept in and the welcome turned to questioning and opposition. Teachers, school management committees, and MCA representatives met early in November to discuss the issue and formed a special committee to seek clarification from the government. The proposal was accepted only after the government had given an explanation and assured the Chinese community of its real intentions.

The explanation given was that the school management committees would be allowed to continue to exercise their powers over their teachers as before, but subject to the approval of the educational authorities. The assurance given was that, in the case of dismissing a teacher, only when the person concerned was thoroughly incompetent, or had behaved so badly as to affect the administration of the school or had been deregistered would he or she be dismissed. Both the explanation and the assurance did not touch on the issue of China orientation.

The Hogan Report and the 1952 Education Ordinance

As mentioned earlier, a special committee led by Attorney-General M.J. Hogan was appointed to present findings on the Second Report of the Central Advisory Committee on Education and to draft legislation to give effect to that report. Hogan submitted his work to the government in October 1952. In the month that followed, what he submitted was accepted and passed by the Federal Legislative Council. The legislation was termed the Education Ordinance, 1952. Below were what Hogan proposed and what was written into the education ordinance:[69]

(1) To establish National Schools. They would be of two kinds, *viz* one using English as the medium of instruction, and the other using Malay.

(2) Present English and Malay schools run by the government, on converting to National Schools, would use English and Malay as their medium of instruction respectively.

(3) English-medium National Schools would teach, as from the third year onwards, Malay as a subject. Malay-medium National Schools would teach, as from the first year onwards, English as a subject.

(4) The National Schools could teach Chinese and Tamil as separate subjects if requested by parents or guardians, and there must be at least fifteen students in the same standard who would study the chosen language.

(5) Government-aided English schools (these were mainly missionary schools) and some government-aided Chinese and Tamil schools should be encouraged to convert gradually to National Schools. Full aid would be given to them, but the Chinese and Tamil schools must abide by all the conditions set for National Schools and must teach English or Malay to their students.

(6) Even when National Schools had been established, the aided English, Chinese and Tamil schools could continue to function.

(7) Non-National Schools must abide by certain conditions pertaining to school premises, equipment, the recruitment and dismissal of students, curricula and medium of instruction, as well as conditions of service for teachers.

(8) In regions where a sufficient number of National Schools had been set up, children in that region between six and twelve years of age must enroll in such schools as a matter of compulsion. But, if there were special reasons, including religious reasons, parents, with permission from the educational authorities, could send their children to other schools. In regions where a sufficient number of National Schools had not been built, children who wished to join English schools would be given preference if they were locally born and of the correct school-going age.

(9) When National Schools were sufficiently built, grants-in-aid to Chinese and Tamil schools should be withdrawn.

(10) National Schools would be interracial. They would instil in the students a sense of Malayan consciousness.

(11) They would charge no fees.

(12) They would be compulsory.

(13) They would offer a course of six years of study.

The education ordinance also gave a definition of the term "National School". It said, "a 'national school' is any school providing for children of all races a six-year course of free primary education with a Malayan orientation and appropriate for children between the ages of six and twelve and using in the main for this purpose the official languages of the Federation and providing facilities for instruction in Kuo Yu and Tamil in accordance with the provisions of this section."

In addition to all the above, Hogan also made provisions for the organization of management committees for the schools, as well as the appointment of teachers and rules for their conduct.

Although accepted and passed by the Federal Legislative Council, Hogan's recommendations and the Education Ordinance could not be implemented. There were several reasons for this. One was that the government was short of finance to see the scheme through. Another was that if the Chinese and Tamil schools were to convert to National Schools straightway, there would not be enough qualified teachers to staff such schools. And a third was the strong opposition from the Chinese and Tamil communities. These were willing to have three languages taught in their schools, but were unwilling to be converted.[70]

Opposition from the Chinese community came as soon as Hogan's findings and draft law were released to the public, but before they were accepted and passed by the Federal Legislative Council. This was led by UCSTA. The opposition climaxed in early November 1952. We have seen earlier that, on that occasion, representatives of Chinese school teachers and school management committees, together with those from the MCA, met to tackle the issue of the New Salary Scheme for Chinese schools. In that meeting, they also discussed the Hogan proposals and his draft law, and sought ways to display their opposition. In fact, the participants were so worked up by Hogan that they spent most of their effort gossiping about him. At the meeting, Tan Cheng Lock, president of the MCA, took a bold stand on Chinese education for his party by saying that a man's native tongue was like his shadow, inseparable from his personality. He stated further that the MCA would fully support the development of Chinese education in the country. The meeting made a number of resolutions with the aim of getting those parts of Hogan's proposals harmful to Chinese education revised before the proposals were accepted and passed by the Legislative Council. A memorandum was to be presented to the high commissioner and members of the council for the purpose and this was done immediately after the meeting. The gathering also issued a declaration to the public to oppose Hogan's proposals as they stood. One other important decision the meeting made was to set up a joint organization of the three parties to work for the better protection and advancement of Chinese education.[71]

The Formation of the Malayan Chinese Association Chinese Education Central Committee

In April the following year, the three parties met again to effect the formation of the proposed joint organization. There was debate between the representatives of the school teachers and school management committees on the one hand, and those from the MCA on the other, on the status of the proposed organization. Should it be an independent body or should it be a subcommittee of the MCA? The teachers and the school management committee members favoured the first idea whereas the MCA was keen on the second. One reason, among several others that the former preferred the first option, was that members of the MCA who sat on the Legislative Council as representatives of the Chinese community did not oppose Hogan's proposals and his draft law when these came up for debate, so they had no confidence that the MCA would really stand up for Chinese education. Tan Cheng Lock went to great lengths to persuade and assure the doubters that the MCA would really be the champion of their cause in the end. Finally, his words were accepted and a decision was made that the joint organization should be put under the control of the MCA. It would consist of representatives from all three parties. Its name would be the Malayan Chinese Association Chinese Education Central Committee, or the MCACECC in short.[72]

Two months after the MCACECC was established, Tan Cheng Lock wrote to the high commissioner, Gerald Templer, to request for the revision of clauses in the 1952 Education Ordinance that were harmful to Chinese education, listing eight reasons for his plea. The high commissioner rebuffed him and rebutted his arguments. In face of this, the MCACECC made a decision to take various steps to continue with the protest, as well as to accept an offer from the Malayan Indian Congress (MIC), a political party which represented the interests of the Indian community, to join hands to combat the Education Ordinance. In May 1953, in the name of Tan Cheng Lock, the president of the MCA, a Memorandum on Chinese Education in the Federation of Malaya was presented to Templer as a response to his reply to Tan. However, the memorandum fell on deaf ears.[73]

The United Chinese School Committees' Association

A very significant event to emerge out of the great turmoil of the opposition to the 1952 Education Ordinance was the birth of the Hua Xiao Dong Shi Lian He Hui Zong Hui [United Chinese School Committee's Association, hereafter the UCSCA] on 22 August 1954. Earlier on, we mentioned the New Salary Scheme for Chinese primary school teachers. The scheme had the projected effect of taking away the powers of school committees to hire, dismiss, promote, or transfer teachers. This upset them a great deal. Immediately, they got together to form associations to defend their powers. Later, the government conceded to their resentment by amending its original proposal, but suspicion, anxiety, and fear prevailed. When the dispute over the 1952 Education Ordinance surfaced, it catapulted the ill feeling into the formation of the UCSCA. The dissatisfaction against the 1952 Education Ordinance was the immediate cause of the UCSCA's formation.[74]

The school management committees had already taken common action, together with the school teachers and the MCA, against the 1952 Education Ordinance and had set up the MCACECC in the process as just mentioned. Now after its establishment, it became an even closer ally of the teachers and MCA. Thereafter, in the common struggle to uphold Chinese education in the years ahead, the three were always referred to as the Three Big Organizations.

Chinese to be an Official Language?

Another development to emerge out of the opposition to the 1952 Education Ordinance was the birth of a clamour from the Chinese community for their language to be recognized as an official language of the country. By the terms of the Federation of Malaya Agreement, a contract made between the British and the Malays, only English and Malay were designated official languages. Chinese and Tamil were not.

In November 1952, after the 1952 Education Ordinance was promulgated, the British deputy high commissioner to the Federation of Malaya at the time, Donald MacGillivray, invited the UCSTA to send representatives to meet him. A delegation of four went, led by Lim Lian Geok. In the meeting, Lim asked MacGillivray whether the Chinese were considered nationals of the country. MacGillivray answered yes. Lim asked further whether the Chinese language could be used to educate these nationals. MacGillivray replied no, in accordance with the terms of the Federation of Malaya Agreement. Lim queried why. MacGillivray said that it was because Chinese was not an official language. The dialogue made Lim realize that to protect Chinese education, it was necessary to get Chinese recognize as an official language in the country.[75]

On 18 August 1954, the committee of the teachers' association in Kuala Lumpur held a meeting. On that occasion, Lim Lian Geok made an appeal to the Chinese community to fight for their language to be made an official language. The response to his appeal was enthusiastic, and the movement, once initiated, lasted for decades to come.[76]

Council Paper No. 67 of 1954 on Educational Policy

It has been noted that the 1952 Education Ordinance could not be implemented as expected, and one of the reasons for this was that the government was short of funds. The government's difficulty arose because in 1953, the prices of rubber and tin, the two most important exports of the country, fell. It was then thought necessary to appoint a committee to find ways to implement the ordinance in the best possible way within a reduced budget. This committee was duly appointed under the chairmanship of the then member for education in the Executive Council, E.E.C. Thuraisingham.

Thuraisingham's findings were released to the public in September 1954, and accepted and passed by the Legislative Council the following month. The recommendations were:[77]

(1) To introduce National School features into vernacular schools, including Malay schools, that is, to run English classes in these schools, in addition to their regular vernacular classes, to which children of all races would be admitted. Such English classes would be regarded as National-Type classes.

(2) By the introduction of such classes, the vernacular schools would be converted gradually to National Schools, using English as the medium of instruction. The procedure would be to start with Primary One classes in the vernacular schools in 1955. Such classes would be taught by trained English teachers. The following year, new Primary One classes would repeat the practice. And this was to go on until finally these English classes would replace the vernacular classes altogether.

(3) To give preference to vernacular schools over government and aided English schools (that is, aided English missionary schools) in the matter of conversion as these were already virtually English-medium National-Type schools.

(4) The general standard of vernacular education was low. The sooner National-Type Education could be provided, the better it would be for everyone.

(5) The provision of National-Type Education was bound to be slow, so vernacular education could continue to provide an education to a portion of the annually increasing school population.

(6) The problem now was how to allow the continuance of vernacular education without detriment to the expansion of National-Type Education, as the ever increasing costs of one type would be at the expense of all other types.

(7) To extend training facilities to teachers.

The member for education also defined what a National School should be: (1) it would admit students of all races to receive a primary education; (2) it must teach English and Malay; (3) it could also teach Chinese and Tamil if a requisite number of students requested for it; (4) it should impart religious or ethical knowledge; and (5) it would provide free and compulsory education.[78]

Thuraisingaham's paper stated too that:

> Government at this stage proposes to seek the agreement of the Council for certain measures in order that the necessary programme to give effect to them may be included in the Budget for 1955, which is to be presented at the next meeting of the Council and the Council will, therefore, be asked to give specific approval for the following:
> (a) The introduction of National School features into vernacular schools, particularly by means of the establishment of English medium classes ...

As expected, the Council Paper No. 67 of 1954 on educational policy — Thuraisingham's recommendations were given this name after they were passed and accepted by the Legislative Council — stirred up a hornet's nest in the Chinese community. Leading in the struggle against the council paper was Lim Lian Geok and his UCSTA. Lim and other representatives from his organization saw the director of education, Whitfield, over the matter and, when given unsatisfactory answers to queries, issued a call first to all Chinese schools in Selangor to resist conversion, and, second, a declaration to Chinese schools in the whole country to resist. The whole Chinese community was aroused.[79]

Regardless of the feelings of the Chinese community, in November that year, Whitfield announced that, in 1955, the government would set aside ten million dollars to establish 250 English classes in the various vernacular schools. He also instructed the state education authorities to find out how many vernacular schools would want to have such classes and how many classes each would have.[80]

Finally, Tan Cheng Lock of the MCA also voiced his protest, and the Malay and Indian communities also rose up to demonstrate their displeasure.[81]

In August 1955, the country achieved self-government, followed quickly by a Malay minister forming a committee to produce a new education report, and soon the Council Paper No. 67 of 1954 on educational policy was given up.[82]

However, before self-government came, attempts were made to pressurize the Chinese schools, as well as the Tamil and Malay schools, to start English classes. One occasion was in January 1955 when three officials from the Education Department in Selangor, accompanied by district officers from the district of Ulu Selangor, met the chairman of the management committee and the headmaster of the Sam Yuk Chinese Primary School in Rawang, as well as the chairmen and headmasters of the Tamil and Malay schools there to try to persuade them to open English classes. The threat was held out that if they refused to cooperate, the government assistance given to them would be affected. The meeting was confidential, but the Chinese press got wind of it and raked up a storm of protest in the Chinese community. The management committee of Sam Yuk reported the matter to the UCSCA and the UCSTA. The UCSCA decided to protest the move and the MCACECC was also dragged in. What followed was that officials from the Education Department visited the management committee of the Sam Yuk Chinese Primary School to explain their real intention. The transaction was again reported to the UCSCA by the Sam Yuk management committee, which instructed it not to trust the words of the officials. The requested English class in the Sam Yuk was, therefore, not opened, and the whole matter was dropped.[83]

Another occasion was a month later when the Ministry of Education announced that any Chinese school with new Chinese classes to be started from that year would be treated as *de facto* new and separate schools. They would not receive any government grants. Besides that, they must be registered with the government as non-aided schools, although the supervisors and management committee members of the original school could also be their supervisors and management committee members. They must have their own separate classrooms; their own separate finances which would be examined by the government; must, on maturity, have their own headmasters; and the teachers of the original school must not also teach in them. The purpose of it all was to discourage these schools from putting newly recruited students into Chinese classes.

As expected, the endeavour also met with strenuous opposition from the UCSTA, the UCSCA, the MCACECC, and the Chinese community at large. Efforts were made to pacific them but to no avail. In the end, the director of education, E.M.F. Payne, met with representatives of the management committee members of the schools to talk things over. Payne moderated his stand. The most important concession he made was to allow the new, non-aided Chinese classes to apply for aid whenever the finances of the government became sound. The other restrictions were also modified so much so that they were no longer restrictions. The commotion died down thereafter.[84]

The Establishment of the Nanyang University

It was a strange phenomenon that while, on the one hand, there was persistent effort from the government to try to convert the Chinese primary schools into National Schools, there was, on the other hand, a cry from the Chinese community to establish a Chinese university to provide further education for students who were graduating from the various Chinese secondary schools.

The need to build a university for graduating Chinese secondary school students came about because of the following developments. Traditionally, such students went to China to join colleges or universities there, but, after 1952, this was no longer possible. This was because in that year the government passed an immigration law which prohibited Chinese from visiting China. This was, of course, a response to the fact that China had since 1949 came under communist rule. Another reason was that the population in Chinese secondary schools, along with that in primary schools, kept increasing. The two factors produced a situation which caused concern.[85]

In 1949, the government set up the University of Malaya, but that was only to accommodate graduates from English secondary schools. Those from Chinese secondary schools, for various reasons, were denied admission. This university was later to start a Department of Chinese Studies for the benefit of Chinese secondary graduates. However, this was not a real solution to the problem.[86]

Even as early as September 1950, Tan Lark Sye, the president of the Hokkien Association in Singapore, had broached the idea of founding such a university. On 16 January 1953, he raised the issue again and pledged five million dollars of his personal wealth for the purpose. Later on, the Hokkien Association donated 500 acres of its land to build the campus. The proposal received widespread support from the Chinese community, including Tan Cheng Lock, president of MCA. Chinese people from all walks of life, from wealthy businessmen to ordinary workers, from students to cabaret hostesses, donated their earnings or helped raise funds for the project.[87]

While Tan Lark Sye was vastly supported by the Chinese community, he was opposed by the British and the Malays. Malcolm MacDonald, the commissioner-general in British Southeast Asia at the time, tried to persuade Tan to go slow. Sydney Caine, vice-chancellor of the University of Malaya, voiced his disagreement and engaged in a debate with Tan Cheng Lock over the issue. E.E.C. Thuraisingham, member for education in the Executive Council, protested that what Tan Lark Sye was trying to do contravened the education policy of the government. Malay dissatisfaction was voiced most loudly by UMNO, which said that the move was an insult to the Malays and would worsen relations between the Chinese and the Malay communities.[88]

Regardless of the commotion created around it, the university was finally established and classes officially began on 15 March 1956. It was named the Nanyang University.[89]

THE MALACCA MEETING AND SELF-GOVERNMENT

It was observed that after the Malayan Union was abandoned and the Federation of Malaya had replaced it, because of Malay opposition, and faced with a rebellion led by the communists, the trend in political development in the peninsula was for the British to yield more and more to Malay pressure until the country was given self-government. That came in July 1955.

The movement to demand self-government from the British was led by Tunku Abdul Rahman, who had replaced Dato Onn as president of UMNO in August 1951. That came about because, that year, Dato Onn suggested to UMNO that it should change its name to the United Malayan Organization so that it could admit non-Malays into its ranks and become a non-racial body. His proposal was rejected, whereupon he left the party and formed the Independence of Malaya Party or IMP, together with Tan Cheng Lock of the MCA. With the departure of Dato Onn, Tunku Abdul Rahman was elected the new president of UMNO.[90]

In 1952, there was an election for the Kuala Lumpur Municipal Council. UMNO took part in the contest, and was joined by the MCA as an ally. By then, Tan Cheng Lock had broken off from Dato Onn and lined up with Tunku Abdul Rahman. The two parties won an overwhelming victory.[91] Two years later, UMNO and MCA were joined by the MIC, and the three formed an Alliance Party.[92]

At the time, the Federal Legislative Council was made up of officials and nominated non-officials. Because the number of non-officials chosen from the IMP was greater than those chosen from UMNO and MCA, Tunku Abdul Rahman in May 1954 led a delegation to London to demand that, by the end of the year, the council should become an elected body in part. He failed in his mission. On its return, the delegation withdrew all their party members from the Legislative Council as well as the various state councils. In face of this, MacGillivray, who had replaced Gerald Templer as the high commissioner, conceded to him and announced that elections to the Legislative Council would be held in July 1955.[93]

To ensure victory in the coming election, Tunku Abdul Rahman felt that he must secure the support of Chinese voters. As UCSTA and UCSCA had great influence over the Chinese community, UMNO and MCA invited the two organizations to send representatives to a meeting to thrash things out, especially the issue of making Chinese an official language. The meeting was to be held on 12 January 1955 in Tan Cheng Lock's residence in Malacca.[94]

Taking advantage of the favourable situation and before sending representatives to attend the Malacca meeting, UCSTA issued a letter to all Chinese school teachers and parents of Chinese students in the country to give support to three demands that it wished to make on candidates in the election. The three demands were: (1) Chinese education should be treated as equal to the education of other races; (2) that free elementary education should be provided in the mother tongue, and, in the case of non-English schools, to have English as a compulsory subject for study; and (3) the Chinese language, used by half of the population in the country, should be made an official language.[95]

When the meeting was held, Lim Lian Geok went further to exert pressure on UMNO by making a number of observations. He stated first that English was not the common language in the country because it was not the language of the greatest number of people. The first common language was Malay and the second was Chinese. And the use of a common language should not obstruct the development of the mother tongue. He next said that unifying the various races physically was not the way to build a new nation, but having common interests among them was. He then went on to ask for the replacement of the 1952 Education Ordinance with a new education policy which every race could accept. Following this, he further pointed out that Chinese education was a product of the effort of the Chinese community itself; that graduates from Chinese schools who went abroad to study did not perform less well than graduates from the English schools; that textbooks used in the Chinese schools were already malayanized and were teaching students to be loyal to Malaya; and that Chinese schools were already teaching students Chinese, English, and Malay and were recognized by the high commissioner as already possessing features of National Schools.[96]

The meeting discussed three main issues, *viz* the Education Ordinance, recognizing Chinese as an official language, and the government giving another two million dollars to support Chinese schools. After much deliberation, the parties agreed on the following:[97]

(1) If the Alliance were to win power, it would revise all education laws unfavourable to the Chinese schools, including the 1952 Education Ordinance and the 1954 Legislative Council paper on educational policy, so that the Chinese could preserve their schools, language, and culture;

(2) In the Alliance's election manifesto, it would be stated that the schools, language, and culture of any race would not be destroyed;

(3) In 1955, the Chinese schools would get two million dollars as aid and development fund; and

(4) That Chinese educationists not raise the issue of getting recognition for the Chinese language as an official language between then and the election at the end of July.

Although there were four items agreed, at the conclusion of the meeting, the negotiating parties chose to reveal only items one and two to the public. The other two were kept under wraps.[98]

On 27 July 1955, the election was duly held. The Alliance Party won fifty-one of the fifty-two seats open to contest. On 9 August, a new government with Tunku Abdul Rahman as chief minister was sworn into office, and the country achieved self-government.[99]

After the formation of the new government, Tunku Abdul Rahman reneged on item three.[100]

It is perhaps noteworthy that, from 1941 to 1955, the Chinese schools, along with them the Chinese language and Chinese culture, in Malaya did not disappear. They actually disappeared for a while during the Japanese Occupation, but were revived and even grew further after the Japanese lost power and gave Malaya back to the British. After the war, for a brief period during the time of the Malayan Union, there was no development which threatened their survival. However, after the establishment of the Federation of Malaya and the outbreak of the Malayan Communist Party uprising, against the international background of the Chinese Communist Party taking over power in China, they began to feel pressure. The factor which worked against them was their China orientation. Soon there emerged a movement to try to convert them, as well as Tamil schools, into National Schools, that is, English or Malay schools. The real danger came with the 1952 Education Ordinance and the 1954 Legislative Council paper on educational policy. Fortunately, they survived and all that they had to concede was to have the textbooks they used malayanized, that is, cleansed of their China orientation. In addition, the Chinese went on to found a university. Also of great significance was the emergence of UCSTA, MCACECC, and UCSCA, which were all born out of the commotion surrounding the proposal to have the Chinese schools converted.

Notes

1. Kua Kia Soong, *A Protean Saga: The Chinese Schools of Malaysia* (Kuala Lumpur, 1985) (hereafter Kua Kia Soong, op. cit. 1), pp. 46 and 48; Cheah Boon Keng, *Red Star over Malaya* (Singapore, 1983), pp. 22–23.
2. Zheng Liang Shu, *Ma Lai Xi Ya Hua Wen Jiao Yu Fa Zan Shi*, vol. 2 (Kuala Lumpur, 1999), pp. 413–15; vol. 3, p. 6.
3. Shu Yun-Tsiao and Chua Ser-Koon, ed., *Malayan Chinese Resistance to Japan, 1937–1945: Selected Source Materials* (Singapore, 1984), p. 52.
4. Kua Kia Soong, *Ma Lai Xi Ya Hua Jiao Fen Dou Shi* (Kuala Lumpur, 1991) (hereafter Kua Kia Soong, op. cit. 2), p. 42; Zheng Liang Shu, op. cit., vol. 2, pp. 416 and 419.
5. Shu Yun-Tsiao and Chua Ser-Koon, op. cit., p. 52.
6. Zheng Liang Shu, op. cit., vol. 2, p. 422.
7. Zheng Liang Shu, op. cit., vol. 2, p. 419.
8. Kua Kia Soong, op. cit. 2, p. 42.
9. V.M. Hooker, *A Short History of Malaysia* (Crows Nest, NSW, Australia, 2003), pp. 186–87.
10. C.M. Turnbull, *A History of Singapore, 1819–1975* (Kuala Lumpur, 1977), pp. 222 and 235.
11. C.M. Turnbull, op. cit., p. 220.
12. Tan Teng Jin et al., *The Chinese Malaysian Contribution* (Kuala Lumpur, 2005), p. 250; James Wong Weng On, *From Pacific War to Merdeka* (Kuala Lumpur, 2005), p. 8; Yang Pei Gen, "Ma Lai Ya zhi Chun, 1945–1958", in *Oriental News*, 2–3 October 2006; Tan Liok Ee, *The Politics of Chinese Education* (New York, 1977), p. 44.
13. Yang Pei Gen, op. cit., 23–24 October 2006 and 8 November 2006; V.M. Hooker, op. cit., pp. 187–88.
14. Yang Pei Gen, op. cit., 8 October 2006, 23–24 October 2006 and 10 November 2006; V.M. Hooker, op. cit., pp. 190–91.
15. V.M. Hooker, op. cit., pp. 188 and 191; Kua Kia Soong, op. cit. 1, p. 52.
16. V.M. Hooker, op. cit., p. 188; Kua Kia Soong, op. cit. 1, pp. 52–53; Zheng Liang Shu, op. cit., vol. 3, p. 80.
17. V.M. Hooker, op. cit., p. 188.
18. Zheng Liang Shu, op. cit., vol. 3, pp. 1–6, 11–14, 18–20 and 33.

19   *Nanyang Siang Pau*, 19 October 1946 and 21 November 1946. Zheng Liang Shu, op. cit., vol. 3, pp. 31–35.

20   *Nanyang Siang Pau*, 1–2 July 1946. Lim Lian Geok, *Feng Yu Shi Ba Nian*, vol. 1 (Kuala Lumpur, 1988) (hereafter Lim Lian Geok, op. cit., vol. 1), p. 22; Zheng Liang Shu, op. cit., vol. 3, pp. 21–30.

21   Adapted from Malayan Union, *Annual Report on Education*, for the years 1946 and 1947 (Kuala Lumpur: 1946 and 1947); and Federation of Malaya, *Annual Report on Education*, for the years 1948 to 1955 (Kuala Lumpur: 1948–55).

22   Adapted from Zheng Liang Shu, op. cit., vol. 3, p. 38.

23   *Council Paper No. 53 of 1946*, reprinted as Appendix XV in Malayan Union, *Annual Report on Education in the Malayan Union for the Period 1st April 1946 to 31st December 1946* (Kuala Lumpur, 1947); Zheng Liang Shu, op. cit. vol. 3, pp. 81–82.

24   Ibid. Tan Liok Ee, op. cit., pp. 47–48.

25   Ibid.

26   Mok Soon Sang, op. cit., p. 45; Zheng Liang Shu, op. cit., vol. 3, p. 82.

27   *Nanyang Siang Pau*, 11 November 1946; Zheng Liang Shu, op. cit., vol. 3, p. 50.

28   *Sin Chew Daily*, 23 December 1947; Zheng Liang Shu, op. cit., vol. 3, pp. 50–60.

29   Zheng Liang Shu, op. cit., vol. 3, pp. 56–57.

30   *Nanyang Siang Pau*, 19 February 1949; Zheng Liang Shu, op. cit., vol. 3, p. 57.

31   *Nanyang Siang Pau*, 3 March 1950; Zheng Liang Shu, op. cit., vol. 3, pp. 58–59.

32   *Nanyang Siang Pau*, 18 March 1951; Zheng Liang Shu, op. cit., vol. 3, p. 136.

33   Zheng Liang Shu, op. cit., vol. 3, pp. 135–36; Francis Wong Hoy Kee and Ee Tiang Hong: *Education in Malaysia*, 2nd edition, (Kuala Lumpur, 1975), pp. 52–55.

34   Zheng Liang Shu, op. cit., vol. 3, p. 59. Francis Wong Hoy Kee and Ee Tiang Hong, op. cit., p. 59.

35   Zheng Liang Shu, op. cit., vol. 3, pp. 59–60.

36   Federation of Malaya, *First Report of the Central Advisory Committee on Education* (Council Paper No. 29 of 1950), Para. 19: Summary of Recommendations; Tan Liok Ee, op. cit., pp. 48–49; Zheng Liang Shu, op. cit., vol. 3, pp. 82–83; UCSTA, *Jiao Zong 33 Nian* (Kuala Lumpur, 1987), p. 293.

37   Federation of Malaya, *First Report of the Central Advisory Committee on Education* (Council Paper No. 29 of 1950), Para. 19: Summary of Recommendations.

38   Zheng Liang Shu, op. cit., vol. 3, p. 83; Tan Liok Ee, op. cit., p. 49.

39   Ibid.

40   Yang Pei Gen, op. cit., 16 November 2006; Zheng Liang Shu, op. cit., vol. 3, pp. 70–71.

41   Federation of Malaya, *Registration of Schools* (Kuala Lumpur, 1950). Zheng Liang Shu, op. cit., vol. 3, pp. 70–77.

42 Ibid.
43 *Sin Chew Daily* & *Nanyang Siang Pau*, 1 June 1950–16 August 1950; Zheng
    Liang Shu, op. cit., vol. 3, pp. 76–77; UCSTA, op. cit., p. 292.
44 Ibid.
45 Zheng Liang Shu, op. cit., vol. 3, p. 65.
46 Ibid., pp. 65–66; *Six-Year Education Plan* in Yu Shu Kuen et al., *Nanyang
    Nian Jian*, third section, pp. 247–48.
47 *Six-Year Education Plan* in Yu Shu Kuen et al., *Nanyang Nian Jian*, third section,
    pp. 246–48.
48 Ibid, p. 66.
49 Ibid, p. 68. *Nanyang Siang Pau*, 15 July 1950.
50 Zheng Liang Shu, op. cit., vol. 3, p. 69.
51 *Nanyang Siang Pau*, 15 July 1950, editorial.
52 Zheng Liang Shu, op. cit., vol. 3, p. 69.
53 Tan Liok Ee, op. cit., p. 116; Tan Teng Jin et al., op. cit., p. 252.
54 *China Press*, 1 January 1951; UCSTA, op. cit., pp. 293–94 and 306; Zheng
    Liang Shu, op. cit., vol. 3, pp. 115–18.
55 UCSTA, op. cit., pp. 294 and 306; Zheng Liang Shu, op. cit., vol 3,
    pp. 118–27.
56 Zheng Liang Shu, vol. 3, op. cit., p. 85; Tan Liok Ee, op. cit., p. 58.
57 Federation of Malaya, *Report of the Committee on Malay Education* (Kuala
    Lumpur, 1951), Chapter XII: Summary of Recommendations and Suggestions;
    UCSTA, op. cit., pp. 306–07 and 855–56.
58 UCSTA, op. cit., pp. 6–8, 12–14, 23–37, 177–79, 295–304, 308–09 and 325.
59 Federation of Malaya, *Report of a Mission Invited by the Federation Government
    to Study the Problems of the Education of the Chinese in Malaya: Chinese Schools
    and the Education of Chinese Malaysians* (Kuala Lumpur, 1951), Chapter VII:
    Conclusion.
60 Zheng Liang Shu, op. cit., vol. 3, pp. 151–56; UCSTA, op. cit., pp. 307–08
    and 325.
61 Tan Liok Ee, op. cit., pp. 59–60; Zheng Liang Shu, op. cit., vol. 3, pp. 157–58.
62 Kua Kia Soong, op. cit. 1, pp. 61–62; Zheng Liang Shu, op. cit., vol. 3,
    pp. 158–62; UCSTA, op. cit., pp. 308 and 325.
63 Zheng Liang Shu, op. cit., vol. 3, pp. 163–68; UCSTA, op. cit., pp. 325–26.
64 Zheng Liang Shu, op. cit., vol. 3, p. 168; UCSTA, op. cit., p. 325.
65 *Sin Chew Daily*, 1 January 1953; UCSTA, op. cit., pp. 321–23; Zheng Liang
    Shu, op. cit., vol. 3, pp. 169–70.
66 Lim Lian Geok, op. cit., vol. 1, pp. 35–42; Zheng Liang Shu, op. cit., vol. 3.
    pp. 175–77.
67 Ibid. *Sin Chew Daily*, 22 December 1951, editorial; UCSTA, op. cit., pp. 321–23
    and 356–57.
68 UCSTA, op. cit., pp. 309–12, 323–25 and 353–56; Zheng Liang Shu, op. cit.,
    vol. 3, pp. 178–89.

69 Federation of Malaya, *Report of the Special Committee Appointed on the 20th Day of September, 1951 to Recommend Legislation to Cover All Aspects of Educational Policy for the Federation of Malaya* (Kuala Lumpur, 1952); Federation of Malaya, *Education Ordinance*, 1952 (No. 63 of 1952) (Kuala Lumpur, 1952), pp. 594–95; UCSTA, op. cit., pp. 325–26 and 857–58; Zheng Liang Shu, op. cit., vol. 3, pp. 189–92.

70 Mok Soon Sang, op. cit., pp. 48–49; Tan Liok Ee, op. cit., pp. 70–73; UCSTA, op. cit., pp. 352–53.

71 UCSTA, op. cit., pp. 312–19, 325–26, 352–53 and 357–59; Zheng Liang Shu, op. cit., vol. 3, pp. 192–11; Tan Liok Ee, op. cit., pp. 134–37 and 144.

72 Lim Lian Geok, op. cit., vol. 1, pp. 61–73; UCSTA, op. cit., pp. 327–36; Tan Liok Ee, op. cit., pp. 137–43; Zheng Liang Shu, op. cit., vol. 3, pp. 235–44.

73 UCSTA, op. cit., pp. 336–48; Zheng Liang Shu, op. cit., vol. 3, pp. 244–50. Tan Liok Ee, op. cit., pp. 144–45.

74 UCSCA, *Dong Zong 50 Nian*; (Kajang, 2004) (hereafter UCSCA, op. cit. 1), pp. 40 and 204; UCSTA, op. cit., p. 348. *Sin Chew Daily*, 23 August 1954.

75 Zheng Liang Shu, op. cit., vol 3, pp. 204–05 and 251–53.

76 Zheng Liang Shu, op. cit., vol 3, pp. 252–53.

77 Federation of Malaya, *Report of the Special Committee Appointed by the High Commissioner in Council to Consider Ways and Means of Implementing the Policy Outlined in the Education Ordinance, 1952, in the Context of Diminishing Financial Resources of the Federation, 1954* (Council Paper No. 67 of 1954) (Kuala Lumpur, 1954), p. 21; UCSTA, op. cit., pp. 858–59; *Nanyang Siang Pau*, 29 September 1954 and 8 October 1954. *Sin Chew Daily*, 7 October 1954; Zheng Liang Shu, op. cit., vol. 3, pp. 260–62.

78 Zheng Liang Shu, op. cit., vol. 3, p. 262.

79 Lim Lian Geok, op. cit., vol. 1, pp. 95–106; *Nanyang Siang Pau*, 13 October 1954, 19 October 1954 and 31 October 1954–15 November 1954; *Sin Chew Daily*, 19 October 1954 and 31 October 1954–15 November 1954; *China Press* and *Xing Bin Ri Bao*, 19 October 1954; UCSTA, op. cit., pp. 348–50, 353, 357–59 and 367–69; Zheng Liang Shu, op. cit., vol. 3, pp. 262–69; Tan Liok Ee, op. cit., pp. 152–53.

80 *Nanyang Siang Pau*, 21 October 1954; Zheng Liang Shu, op. cit., vol. 3, p. 269.

81 *Nanyang Siang Pau*, 8 November 1954 and 25 December 1954; *Sin Chew Daily*, 25 December 1954 and 14 January 1955; *China Press*, 1 January 1956; UCSTA, op. cit., p. 369; Tan Liok Ee, op. cit., pp. 153–54; Zheng Liang Shu, op. cit., vol. 3, pp. 271–72.

82 Various Chinese newspapers of 15 September 1955; UCSTA, op. cit., p. 367.

83 UCSTA, op. cit., pp. 368–69; Zheng Liang Shu, op. cit., vol. 3, pp. 344–49.

84 UCSTA, op. cit., pp. 370–71; Zheng Liang Shu, op. cit., vol. 3, pp. 349–58.

85 Zheng Liang Shu, op. cit., vol. 3, pp. 212–17.

86 Zheng Liang Shu, op. cit., vol. 3, pp. 217–18.

[87] UCSCA, *Feng Yun Ji Dang Yi Bai Ba Shi Nian* (Kajang, 2001), pp. 16–18 (hereafter UCSCA, op. cit. 2); *Nanyang Siang Pau*, 10 September 1950, 10 November 1952 and 17 January 1953; *Sin Chew Daily*, 10 November 1952 and 17 January 1953; *China Press*, 10 November 1952 and 20 January 1953; *Xing Bin Ri Bao*, 10 November 1952; Zheng Liang Shu, op. cit., vol. 3, pp. 218–32.

[88] Zheng Liang Shu, op. cit., vol. 3, pp. 227–29.

[89] Zheng Liang Shu, op. cit., vol. 3, p. 234; UCSTA, op. cit., pp. 14–20.

[90] V.M. Hooker, op. cit., pp. 191 and 204.

[91] V.M. Hooker, op. cit., p. 204.

[92] Ibid.

[93] Tan Liok Ee, op. cit., pp. 71–72.

[94] UCSTA, op. cit., p. 369; Zheng Liang Shu, op. cit., vol. 3, pp. 273–74; Tan Liok Ee, op. cit., p. 155.

[95] UCSTA, op. cit., pp. 350–51.

[96] Lim Lian Geok, op. cit., vol. 1, pp. 108–09; UCSTA, op. cit., pp. 276–79; Tan Liok Ee, op. cit., p. 156.

[97] Lim Lian Geok, op. cit., vol. 1, pp. 110–13; UCSTA, op. cit., pp. 361–64 and 370; Zheng Liang Shu, op. cit., vol. 3, pp. 279–88; Tan Liok Ee, op. cit., pp. 156–57.

[98] *Nanyang Siang Pau*, 13 January 1955; Lim Lian Geok, op. cit., vol. 1, pp. 111–13.

[99] Lim Lian Geok, op. cit., vol. 1, p. 115; Zheng Liang Shu, op. cit., vol. 3, p. 293; V.M. Hooker, op. cit., p. 205.

[100] Lim Lian Geok, op. cit., vol. 1, pp. 115–18; Zheng Liang Shu, op. cit., vol. 3, p. 293.

3

TOWARDS THE "ULTIMATE OBJECTIVE" OF ONE-MEDIUM EDUCATION

The self-government granted by the British to the Alliance Party in 1955 was returning partial power to the local people of the country. This was followed two years later by the British relinquishing power altogether and Malaya becoming independent.

As to be expected, the political changes, like in previous times, had ramifications in the educational field. The Alliance Party was led by UMNO, a Malay organization. With power in its hands, UMNO aspired and took steps to pursue an "ultimate objective" in education, which was to use the Malay language as the main medium of instruction in all schools. This objective still holds today.

The objective was called ultimate because UMNO realized, for various reasons, that this could not be achieved overnight. It was ready to accommodate these various reasons and aimed to reach the objective only ultimately.

This chapter will attempt to chart the course which UMNO pursued to achieve its goal, as this impacted on Chinese education from the year 1955, when self-government was realized, to 1969, which was a turning point in the history of the country after which there were momentous changes again in the field of education. The Alliance Party was able to wrest self-government at first, and finally, even independence from the British because its component parties, UMNO, the MCA, and MIC, could reach a compromise amongst themselves on what should be the respective status of the Malay, Chinese, and Indian races in a new country. The understanding worked well for many years, but by 1969 each community had become dissatisfied with what the others were enjoying and an explosion occurred. Racial riots broke out.

TOWARDS INDEPENDENCE

Between 1955 and 1957, the Alliance Party led by Tunku Abdul Rahman, negotiated with the British for independence. The talks were successful and the country became independent on 31 August 1957, with the Tunku as the prime minister.[1]

In 1955, soon after obtaining self-government, Tunku Abdul Rahman also negotiated with the communists for an end to their uprising. By this time, the fight of the communists had got nowhere. The two sides could not agree on the terms of peace, however, and the talks failed. The posture adopted by the Tunku towards the communists, insisting on the dissolution of their party and the wounding up of their movement, satisfied the British, which contributed significantly to their agreeing to let Malaya become independent.[2]

During the process of the negotiations between the Alliance Party and the British, the latter appointed a commission, headed by a Lord Reid, to prepare a constitution for an independent Malaya. Simultaneously, the component parties in the Alliance Party negotiated among themselves on what status each of the communities which they represented should have in the projected new political set-up. Reid's commission took into account their compromises and agreements.[3]

In brief, what UMNO, the MCA, and MIC agreed on was that the Malays would enjoy political dominance in the country with the right to raise their economic position, while the Chinese and the Indians could continue with their business and other economic activities as before.[4]

THE ULTIMATE OBJECTIVE AND NEAR PARITY TREATMENT FOR SCHOOLS OF ALL LANGUAGE STREAMS

The Razak Report, 1956, and the Education Ordinance, 1957

Because of the burning urge to achieve the "ultimate objective" in education, the new government, after the electoral victory in 1955, promptly appointed a committee to review the education system in the country and devise a new set-up. It was headed by the then minister for education, Abdul Razak, and consisted of members from the component organizations of the

Alliance Party. The committee's report was accepted by the Legislative Council in June 1956 and became the basis for the enactment of an Education Ordinance in July the following year, just one month before the country became independent.[5] The report and the act took into account the agreements reached between UMNO and the Chinese educationists at the Malacca meeting in 1955, and the various promises on education reflecting those agreements, and declared in campaigning by the Alliance Party in the election later the same year.

The salient points of the report and the act were as follows.[6]

(1) Objective of Educational Policy

In the words of the report itself,

> ... the ultimate objective of educational policy in the country must be to bring together the children of all races under a national educational system in which the national language [that is, the Malay language] is the main medium of instruction, though we recognize that progress towards this goal cannot be rushed and must be gradual.

Why the ultimate objective could not be immediately realized and had to be achieved only gradually was obviously because of the undertakings given to the Chinese educationists at the Malacca meeting. Another reason was, perhaps more importantly, that there were at that point of time only enough trained Malay teachers to staff, and textbooks in the Malay language for use in, primary schools using Malay as the main medium of instruction. Beyond that, both Malay teachers and textbooks were in short supply.

Nevertheless, when Lim Lian Geok discovered this provision in Razak's Report, he became highly agitated and took the matter up with the minister for education. Due to his pressure, Abdul Razak agreed not to have this "ultimate objective" written into the coming education ordinance.[7]

Meanwhile, there would be near parity treatment of schools from all language streams.

(2) Types of Primary School

Primary schools were to be of two types, those assisted by the government, and those that were not, which would be regarded as independent. Those which were assisted would again be divided into two kinds, that is, Standard Primary Schools, and Standard-Type Primary Schools.

Standard Primary Schools would use the national language, that is Malay, as the medium of instruction. English would be taught as a compulsory subject. Chinese or Tamil could also be taught if the parents of fifteen students requested for such. Standard-Type Primary Schools would use English, Chinese, or Tamil as the main medium of instruction. Standard-Type English Primary Schools must teach Malay as a compulsory subject. They could also, like the Standard Primary Schools, teach Chinese or Tamil if the parents of fifteen students requested for such. Standard-Type Chinese and Tamil Primary Schools must teach Malay and English as compulsory subjects.

(3) Types of Secondary School

Secondary schools, as in the case of primary schools, would also be of two types. There would be, in the first instance, institutions assisted by the government. Those that were not would be regarded as independent. Of the former, again there would be two kinds, namely National Secondary Schools, and National-Type Secondary Schools.

In National Secondary Schools, the study of the national language and English would be compulsory. But there would be sufficient flexibility in the curriculum to allow schools or parts of schools to give particular attention to various languages and cultures (that is, Chinese and Tamil).

At the time, there were no secondary schools which used Malay as the main medium of instruction in existence yet, but the intention was to start such schools as soon as possible.

In National-Type Secondary Schools, the language to be used as the medium of instruction was not of first importance. Indeed, more than one medium could be used. There would also be sufficient flexibility in the curriculum to allow schools or parts of schools to give special attention to particular Malayan languages and cultures. In the case of those which were using Chinese as a general medium, even three languages could be taught, that is, other than Chinese, Malay and English also.

(4) Common Content in Syllabuses

All schools must use a common content in their syllabuses. This was to orientate them to a common Malayan outlook.

(5) Common Examination

The report specified that in the National Secondary Schools, "pupils [would] work towards a common final examination" and in the National-Type Secondary Schools, "All ... will work ... for common examinations".

However, in what language and languages such examinations would be conducted was not spelt out. Chinese educationists saw the minister for education on this and were given a verbal undertaking that students from Chinese-medium National-Type Schools would sit for their examinations in Chinese.[8]

(6) Assisted and Direct Grant School

Standard-Type Primary Schools were given government assistance, and National-Type Secondary Schools given grants. The report recommended that "All assisted and direct grant schools to be treated alike as regards grants".

(7) Ordinance and Council Paper Revoked

The Education Ordinance of 1952 and the Council Paper No. 67 of 1954 on education policy were both revoked.

Thus, the previous attempts to try to convert Chinese-medium and Tamil-medium schools were given up. The achievement of the new system of education thus recommended and devised, using the terms of reference of the Razak committee itself, was

> ... having regard to the intention to make Malay the national language of the country whilst preserving and sustaining the growth of the language and culture of other communities living in the country.

As the Razak Report made such fundamental concessions to the Chinese and Indian communities, it met with severe criticism and opposition from some quarters in the Malay community. But this was eventually assuaged by Dr Ismail bin Dato Abdul Rahman, the industry and commerce minister, who pointed out that the attitude of these people "was tantamount to posing as imperialists with no consideration for the Chinese and Indians".[9]

The Chinese and Indian educationists and communities, including Lim Lian Geok, were satisfied with Razak's report, and its consequence, the 1957 Education Ordinance.[10]

Chinese Schools to Measure Up to English Schools

In spite of the fact that the Razak Report was accepted and passed by the Legislative Council, attempts were still made to try to make the Chinese schools as alike to the English schools as possible. This was because the education establishment at that time was still staffed by many British officers. And the newly installed self-governing and later independent administration went along with them because between a pure and an anglicized Chinese school, the latter was the lesser evil. This can also be viewed against the development that the pending constitution for an independent Malaya would allow the continued use of English as an official language for ten years after the country became independent.

Via New Syllabuses and a New School System for the Chinese Schools

After the Razak Report was passed, the government appointed a committee to deal with the matter of unifying the content of syllabuses in all the schools. The committee was called the Syllabus and Time-Table Committee. It was chaired by Dr Lim Chong Eu from MCA, and among its members were presidents of teacher associations of all the four language streams of education. Lim Lian Geok, as president of UCSTA, sat on the committee and was later joined by Dr Yan Yuan Zhang, UCSTA's adviser. Although in name the committee was led by Lim Chong Eu. a local person, it was actually dominated by one of the then deputy directors for education, a British officer.[11]

There was a subcommittee to deliberate on the syllabus content for Chinese secondary as well as primary schools. Its membership comprised the head of the Chinese department from the University of Malaya; for a while, another academic from Taiwan; a secondary Chinese school teacher; the supervisor of Chinese schools in the Ministry of Education; and a Chinese primary school headmaster. The last two persons, in shaping the required new syllabus content for Chinese secondary schools, tried to take into account more of what was then being taught in English schools rather than in Chinese schools. This was perhaps because of the impact of Malay nationalism and the talk about the "ultimate objective". Even what was suggested for the subject of Chinese language was to follow what was established for the Overseas School Certificate for English secondary schools designed by Cambridge University.[12] The moves were opposed by Lim and Yan, resulting in Yan taking over the subcommittee as its chairman and reconstituting it with new members. For the subject of history, which had a decisive influence on the political thinking of students, there was at first also an attempt to dilute as much as possible "Chinese-ness" from its content. It was only after a hard struggle put up by Lim Lian Geok that the final decision was made that one-third of it should be on Malaya, another third on China, and the last one third on India and the rest of the world.[13] The apportionment of different sectors for geography followed a similar pattern.[14]

When it came to the new syllabus for Chinese primary schools, the Ministry of Education at first wanted the schools to start teaching English to students as early as Primary One. Lim and Yan put up a hard fight against this, and it was finally changed to starting from Primary Three instead[15]

English secondary schools at that time followed a system with one year of Remove Class, three years of Lower Secondary, two years of Higher Secondary, and two years of University Preparatory Class. Chinese secondary schools, however, had a different pattern. They had three years of Lower Secondary as well as three years of Higher Secondary. The decision was made, in the face of strenuous opposition from Lim Lian Geok, that the Chinese secondary schools should follow the English schools. However, when subsequently the Chinese secondary schools ignored the decision and persisted in keeping to their tradition, the authorities did not interfere.[16]

Lower Certificate of Education Examination and Malayan Certificate of Education Examination

On 21 May 1956, merely a week after the Razak Report was passed by the Legislative Council, but before it had become the Education Ordinance, the controller of Examinations, G.D. Muir, announced that the first Lower Certificate of Education examination to be held in the country would be conducted in November. Students who wished to sit for the examination should register by 26 May. The examination would be conducted in English. Students from Chinese secondary schools who wanted to participate must be from Higher Secondary One, the fourth year in the Chinese secondary school system, but students from English secondary schools would be from Form Three, the third year in the English secondary school system.[17] Muir explained that the reason Chinese secondary school students were invited to take part in an English-medium examination was to help them acquire a certificate which would secure them employment more easily after graduation. And the reason Chinese Higher Secondary One was equated with English Form Three was that the academic standard of the Chinese secondary schools was lower than that of the English schools.[18]

Led by Lim Lian Geok, the Chinese community came out in arms against the move. Chinese secondary school students studied their lessons in Chinese and now they had to sit for the examination in English. This was absolutely unreasonable. To equate Chinese Higher Secondary One with English Form Three was to debase the Chinese schools.

On 12 June, the minister for education came out with an explanation to say that the projected examination was not compulsory for Chinese secondary school students to take. If the Chinese community so wished, the authorities could conduct a Lower Secondary examination for them in the Chinese language. However, a certificate acquired through such an examination would only qualify a student for teacher training, that is, training to be a primary school teacher, but not for other government employment. Also, the Malayan Certificate of Education examination which Chinese Higher Secondary Three students could sit for would be conducted only in the country's official languages, that is, English and Malay.[19]

When the Lower Certificate of Education examination was finally held in November, only twenty out of the thousands of Chinese secondary school students in the country took part. This was in answer to a call by UCSTA to boycott the examination.[20]

Obviously, this move on examinations on the part of the government was to manouevre Chinese secondary schools into converting to English.

Malayan Secondary School Entrance Examination

In 1956, on the basis of recommendations in the Razak Report, the education authorities issued notices to the various Chinese primary schools to get their Primary Six school leaving students to sit for the Malayan Secondary School Entrance Examination. This examination would be conducted in the Chinese language. In Negeri Sembilan, the schools were told that successful candidates would qualify to be selected to join Form One in an English secondary school. In Malacca, they were told that participating in the examination was optional and students who passed could apply for admission into any kind of secondary school they wished. And in Selangor, the notice was that students must sit for the examination. Otherwise, they would not be allowed to join any secondary school at all. Subsequently, a number of conditions were, in succession, imposed on those ready to take part in the examination. This resulted in some observers drawing the conclusion that the purpose of holding the examination was to select outstanding students from the Chinese primary schools to join English secondary schools, as well as to weed out overage students from the education process.[21]

The proposed measure got UCSTA and the MCACECC so agitated that they took the matter up with the education authorities. On their representation, they were told that the purported examination was only to give school leaving primary students a test and would not serve as a sifting process for them to go for higher studies. On this understanding, UCSTA and the MCACECC told students to go ahead and take the examination. A strange thing that happened subsequently was that only some parts of the country released the results of the test while others announced no results at all.[22]

Some Chinese Secondary Schools Converted to English

In 1956, a Chinese secondary school in Penang transformed itself into a near-English school not by compulsion from, or manoeuvring by, the government, but of its own accord. This was the Zhong Ling High School.

All along, the Zhong Ling, though a Chinese school, had given great emphasis to the learning of English. In 1954, for instance, in its Lower Secondary classes, only the Chinese language, history, geography, and civics were taught in Chinese, but mathematics, physics, and chemistry were taught in English. Textbooks used for the latter subjects were also in English. In the Higher Secondary classes, only the Chinese language was taught in Chinese, but all other subjects were taught in English, using English textbooks. So, in essence, the Zhong Ling was already not vastly different from an English school.[23]

At the time, the government was giving more assistance to English secondary schools than to Chinese schools. The MCACECC then undertook negotiations with the government to have grants given to Chinese secondary schools doubled. The chairman of Zhong Ling's management committee, Wang Jing Cheng, and the principal, Waung Yoong Nien, were members of the MCACECC and UCSTA respectively.[24] Disregarding what the MCACECC was doing at the time, because of the special nature of their school, which was obviously a winning point, and its disturbing poor finances, Wang and Waung on their own took action separately and approached the government to request for equal treatment with the English schools. Talks were opened in January 1953.[25]

On 6 July 1955, Waung Yoong Nien at a gathering disclosed to both staff and students the news that the management committee of the school was negotiating with the education authorities for additional assistance to be given to Zhong Ling. He gave the assurance that there would be no diluting of the powers of the management committee, and no change in either the policy or the curriculum of the school.[26] The disclosure took the teachers and the students by complete surprise and, when publicized, also shocked the whole Chinese community. In spite of Waung's assurance, the feeling was that he and Wang should not have disregarded the MCACECC and take separate action by themselves. It was suspected that they would cave in to unfavourable conditions set by the government in exchange for increased funding.[27]

The students of the school itself were the first to mount a protest. Speedily, they sent a memorandum to the school management committee and the principal requesting them not to take separate action which would weaken the unity and strength of Chinese schools. They even proposed hiking the fees they had to pay for their schooling to help relieve the financial burden of the school.[28] The teachers protested the move too, and both the MCACECC and the UCSTA pressured Wang and Waung to reveal the conditions that they would be accepting from the government.[29]

On 12 August, early in the morning, news spread that the police in Penang had arrested twelve students, seven of whom were from Zhong Ling. This happened, it was understood, because the students were making secret plans to oppose Wang's and Waung's move. The event was to trigger an initiative by more than a thousand students in Zhong Ling that morning not to take their examinations, which were scheduled for that morning.[30]

In November, UCSTA issued a call to all Chinese secondary schools not to go the Zhong Ling way, but to wait for the outcome of talks which it was going to have with the government and then take steps together. Later, Lim Lian Geok, accompanied by the deputy minister for education, Too Joon Hin, a member of the MCA, met up with the minister for education, Abdul Razak, to discuss the issue. The meeting concluded with Abdul Razak deciding to suspend making a decision on Zhong Ling's plea for increased aid until he had completed preparing his report for a new education system.[31]

Razak's report was passed by the Legislative Council in May 1956, and, in the month that followed, the government announced that it would grant Zhong Ling increased assistance on its conversion and that Zhong Ling would become a fully-aided school.[32]

The announcement astounded the whole Chinese community and soon posters were seen put up in many places in the city to criticize the Zhong Ling authorities.[33] Also, because of this and several other issues, on 23 November, the students of Zhong Ling assembled in the school and presented a list of demands to the school management committee. One of the demands was to disclose the conditions imposed on Zhong Ling by the government for giving it extra money, and another was to ask Waung why two teachers had to resign from their posts. In the midst of it all, they were suddenly set upon by the police who fired tear gas at them to get them dispersed. It was then also announced that the school would be closed for twenty-one days.[34] Following the event, sixty-nine students were expelled from the school. On appeal, sixteen were rehabilitated but they had to transfer to other schools to continue their studies.[35]

Amidst all the commotion ignited by the Zhong Ling incident, on 29 December 1956, the director for education, E.M.F. Payne, notified all Chinese secondary schools in the country that if they followed in Zhong Ling's footsteps, on fulfilling twenty conditions which were spelt out, they would obtain full assistance.

Among those conditions were two which stipulated that Lower Secondary students must sit for the Lower Certificate of Education, and Higher Secondary students must sit for the Malayan Certificate of Education examinations, both of which would be conducted in English. The latter could, in lieu of the Malayan Certificate of Education examination, sit for the Overseas School Certificate examination conducted by Cambridge University. Quite clearly, this was to force the schools to change from using Chinese as their medium of instruction to using English, and to substitute Chinese textbooks with English books. The schools accepting this would also have to sign agreements with the Ministry of Education by which the ministry could send its people to be members of their management committees as well as deploy British teachers to be their subject advisers.[36]

UCSTA, UCSCA, and the MCACECC stepped in to counter Payne. They called on the schools not to make any separate move, and convened meetings by which they devised fifteen proposals to counter any conversion. The country became independent on 31 August 1957, after which Khir Johari replaced Abdul Razak as the minister for education. Early in November that year, a delegation from the three organizations met with the new minister to present him their ideas. On the question of Chinese schools accepting full aid, the minister offered an explanation that was not different from Payne's stipulations. He stated that, on accepting such aid, students from those schools must sit for the Lower Certificate of Education and the Malayan Certificate of Education examinations, both of which would be conducted in English; all textbooks used, except those for Chinese language, must be in English; and school administration must follow that of English schools.[37]

Early in April 1957, the students of Zhong Ling were to sit for their examinations. Several of them went around the school to tell their friends not to do so. Waung Yoong Nien immediately dismissed them, and later sacked another ten. Because of the disturbance, students from two classes refrained from sitting for the examinations. Then more than a hundred of them assembled and presented several demands on the school, one of which was to stop accepting additional assistance from the government, and another was to rehabilitate the sixty-nine students expelled in November last year. They also unfurled banners on which the slogans "Love our Zhong Ling!" and "Love our Chinese language!" were written in blood. Waung responded by immediately closing the school for holidays.[38]

The students' frenzy quickly spread to other schools. Students in the Han Jiang High School and the Zhong Hua High School also assembled to show support for their compatriots in Zhong Ling. In the former, many students also bit their fingers to write in blood on white cloth the slogan "Protect our Chinese schools!" The acting principal of the Bin Hua Girls' School, on hearing of the disturbances, straightway ordered her school to disperse and go on holiday.[39]

In October 1957, the news came that two more Chinese secondary schools had gone the Zhong Ling way and accepted full aid from the government. One was the Zhen Hua in Seremban and the other was the Zhong Hua in Segamat. The students of Zhen Hua protested, but to no avail.[40]

Following the steps taken by Zhen Hua and Zhong Hua in conversion, rumours flew that there would be student disturbances in Penang again. This time, student agitation would not be over conversion alone, but also over another move on the part of the government which required overage students in schools of all language streams — such students were the most numerous in Chinese schools — to give up schooling and leave their schools. This measure was mandated by the Razak Report which will be explained a few pages later. What eventually happened was that disturbances broke out not only in Penang, but in six other states as well. The schools that took part in showing off their discontent numbered more than a dozen and involved thousands of students in the end. The forms of protest were strikes, assemblies, and processions through the towns. They were met by the police who got many of them arrested, shot tear gas at them, and had their houses searched in some instances. Some of them were dismissed by their school authorities. The commotion lasted for more than a month, from November to December 1957.[41]

On 19 December 1957, the Foon Yew High School in Johor Bahru announced that it would not change to an English school, and from January the following year, it would accept no aid from the government and would raise its own finances. Later, the Foon Yew was followed by the Zhong Hua in Seremban. These two were the first to become what came to be known as independent schools in the country.[42]

A Special Examination to Assess the Standard of Chinese Primary School Teachers: The Teachers' Qualifying Test

Also just after the passing of the Razak Report by the Legislative Council, but before it became the Education Ordinance, on 24 July 1956, the government announced that it would conduct a special examination, called the Teachers' Qualifying Test, the following year for serving Chinese primary school teachers. This was to determine whether they were qualified to be teachers in Standard-Type Chinese primary schools, to which existing Chinese primary schools would be converted. These teachers would joined a new salary scheme which would be devised for all schools. A primary school found staffed by deficient teachers would be classified as a Non-Standard Primary School, and the deficient teachers would not be placed on the new salary scheme, although the government would continue to extend financial assistance to these schools.[43]

Previously, the qualifications required of teachers who served in Chinese primary schools were that they must have graduated from Lower Secondary Three in a Chinese secondary school, and have had two years of teaching training in a Senior Normal Class, which was run by the education authorities. The Razak Report envisaged that, in future, teachers in Standard Primary or Standard-Type Primary Schools must have had at least three years of secondary schooling, as well as three years of teacher training. It was understood that the three years of secondary schooling meant having obtained the Lower Certificate of Education. As students from Lower Secondary Three in a Chinese school were not considered good enough to sit for the examination to acquire the Lower Certificate of Education, but only those from Higher Secondary One were, the standard of presently serving teachers became a matter of doubt. Moreover, they only had two and not three years of teacher training.[44] So a special examination to assess their capacity was deemed necessary.

It was also made known that serving teachers who came from Higher Secondary Three in a Chinese secondary school could, on application, be exempted from having to sit for the test in the Chinese language. Each application would be considered individually. Those who came from Standard Nine in an English secondary school and had the Overseas School Certificate issued by Cambridge University would automatically be xempted.[45]

Again, the thrust of the exercise had the effect of debasing the academic standard of the Chinese stream of education. It also had the effect of showing that this stream should measure up to the English stream.

The move again hurt the feelings of Chinese educationists. Led by Lim Lian Geok, UCSTA, UCSCA and the MCACECC called on all Chinese primary school teachers not to sit for the examination, but to boycott it. The call fell on willing ears.[46]

So, eventually, the Teachers' Qualifying Test could not be held.[47]

"Operation Torch" and an Attempt to Sideline Chinese Primary Schools

On 2 August 1956, the government announced that it would launch an "Operation Torch" during the coming school holidays to enable parents of children of the correct ages to register them for primary schooling. The choice of which kind of school their children should join, whether English, Malay, or any other, would depend entirely on the wishes of those parents. The exercise would last for a month, from the end of August to the end of September. Statistics collected would help the education authorities plan in advance what kind of, and how many new schools to build, as well as the required teachers to train for staffing the new institutions.[48]

Following the announcement, the education authorities notified English and Malay schools a month before the end of August to get themselves ready as registration stations, and to alert parents to carry out the exercise. However, they failed to do so with the Chinese schools. Not only were notification letters not dispatched to the Chinese schools, such letters were written in English and even barred from being translated into Chinese. The purpose of the stealthy move was to get parents to send their children to English or Malay schools instead of Chinese schools. The Chinese schools were to be kept in slumber.[49]

Lim Lian Geok, on discovering the unusual move, took action immediately to regain lost ground. He mobilized UCSTA, UCSCA, the MCACECC, the Chinese press, and the whole Chinese community to get Chinese schools as well as organizations opened as registration centres, and parents to bring their children in for registration to study in Chinese schools. School principals, teachers, as well as students, were told to advise parents to send their children to Chinese schools instead of English or Malay schools. He also went around the country giving talks. Work teams were organized to go everywhere, including the countryside, to visit parents. The slogan "Chinese children should study Chinese!" was put out.[50]

Eventually, Lim Lian Geok's campaigns were successful. It was seen that Chinese registration centres were packed with parents registering their children for Chinese schools, and the English schools were quite quiet. And many of those who went to English centres to register also chose Chinese schools for their children instead of English schools.[51]

After the registration exercise ended, the government did not publish the statistics collected. It also did not say anything more about setting up new schools and training new teachers to staff them.[52]

Overage Students to be Evicted from School, and the Possibility of Chinese Schools Closing Down

Towards the end of 1956, an incident occurred which was not related to the issue of the "ultimate objective", that is, of making Malay the main medium of instruction in all schools in Malaya. It did, however, pose the danger of bringing about the closure of three quarters of all Chinese schools, primary and secondary, and tens of thousands of students being thrown out of schools in the country. The Chinese community was alarmed and felt threatened.

The issue was about overage students in the schools. The Razak Report envisaged that the ideal age of Primary One students in all schools should be six years old and should not be more than eight years old. That of Lower Secondary One or Form One students should be twelve years old and should not be more than fourteen.[53] At that time, there were many overage students in schools of all language streams, but it was the worst in Chinese schools. According to findings, the percentage of overage students in Chinese schools was 75, in Malay schools 30, and in English schools 20.[54]

The Ministry of Education, like in several other areas, sought to implement the ideas of the Razak Report immediately. On 13 December 1956, order was given out in Perak that from January the following year, students over the age of seventeen in primary schools, and over twenty-three in secondary schools, must stop studying and leave school. At the same time, new students to be recruited for Primary One and Lower Secondary One or Form One must keep to the ideal ages. Similar orders were issued in Selangor in January and in all other states in July 1957. The penalty for not complying with the orders was withdrawal of government assistance. Why overage students had to be evicted was that they were taking up too many of the places in the schools so that children of the correct age had no opportunity of joining the schools to start their schooling.[55] The announcement shocked the country.

UCSTA, UCSCA and the MCACECC took the matter up with the government. On 16 October 1957, Khir Johari, the new minister for education after independence, wrote to the MCA to offer starting afternoon and night classes to accommodate the overage students. But doubts regarding the implementation remained. Such classes could be started in urban centres where there were many students. But could they also be started in the countryside where there were few students? Also graduating students from Chinese secondary schools had to sit for the Lower Certificate of Education examination which would be conducted in English. Could they cope?[56]

Before such questions could be answered, widespread disturbances broke out among many Chinese secondary schools in the country between November and December. We have earlier discussed those disturbances. The reason for the commotion was the discontent aroused over the conversion of Chinese secondary schools into English. Another cause of the rebellious action was the eviction of overage students.[57]

UCSTA Got Many Chinese to Become Citizens of Independent Malaya: Better Prospects for Chinese Education

Whether a person was a citizen of independent Malaya was a matter of crucial importance. As a citizen, he could through his political rights influence the outcome of any election, send his children to study in government-aided schools, and so on. Non-citizens were deprived of all these privileges.

After 31 August 1957, the government of newly independent Malaya allowed all those who qualified, by the terms of the country's constitution as drawn up by Lord Reid, to apply to become citizens during the period from 1 Septembet 1957 to 31 August 1958.[58] Lim Lian Geok and UCSTA promptly suggested to the MCA to set up a committee in common with the various Chinese public organizations to help the Chinese apply.[59] The committee was not subsequently formed, however, because there was a rift in the MCA. In view of this, Lim and UCSTA took it upon themselves to mobilize the Chinese. They advised their twenty-nine branches throughout the country to urge all Chinese school principals and teachers to help the parents of students to apply. Due to their efforts, by the time the next election was held in the country in 1959, the number of Chinese who had citizenship status totalled 900,000. In 1955, when an election was first held for the Legislative Council, the number was no more than 140,000.[60] The improvement in the political position of the Chinese was to have, in the days ahead, a great bearing on the language policy of the country, as well as on the development of the Chinese schools.

A Parting of the Ways for the MCA and Chinese Educationists, an Event of Misfortune for Chinese Education

In December 1956, there was an election for the Georgetown Municipal Council in Penang, a Chinese-majority town, in which the MCA and the Labor Party, both Chinese-based organizations, engaged each other. The former lost to the latter by five seats. The MCA was defeated because Chinese voters were disenchanted with it over the conversion of the Zhong Ling High School into an English school. The MCA was a member of the MCACECC which did not support the conversion. However, the fact that the Alliance government, of which the MCA was a member, accepted Zhong Ling's conversion did not go down well with the voters. After its victory, the Labor Party merged with a Partai Rakyat, a Malay-based organization, into the Socialist Front. The Socialist Front spread its wings into Selangor, Negeri Sembilan, and Malacca, and posed a serious threat to the MCA.[61] In November 1957, there was a by-election in Menglembu, Ipoh, again a Chinese-majority town, and the MCA contestant was trounced by D.R. Seenvisagam, a leader of the People's Progressive Party. It will be recalled that in November and December there were Chinese school student disturbances in the greater part of the country. While the Alliance government, of which the MCA was a part, took action to suppress the students, the People's Progressive Party sympathized with them and got students who were arrested bailed out from jail. The MCA also lost influence in Menglembu.[62]

In March 1958, the leadership of the MCA was reconstituted. Tan Cheng Lok was ailing, and a younger man was elected to replace him. The new president chosen was Dr Lim Chong Eu. Too Joon Hin, who was then deputy minister for education, was made the secretary-general. Both men were considered able to protect and advance Chinese interests, including Chinese education, and save the fortunes of the MCA. Both had a close relationship with Lim Lian Geok. Lim Chong Eu had served together with Lim Lian Geok in the Syllabus and Timetable Committee, and Too Joon Hin, as deputy minister for education, also had dealings with Lim Lian Geok.[63]

It was seen earlier that in 1956 the government conducted, for the first time, the Lower Certification of Education examination in English for students in the country, in which Chinese pupils could take part. On protest from Lim Lian Geok, the government explained that the examination was not compulsory for Chinese secondary school students and, if they so wished, the government could hold Lower Secondary Three examination in the Chinese language for Chinese secondary school students. However, the certificate obtained through such an examination would entitle the graduate to be recruited only for training to be a teacher in Chinese primary schools, but not for other government employment. Obviously, there was discrimination. Lim Lian Geok was not keen to accept such a compromise. However, in June 1958, in a meeting of the MCACECC, UCSTA and UCSCA, Lim Chong Eu persuaded Lim Lian Geok to accept the proposal for the time being until he could get the situation remedied. This was one occasion in which Lim Chong Eu was seen planning to do something for Chinese education.[64]

Following this, Lim Chong Eu began to voice demands openly on behalf of Chinese education. Three months after the above meeting, the MCACECC convened an all-nation conference on Chinese education which had the purpose of, besides others, devising a new common syllabus content for schools of all language streams in the country so as to enable mother tongue education to flourish freely. In this meeting, Lim Chong Eu made an open stand for one of Lim Lian Geok's cherished dreams which was anathema to UMNO. Lim Chong Eu was found to state: "If the government persisted that only official languages [Malay and English] could be used as media for public examinations, then the government should forthwith recognize Chinese as an official language."[65]

In April 1959, on the eve of the first general election to be held after Malaya gained independence, the MCACECC, UCSTA, and UCSCA, together with other Chinese public organizations with a total of 747 names and made up of 1,209 delegates, met at another conference on Chinese education, with Lim Chong Eu as the chair. The meeting issued a manifesto on Chinese education in which four main demands, called appeals, were made on the government. These were:

(1)   The education of the different races should use their different mother tongues as their different medium of instruction, and schools of the different language streams should be treated equally;

(2)   The government should increase its present assistance given to Chinese secondary schools by 100 per cent; and

(3)   The government should set up a Chinese Education Advisory Council, made up of delegates from representative Chinese educational organizations to help it resolve problems pertaining to Chinese education.[66]

The demands were clearly designed to exert pressure on UMNO just before the general election, as it had to depend to a great extent on the Chinese vote to win.

Before nomination day for the general election, Lim Chong Eu sent a private letter to Tunku Abdul Rahman, the president of the Alliance Party, which, on the basis of the different racial compositions among the country's voters, set out the following requests:

(1) To allocate at least forty constituencies to the MCA, and
(2) To list out in the election manifesto of the Alliance Party an undertaking to review the present education policy of the country.[67]

The propaganda chief for the MCA, Yong Pung How, released Lim's letter to the press. Tunku Abdul Rahman was infuriated, considering Lim's move as stabbing him in the back and delivering to him an ultimatum.[68] Countering this, the Tunku laid down his cards:

(1) The MCA would be allocated only thirty-two constituencies, and
(2) All candidates for the election would have to be personally selected by him.

It would be up to the MCA to accept the offer or leave the Alliance Party.[69]

The Central Committee of the MCA made a decision to go along with Tunku Abdul Rahman upon which Lim Chong Eu, Yong Pung How and two other MCA leaders, Too Joon Hin and Chin See Yin, left the MCA. Lim Chong Eu was succeeded by Dr Cheah Toon Lok as acting president. Cheah stayed in that position until 1961 when Tan Siew Sin was elected to replace him as the president. Both Cheah and Tan had no interest in Chinese education and were not sympathetic to UCSTA and UCSCA. So with the departure of Lim Chong Eu and his colleagues from the MCA, UCSTA and UCSCA lost a channel through which they could struggle with UMNO to protect and advance the interests of Chinese education. The MCA and Chinese educationists no longer walked the same path, which was a misfortune for Chinese education.[70]

The general election was held on 19 August 1959 and of the 31 constituencies allocated to the MCA (the original 32 given by Tunku Abdul Rahman had now been reduced to 31), only 19 were won. The rest were lost to opposition parties. But the Alliance Party, as a whole, won 74 of all the 104 seats contested. So it formed the new government.[71]

THE ULTIMATE OBJECTIVE FORWARD
The Talib Report, 1960, and the Education Act, 1961

The Alliance Party won the 1959 election and formed the government. With this victory, it felt that it could take a step further towards realizing the "ultimate objective" in education. Consequently, in 1960, it appointed a committee, headed by the new minister for education, Rahman Talib, and consisting of representatives from all three components of the Alliance Party, to review among other things the Razak Report and its consequent 1957 Education Ordinance, their implementation thus far and in the future, and to make recommendations. After Talib had submitted his report to the Legislative Council, an Education Act was enacted in 1961.[72]

In summary, what was recommended and then passed into law was as follows.[73]

(1) Primary School

Concerning primary schools, the system devised by Abdul Razak was to continue. It will be recalled that under that system, primary schools were first divided into aided and independent institutions. The former was again separated into two kinds, Standard Primary Schools and Standard-Type Primary Schools, which would be renamed National Primary Schools and National-Type Primary Schools respectively.

Innovations were also introduced. The first was "Where at any time the Minister is satisfied that a national-type primary school may suitably be converted into a national primary school he may by order direct that the school shall become a national primary school". The second was "primary education in Malay must ... be made available to more children by the introduction, for a start, of Malay-medium streams in what were formerly Government English primary schools". Both new departures were designed to bring closer the realization of the "ultimate objective".

Under the Razak's system, the Standard Primary Schools were fully assisted by the government, but the Standard-Type Primary Schools were only partially funded. Now the latter would also become fully aided.

(2) Secondary School

For secondary schools, like in primary schools, there were firstly two varieties, that was, aided secondary schools and independent secondary schools. And of the former, there were also two kinds, that was, National Secondary Schools and National-Type Secondary Schools.

Now, something new was created for the National-Type Secondary Schools. From henceforth, only those which used English as the main medium of instruction would be recognized. Those which were based on the Chinese or Tamil languages must convert to English. If they converted, they would be fully aided, just like the National Secondary Schools. If they did not do so, they would be regarded as independent institutions and would receive no aid.

"An essential requirement ... is that public examinations at secondary level should be conducted only in the country's official languages", which were Malay and English. Hitherto, the government had conducted examinations for both Lower Secondary Three and Higher Secondary Three in Chinese secondary schools in the Chinese language. This would henceforth be discontinued.[74]

Independent schools "must observe statutory requirements ... as much ... as ... assisted schools ... inter alia, those relating to Board of Governors ... the registration requirements of the Education Ordinance, 1957, the observance of common syllabuses, timetables and courses of studies laid down by the Minster, the Education (School Discipline) Regulations, 1959, and statutory health requirements".

And the reason independent schools were allowed to exist was due to some special considerations. "They do in fact serve a useful purpose. In the main they cater for pupils who are unable to obtain admission to fully assisted secondary schools because they are overage ... or have not qualified ... through the Malayan Secondary Schools Entrance Examination. Some of them do not qualify for assistance because their teachers are not appropriately qualified or because their buildings are inadequate."

Soon after the Education Act was enacted, the minister for education and three MCA members of parliament (as the Legislative Council was renamed after Malaya became independent in August 1957), Lee San Choon, Lee Siok Yew, and Li Yun Tian, went on radio to persuade Chinese National-Type Secondary Schools to convert to English. After conversion, the schools could use two-thirds of their teaching time to teach the Chinese language. Posters with the same message were also distributed. On 19 October 1961, the minister made a statement in parliament to guarantee that the Chinese language would be taught and examined as a subject in both National Secondary and National-Type Secondary Schools and one-third of learning time would be devoted to its study. Also, the Chinese language could be taught in Form Six and students could sit for it in the Higher School Certificate examination.[75]

Lim Lian Geok took great exception to Rahman Talib's report after it was passed in parliament. He wrote to the press to say that the Alliance Party was breaking the promises it had made to him at the 1955 Malacca meeting and was set on a path to destroy Chinese education. Leong Yew Koh, one of the MCA members on the Rahman Talib committee, responded and a "pen-war" in the Chinese press ensued between the two men which lasted for as long as eight to nine months. The Chinese newspapers were warned not to publish Lim's words, which resulted in Lim buying advertisement space in the newspapers with his own money to air his views.[76] On 12 August 1961, the government charged Lim for distorting its education policy and being chauvinistic, and his Malayan citizenship was revoked. This was followed on the 21 August by his teaching registration being cancelled. In August 1963, a book by him entitled *Hui Yi Pian Pian Lu* [Reminiscences] was also gazetted as banned. And a teachers' magazine which had printed extracts from the book was prohibited from being sold.[77] On 6 September 1962, Dr Yan Yuan Zhang, adviser to Lim's UCSTA, was expelled from the country.[78] Lim took the revocation of his citizenship to the courts, but after prolonged litigation, lost the battle. On 23 October 1964, the final verdict of the judges upheld the government's decision.[79]

On 30 May 1961, there was a by-election in Teluk Anson, Perak. Too Joon Hin stood in the contest as an independent against an MCA candidate. As seen, Too had left the MCA earlier on and along with that he had also lost his position as deputy minister for education. Too campaigned against the Talib Report. He won against the MCA by an overwhelming majority.[80]

D.R. Seenivasagam, leader of the People's Progressive Party, who sat in the opposition in Parliament, charged the Talib Report for violating clause 152 of the Malayan constitution for failing to respect the languages of the non-Malay races. On 21 October 1961, when the Education Act was enacted, he pronounced that the Chinese and Tamil languages and cultures were executed on that day. He vouched that the Chinese and the Tamils would fight, using constitutional means, to uphold their rights.[81]

The Situation of the Chinese Schools After the Talib Report and the Education Act

In January 1962, the minister for education announced that fifty-four Chinese National-Type Secondary Schools accepted conversion.[82] Seventeen chose to become independent. It is perhaps pertinent and interesting to see how many independent schools, together with the numbers of students, there were from then until 1969. Table 3.1 gives the picture:[83]

Table 3.1
Number of Independent Chinese Secondary Schools and their Students, 1962–69

Year	Number of Schools	Number of Students
1962	77	34,410
1963	84	35,789
1964	78	35,507
1965	73	30,470
1966	69	26,141
1967	59	22,221
1968	50	19,507
1969	45	18,476

Source: See note 83.

There was an increase in the numbers between 1962 and 1963, and thereafter, there were continuous declines. The increase came about because new schools were opened. For instance, the Yuk Choy and the Poi Nam National-Type Secondary Schools in Ipoh, Perak, after converting from the Chinese stream to the English stream, started independent schools. The declines from 1964 onwards were because the government abolished the Malayan Secondary School Entrance Examination that year and allowed the automatic promotion from primary to secondary schools.[84] Because of that, many parents chose to send their children to National-Type Secondary Schools, rather than to independent Chinese secondary schools, after their primary education. Previously, with the Malayan Secondary School Entrance Examination, only about 30 per cent of the candidates would pass and the rest had to enrol in independent Chinese secondary schools to further their studies. The reason for this preference for National-Type Secondary Schools over independent Chinese secondary schools was, firstly, that studying in the former would enable students to obtain the Lower Certificate of Education more easily. The students would be exposed to the English language rather than Chinese, which was the case in the independent Chinese secondary schools. Secondly, the National-Type Secondary Schools charged lower fees than the independent Chinese secondary schools.

The decline in the number of independent Chinese secondary schools caused Chinese educationists great anxiety. The possibility that such schools could totally vanish in the future stared them in the face. During the 1970s, a vigorous attempt was made to reverse the trend to which we shall return in the next chapter.

It is useful too to take a look at the situation of the Chinese National-Type Primary Schools, as well as the Chinese independent primary schools under the Talib Report and the Education Act. Table 3.2 tells what that situation was like.[85]

Table 3.2
Number of Students in Chinese National-Type Primary Schools and Chinese Independent Primary Schools, 1960–67

Year	Number of Students in Chinese National-Type Primary Schools	Number of Students in Chinese Independent Primary Schools
1960	354,474	28,744
1961	352,345	25,686
1962	348,171	14,250
1963	339,829	11,025
1964	340,845	7,990
1965	340,724	6,762
1966	347,061	5,456
1967	355,771	4,814

Source: See note 85.

It will be noticed that the numbers in both columns kept on declining over the years. Only in the first column was there a reversal in the last two years. There was a reason for this. Students from these schools found it difficult to cope with the English language when they joined the English National-Type Secondary Schools. Many of them failed in the Lower Certificate of Education examination after their third year of schooling.

No doubt, the government had provided for them to study in a one-year Remove Class to improve their command of the English language before they were placed in Form One, but that did not do them any good. In the end, the parents decided to send their children to begin their education in English National-Type Primary Schools instead of Chinese schools. This development was not favourable to Chinese education.

The Struggle to Make Chinese Language an Official Language

Because Chinese educationists were alarmed at the decline of both Chinese secondary and primary schools, they soon revived the struggle to get the government recognize the Chinese language as an official language of the country, just like the Malay and English languages. If successful, that would reverse the fortunes of Chinese education. Public examinations could then be held in Chinese, besides Malay and English, and that would stem the tide of Chinese students abandoning schools of their own language, as well as ease the pressure on Chinese schools to convert to English or Malay. This would also entitled the Chinese independent schools to aids from the government, and not be regarded as independent.

At the time when the struggle was revived, there were other developments which acted as catalysts to bring this about. One was the formation of Malaysia by merging Malaya with Singapore, Sarawak, and Sabah to become a new entity. After the merger, the number of Chinese became larger than the number of Malays in the country. The Chinese formed 42.2 per cent of the total population and the Malays only 40.6 per cent.[86] This gave Chinese educationists a *raison d'etre* to put forth their demand. Next, on their part, Malay educationists and culturists were also pushing very hard to forward the cause of the national language, which was the Malay language. After the Razak Report was passed and the Education Ordinance enacted, the Kesatuan Guru-guru Melayu Semananjung [Malay Teachers' Union of the Peninsula] campaigned the government to fulfil the targets enunciated in the report and the ordinance, including the setting up of Malay secondary schools. This stimulated Chinese educationists to match move with move.[87]

It will be remembered that the struggle to get Chinese acknowledged as an official language was first started by Lim Lian Geok in 1954 as a consequence of the campaign to oppose the 1952 Education Ordinance.[88] At the 1955 meeting in Malacca, Lim also pressed the issue on Tunku Abdul

Rahman.[89] This time, it was picked up because of the following development. In August 1964, the government announced that it would start a new kind of secondary school called the comprehensive secondary school which would teach arts, science, as well as technical subjects. The medium of instruction in this kind of school would be Malay and English. Chinese as a medium of instruction was not mentioned. This could happen because Chinese, unlike Malay and English, was not an official language. Reacting immediately, UCSTA called for a conference of Chinese registered organizations to press the following demands on the government: recognize Chinese as an official language, start Chinese-medium integrated secondary schools, and recognize the degrees of Nanyang University.[90]

This move on the part of Chinese educationists at once drew fire from Malay educationists and culturists. The attack was so intense as to cause a group of them in Perlis to demand that all signboards in Chinese in government buildings, business places, and schools be taken down and replaced by signboards in Malay. A counter-attack was mounted by the acting president of UCSTA, Sim Mow Yu, who instructed the Chinese schools not to change their signboards. Sim at the time was also the deputy head of the youth wing of MCA, of which he was the founder. He was very different from Dr Cheah Toon Lok and Tan Siew Sin.[91]

At the time when the Malay and Chinese educationists and culturists were exchanging fire, the People's Action Party from Singapore championed for a "Malaysian Malaysia" to fight for equality for all races in Malaysia. This party was the ruling party in Singapore and was a Chinese-majority organization. The slogan of this party poured oil on the fire.[92]

Sim Mow Yu pressed ahead hard with his campaign. He was involved in many activities, the highpoint of which was drawing up a memorandum on the issue, together with representatives from various Chinese registered organizations, to present to the prime minister as well as all ministers and deputy ministers. There was also the move to get Chinese organizations to sign their names or stamp their seals on a document to show support for the memorandum, which was, however, not submitted to the government. Sim was also involved in a dispute with Tan Siew Sin who announced that he would fight for Chinese to be made an official working language.[93]

On 27 September 1965, in a speech at a Chinese festive occasion, Prime Minister Tunku Abdul Rahman made the statement that if the non-Malays supported the country's constitution in accepting the Malay language to be the national language, he would grant them mutually beneficial arrangements and concessions. He would respect the use of the languages of the non-Malays in the country. This evoked Sim to respond by saying that he wished to show his deep respect to the prime minister for his magnanimous attitude.[94]

While on the one hand, the prime minister's statement pleased the Chinese, on the other, it drew ire from Malay educationists and culturists. The head of the Dewan Bahasa dan Pustaka and leader of a National Language Action Front, Syed Nasir, expressed the sentiment that he hoped what the prime minister stated was not a sign that there would be compromises on the nation's language policy. The minister for information and broadcast, Senu, warned that anyone who championed another language to be also made an official language would be violating the country's constitution and must bear the consequences.[95]

On 1 April 1966, Sim Mow Yu came out with a set of proposals about the issue which ran as follows:[96]

(1) The first aim: struggle for the Chinese language to be made an official language.
(2) The second aim: failing the first aim, to struggle for the Chinese language to be made a *fu zhu* (supplementary) language or a second language.
(3) The third aim: failing the second aim, to struggle for the Chinese language to be an official *ying yong* (used) language.

The proposals were sent not only to the Central Committee of the MCA for its consideration and action, but also to its various divisions and branches. They received widespread support among the lower rungs of the party.

On 18 October 1966, Sim Mow Yu was expelled from the MCA. The first charge against him was that in fighting for the Chinese language to be made an official language, he violated Clause 152 of the country's constitution. Other charges were that he also violated party discipline, treated the party leadership with contempt, and openly opposed the party's policy decisions.[97]

On 3 March 1967, the National Language Act was passed. The act permitted the non-Malay languages to be used for translation purposes, that is, for translating official documents or communications, and so on. The dismissal of Sim Mow Yu from the MCA, together with the passing of this act, quietened down the struggle to make Chinese an official language.[98]

Another Step Towards the Ultimate Objective

The National Language Act, 1967, and the Conversion of English Schools to Malay

The constitution devised for Malaya when it became independent in 1957 provided for the continued use of the English language for ten years, or longer, if parliament permitted, in parliament itself, in the Legislative Assembly of every state, and for all other official purposes. It would be regarded as an official language, just like Malay. By 1967, the ten-year period came to an end and parliament passed an act, called the National Language Act, to terminate the special privilege granted to it.[99]

Following the enactment of the act, from 1968 till 1982, the government took steps to convert all National-Type English Primary as well as Secondary Schools into Malay National Primary and Secondary Schools.[100] This did not affect the National-Type Chinese Primary Schools or the Chinese independent secondary schools. However, there are two interesting points to note about the Chinese schools in connection with this development. One was that the 1961 Education Act had provided for the minister for education to convert National-Type Primary Schools of any language stream into Malay-medium National Primary Schools whenever he deemed fit. The minister could use that power only on the National-Type English Primary Schools, but not on the National-Type Chinese Primary Schools. The latter were spared the axe. A second point was that all the previous National-Type Chinese Secondary Schools which had converted to become National-Type English Secondary Schools under the 1961 Education Act now got converted a second time into Malay-medium schools but they were allowed to retain their names as National-Type Secondary Schools.

An Attempt to Deny Chinese Secondary Students Opportunities of Higher Education

Merdeka University versus Rahman College

All along, graduates from the Chinese independent secondary schools had been going to the Nanyang University in Singapore or abroad to further their studies. In August 1965, Singapore separated from Malaysia and became an independent country. As a result, the Nanyang University became a foreign university. This impelled some Chinese educationists to harbour the desire to establish a university for such students in Malaysia itself. Then on 21 September 1967, the minister for education, Khir Johari, announced that secondary school graduates who wished to go overseas for higher studies must now have the Malaysian Certificate of Education or the Overseas School Certificate from Cambridge University before they would be allowed to proceed. Those two certificates, as noted, were awarded on the basis of the examinations being conducted in the English language. Few of the graduates of the Chinese independent secondary schools had such certificates. They could not go to the Nanyang University in Singapore. The announcement catapulted Chinese educationists into initiating a movement to found a Chinese university in Malaysia.[101]

On 7 December 1967, the vice-president of UCSTA, Loot Ting Yee, inspired by Lim Lian Geok, made an open proposal to found such a university. His organization, which represented Senior Normal teachers, voted total support for him, and this was soon followed by the whole Chinese community. On 14 April 1968, a meeting of sponsors of the university was convened, which was attended by 218 registered organizations and more than 700 representatives. The conference adopted a draft organization plan for the university as well as a manifesto. A limited company was to be established to manage the university, which would apply to the government for registration. Steps would be undertaken immediately to raise funds to finance the project. The proposed institution was to be called the Merdeka University.[102]

The Alliance government, UMNO, and the MCA were all against the founding of such a university. To ease the unhappiness, the minister for education withdrew his requirement that students proceeding abroad for higher studies must possess either the Malaysian Certificate of Education or the Overseas School Certificate. But his move was to no avail. The Chinese, once aroused, refused to be placated, but pushed on with their campaign. On 14 July 1968, the acting president of the MCA, Khaw Kai Boh, announced that a Rahman College would be founded to counter the Merdeka University. Following him, the minister for education made it known that qualifications conferred by the Rahman College would be recognized by the government.[103] The difference between the Merdeka University and the Rahman College was that whilst the former would use Chinese as its main medium of instruction, the latter would use Malay and English.

In May 1969, a general election was to be held in the country. In order to win the support of Chinese voters, the government approved the application of the Merdeka University Limited Company to be registered.[104] The election was duly held which, however, eventuated into a bloody showdown between the Malays and the Chinese. The Merdeka

University was prohibited from raising funds and the attempt to start it was suspended.

GENERAL ELECTION, RACIAL RIOTS, AND A NEW ERA

On 10 May 1969, the general election was held. Three days later, riots broke out between the Malays and the Chinese. Malaysia entered into a new era in its politics.

When the results of the election were announced, it was found that for the national parliament the Alliance Party polled only 48 per cent of all votes, down by 10 per cent from 1964, when an earlier general election was held. And for the legislative assemblies of the various states, its harvest was only 47 per cent, also down by 10 per cent from 1964. The Parti Islam Se Malaysia (PAS), a Malay party more racial in nature than UMNO, eroded UMNO's Malay voter support, and the Gerakan Rakyat Malaysia (Gerakan), the Democratic Action Party (DAP), and the People's Progressive Party (PPP) also more racial in nature than the MCA, made inroads into its Chinese base. PAS kept the state of Kelantan, and Gerakan secured Penang. In Perak, the PPP, the DAP, and the Gerakan shared equal power with the Alliance Party; and in Selangor, the DAP and the Gerakan also shared seats equally with the Alliance Party. The probability that in both Perak and Selangor, Chinese parties could become the ruling parties rubbed hard on the Alliance Party and the Malay populace.[105]

That the PAS could take away Malay support from UMNO was because many Malay voters were dissatisfied with the continued dominance of the Chinese in the economy. And that the Gerakan, the DAP, and the PPP could profit at the expense of the MCA was because many of the Chinese electorate chafed at the continued political dominance of the Malays.[106]

On 12 May 1969, the triumphant Chinese opposition parties staged a victory procession in Kuala Lumpur. They taunted Malay bystanders with their victory slogans which evoked retaliation from them. The following day, the Malays also organized a procession. Riots between the races ensued, resulting in many casualties. The government declared a state of emergency in the country, suspended parliament, and established a National Operations Council, headed by Abdul Razak, to run the country's administration. Democratic rule was not restored until two years later.[107]

That the unsavoury situation could come about was blamed on Tunku Abdul Rahman by radicals in his party who charged him for being too compromising with the Chinese. Consequently, he resigned from his posts as president of UMNO and as prime minister of the country, and Abdul Razak took over from him.[108]

The general election of 1969 and the consequent racial riots were a watershed in the political development of the country. Thereafter, things changed.

It was seen in Chapter 2 that during the years between 1945 and 1955, in spite of the various challenges, the Chinese schools survived. However, from 1955 to 1969, they were not so fortunate. They still manage to survive, but not without substaining serious bruises. Given the pursuit of the "ultimate objective" on the part of the authorities, these Chinese schools could only maintain their primary schools intact. Their secondary schools were compelled to give up using the Chinese language as the main medium of instruction, or had to become independent by which they would not receive any government assistance. The independent schools, together with the Chinese primary schools, slipped into decline which stimulated Chinese educationists to revive a campaign to have the Chinese language made an official language. The effort ended in failure. Eventually, there was even an attempt to have the independent schools wither away by denying their graduates opportunities for higher studies, which spurred the community to found a university to meet the challenge. Another stroke of ill fortune to befall Chinese schools during these years was the MCA breaking ranks with Chinese educationists in the latter's effort to protect and advance the interests of Chinese education. Because of the tensions built up between the Chinese and the Malays over education problems as well as over other issues, a showdown between them broke out eventually which ushered in a new era in the political development of the country.

Notes

1   The *Star*, 25 March 2007, Special III: Tunku Abdul Rahman, *As I See It*; Ruslan Zainuddin, *Sejarah Malaysia*, Edisi ke-2 (Selangor, 2006), pp. 649–55.

2   Lee Ting Hui, *The Open United Front: The Communist Struggle In Singapore, 1954–1966* (Singapore, 1996), pp. 18–19.

3   Jim Baker, *Crossroads: A Popular History of Singapore & Malaysia* (Singapore, 1999), pp. 249–52; Ruslan Zainuddin, op. cit., pp. 652–58.

4   Ibid.

5   UCSTA, *Jiao Zong 33 Nian* (Kuala Lumpur, 1987) (hereafter op. cit. 1.), pp. 859–61; Federation of Malaya, *Report of the Education Committee, 1956*

(Kuala Lumpur, 1956) (Razak Report), p. 3 and pp. 873–74; Federation of Malaya, *Education Ordinance*, 1957 (No. 2 of 1957) (Kuala Lumpur, 1957), pp. 34–35 and 47; Tan Liok Ee, *The Politics of Chinese Education in Malaysia, 1945–1961* (Kuala Lumpur, 1997), pp. 169–80; Mok Soon Sang, *Ma Lai Xi Ya Jiao Yu Shi, 1400–1999* (Kuala Lumpur, 2000) (hereafter, Mok Soon Sang, op. cit. 1), p. 66.

[6]   Ibid., Mok Soon Sang, op. cit. 1, pp. 64–66.

[7]   UCSCA, *Feng Yu Ji Dang Yi Bai Ba Shi Nian* (Kuala Lumpur, 2001) (hereafter op. cit. 1) p. 22; Lim Lian Geok, *Feng Yu Shi Ba Nian*, vol. 2 (Kuala Lumpur, 2001), pp. 146–47.

[8]   Zheng Liang Shu, *Ma Lai Xi Ya Hua Wen Jiao Yu Fa Zan Shi*, vol. 3 (Kuala Lumpur, 2001), p. 319.

[9]   Tan Liok Ee, op. cit., pp. 178–79; Cheah Boon Kheng, *Malyasia: The Making of a Nation* (Singapore, 2004), p. 88; Zheng Liang Shu, op. cit., vol. 3, pp. 313–15.

[10]   Zheng Liang Shu, op. cit., vol. 3, pp. 312–14.

[11]   Lim Lian Geok, op. cit., vol. 1, pp. 146–49.

[12]   Lim Lian Geok, op. cit., vol. 1, pp. 150–53.

[13]   Lim Lian Geok, op. cit., vol. 1, pp. 154–59.

[14]   Lim Lian Geok, op. cit., vol. 1, pp. 162–63.

[15]   Lim Lian Geok, op. cit., vol. 1, pp. 164–67.

[16]   Lim Lian Geok, op. cit., vol. 1, pp. 174–77.

[17]   *Sin Chew Daily*, 22 May 1956, p. 8; Zheng Liang Shu, op. cit., vol. 3, p. 358; Tan Liok Ee, op. cit., p. 180.

[18]   *Sin Chew Daily*, 25 July 1956; *Nanyang Siang Pau*, 25 July 1956; Zheng Liang Shu, op. cit., vol. 3, pp. 363–64.

[19]   Tan Liok Ee, op. cit., pp. 183–86.

[20]   Zheng Liang Shu, op. cit., vol. 3, pp. 362–65.

[21]   *Sin Chew Daily*, 30 May 1956, p. 9; UCSTA, op. cit. 1, pp. 386–87; Zheng Liang Shu, op. cit., vol. 3, pp. 365–67.

[22]   Ibid.

[23]   Mok Soon Sang, op. cit. 1, p. 67; Tan Liok Ee, op. cit., pp. 180–81; Zheng Liang Shu, op. cit., vol. 3, p. 393.

[24]   Zheng Liang Shu, op. cit., vol. 3, pp. 398–99.

[25]   UCSTA, op. cit. 1, p. 390; Zheng Liang Shu, op. cit., vol. 3, p. 398.

[26]   Lim Lian Geok, op. cit., vol. 1, pp. 181–83; UCSTA, *Hua Wen Zhong Xue Gai Zhi Zhuan Ji* (Kuala Lumpur, 2000) (hereafter UCSTA, op. cit. 2), p. 7; Zheng Liang Shu, op. cit., vol. 3, pp. 399–400; Tan Liok Ee, op. cit., p. 209.

[27]   Zheng Liang Shu, op. cit., vol. 3, pp. 398–99.

[28]   *Sin Chew Daily*, 8 July 1955; UCSTA, op. cit. 1, p. 397; Zheng Liang Shu, op. cit., vol. 3, pp. 399–400.

[29]   UCSTA, op. cit. 1, p. 390; Zheng Liang Shu, op. cit., vol. 3, pp. 400, 402–03 and 406–07.

30   Zheng Liang Shu, op. cit., vol. 3, pp. 402 and 409.

31   Lim Lian Geok, op. cit., vol. 1, pp. 181–83.

32   Mok Soon Sang, op. cit. 1, p. 67; Tan Liok Ee, op. cit., pp. 180–81; Zheng Liang Shu, op. cit., vol. 3, pp. 407–08.

33   UCSTA, op. cit. 1, p. 390; Zheng Liang Shu, op. cit., vol. 3, pp. 408–09.

34   UCSCA, op. cit. 1, p. 23; Zheng Liang Shu, op. cit., vol. 3, pp. 409–13.

35   Zheng Liang Shu, op. cit., vol. 3, pp. 422–24.

36   *Sin Chew Daily*, 30 December 1956; Zheng Liang Shu, op. cit., vol. 3, pp. 403–04 and 415–18.

37   *Sin Chew Daily*, 14 January 1957 and 19 January 1957; Zheng Liang Shu, op. cit., vol. 3, pp. 418–22 and 432–33.

38   UCSCA, *Hua Guang Yong Yao* (Kuala Lumpur, 1993) (hereafter UCSCA, op. cit. 2), p. 11; Zheng Liang Shu, op. cit., vol. 3, pp. 424–25; Tan Liok Ee, op. cit., pp. 234–35.

39   Zheng Liang Shu, op. cit., vol. 3, pp. 425–26.

40   UCSTA, op. cit. 2, pp. 11–16; UCSCA, op. cit. 1, pp. 24–25; Zheng Liang Shu, op. cit., vol. 3, pp. 429–31.

41   Zheng Liang Shu, op. cit., vol. 3, pp. 435–42.

42   UCSCA, op. cit. 1, p. 25; Zheng Liang Shu, op. cit., vol. 3, p. 442.

43   UCSTA, op. cit. 1, pp. 387–88; Zheng Liang Shu, op. cit., vol. 3, pp. 367–69.

44   Zheng Liang Shu, op. cit., vol. 3, p. 367.

45   Zheng Liang Shu, op. cit., vol. 3. pp. 371–72.

46   Zheng Liang Shu, op. cit., vol. 3, pp. 372–74; UCSTA, op. cit. 1, p. 388.

47   Zheng Liang Shu, op. cit., vol. 3, p. 374.

48   *Guang Hua Ri Bao*, 3 August 1956; *China Press*, 3 August 1956; UCSTA, op. cit. 1, p. 389; Zheng Liang Shu, op. cit., vol. 3, pp. 375–76.

49   Zheng Liang Shu, op. cit., vol. 3, pp. 375–77. Zheng mentions Lim Lian Geok's banned *Hui Yi Pian Pian Lu*. See Lim Lian Geok, op. cit., vol. 2, pp. 91–95.

50   Ibid. UCSTA, op. cit. 1, p. 389; Zheng Liang Shu, op. cit., vol. 3, pp. 376–79; Mok Soon Sang, op. cit. 1, pp. 67–68.

51   UCSTA, op. cit. 1, p. 389; Zheng Liang Shu, op. cit., vol. 3, pp. 379–80; Mok Soon Sang, op. cit., p. 68.

52   Zheng Liang Shu, op. cit., vol. 3, p. 380.

53   Lim Lian Geok, op. cit., vol. 1, pp. 201–07; Zheng Liang Shu, op. cit., vol. 3, pp. 380–82.

54   Lim Lian Geok, op. cit., vol. 1, p. 204; UCSTA, op. cit. 1, pp. 415–17.

55   Zheng Liang Shu, op. cit., vol. 3, pp. 381 and 386–88.

56   Zheng Liang Shu, op. cit., vol. 3, p. 390.

57   *China Press*, 17 November 1957; Lim Lian Geok, op. cit., vol. 1, pp. 209–11; UCSTA, op. cit. 1, p. 418; UCSCA, op. cit. 1, p. 30; UCSCA, *Dong Zong 50 Nian (1954–2004)* (Kajang, 2004) (hereafter UCSCA, op. cit. 3), pp. 810–12; Tan Liok Ee, op. cit., pp. 248–50.

58   Lim Lian Geok, op. cit., vol. 2, p. 158; Ruslan Zainuddin, op. cit., p. 657.

[59] Lim Lian Geok, op. cit., vol. 2, p. 159.

[60] Lim Lian Geok, op. cit., vol. 2, pp. 158 and 168.

[61] Tan Liok Ee, op. cit., p. 251.

[62] Ibid., Kua Kia Soong, *A Protean Saga: The Chinese Schools in Malaysia* (Kuala Lumpur, 1985), p. 99.

[63] Lim Lian Geok, op. cit., vol. 2, pp. 117–23; Tan Liok Ee, op. cit., pp. 254–55 and 260–61.

[64] Tan Liok Ee, op. cit., pp. 255–56.

[65] Tan Liok Ee, op. cit., pp. 256–57.

[66] UCSTA, *Hua Wen Jiao Yu Shi Liao* (Kuala Lumpur, 1984) (hereafter UCSTA, op. cit. 3), vol. 1, p. 59; Zheng Liang Shu, op. cit., vol. 4, pp. 4–6.

[67] Zheng Liang Shu, op. cit., vol. 4, p. 9; Cheah Boon Kheng, op. cit., pp. 91–92; Tan Liok Ee, op. cit., p. 263, who says that Lim Chong Eu asked for thirty-five constituencies and not forty.

[68] Zheng Liang Shu, op. cit., vol. 4, p. 11; Cheah Boon Kheng, op. cit., p. 91; Tan Liok Ee, op. cit., pp. 263–64.

[69] Tan Liok Ee, op. cit., p. 264.

[70] Loot Ting Yee, *Wo Men de Zhe Yi Tiao Lu* (Kuala Lumpur, 1993), p. 26, says in effect: "The resignation of Lim Chong Eu ... Tan Siew Sin's leaning towards the UMNO ... Chinese education faces a greater ill fate". Lim Chong Eu went abroad for medical treatment and rest. When he returned to Malaya, he undertook to organize the United Democratic Party to carry on fighting for his political ideals. See Ibrahim Saad, *Pendidikan dan Politik di Malaysia* (Kuala Lumpur, 1977), p. 59; Tan Liok Ee, op. cit., pp. 264–65.

[71] Ruslan Zainuddin, op. cit., pp. 716–18; Cheah Boon Keng, op. cit., p. 92.

[72] UCSTA, op. cit. 1, pp. 861–64; Federation of Malaya, *Report of the Education Review Committee, 1960* (Kuala Lumpur, 1960) (Talib Report); *Education Act, 1961* (Kuala Lumpur, 1961); Mok Soon Sang, op. cit. 1, pp. 78–80.

[73] Ibid. Zheng Liang Shu, op. cit., vol. 4, pp. 20–26.

[74] Zheng Liang Shu, op. cit., vol. 4, pp. 22–23; UCSCA, op. cit. 1, p. 33.

[75] *China Press*, 24 October 1961; UCSTA, op. cit. 2, pp. 22–25 and op. cit. 3, pp. 22–25; Zheng Liang Shu, op. cit., vol. 4, pp. 34–38 and 43–45.

[76] UCSTA Secretariat, *Lim Liang Gong An* (Kuala Lumpur, 1987), pp. 97–103; Lim Lian Geok, op. cit, vol. 2, pp. 79, 83 and 85–86.

[77] UCSCA, op. cit. 1, pp. 36–38; UCSTA, op. cit. 3, mid vol., p. 51; Lim Lian Geok, op. cit., vol. 2, pp. 90–94.

[78] UCSCA, op. cit. 1, p. 38.

[79] UCSTA Secretariat, *Lim Lian Geok Gong Min Quan An* (Kuala Lumpur, 1989); Lim Lian Geok, op. cit., vol. 2, pp. 96–115; UCSTA, op. cit. 3, mid vol., pp. 51–53.

[80] Lim Lian Geok, op. cit., vol. 2, p. 125; K.J. Ratnam, *Communalism and the Political Process in Malaya* (Kuala Lumpur, 1963), p. 26; Kua Kia Soong, op. cit., pp. 118–19.

81　Kua Kia Soong, op. cit., pp. 109–10.

82　UCSTA, op. cit. 1, p. 749; Mok Soon Sang, op. cit. 1, p. 82.

83　Chai Hon Chan, *Education and Nation Building in Plural Societies: The West Malaysian Experience* (Canberra, 1977), p. 94; Mok Soon Sang, op. cit. 1, p. 83.

84　Wong Hoy Kee and Ee Tiang Hong, *Education in Malaysia*, 2nd edition (Kuala Lumpur, 1975), pp. 99–100.

85　Ministry of Education, *Educational Statistics of Malaysia, 1958–1967* (Kuala Lumpur, 1968).

86　Gordon P. Means, *Malaysian Politics* (London, 1976) p. 429; Zheng Liang Shu, op. cit., vol. 4, p. 117.

87　Zheng Liang Shu, op. cit., vol. 4, pp. 115–17.

88　See Chapter 2.

89　Ibid.

90　Zheng Liang Shu, op. cit., vol. 4, pp. 118–20.

91　Zheng Liang Shu, op. cit., vol. 4, pp. 118–21.

92　Zheng Liang Shu, op. cit., vol. 4, p. 120.

93　Sim Mow Yu, *Shi Zai Huo Bu Mie* (Kuala Lumpur, 1996), pp. 9–13; UCSCA, op. cit. 1, p. 44; Zheng Liang Shu, op. cit., vol. 4, pp. 120–41.

94　*China Press*, 28 September 1965; Zheng Liang Shu, op. cit., vol. 4, pp. 130–31.

95　Zheng Liang Shu, op. cit., vol. 4, p. 131; *Sin Chew Daily*, 2 October 1965.

96　Sim Mow Yu, op. cit., pp. 14–19; Zheng Liang Shu, op. cit., vol. 4, pp. 134–136.

97　Sim Mow Yu, op. cit., pp. 74–75; *Sin Chew Daily*, 19 October 1966; *Berita Harian*, 20 October 1966.

98　Kua Kia Soong, op. cit., p. 123; Zheng Liang Shu, op. cit., vol. 4, pp. 140–41.

99　UCSTA, op. cit. 3, mid volume, pp. 58 and 71; Zheng Liang Shu, op. cit., vol. 4, p. 140; Kua Kia Soong, op. cit., pp. 121 and 123.

100　Mok Soon Sang, *Pendidikan di Malaysia*, Edisi ke-7 (Selangor, 2006) (hereafter Mok Soon Sang, op. cit. 2), pp. 302–05, Appendix II; Alis Puteh, *Language and Nation Building* (Selangor, 2006), pp. 115–16; UCSTA, op. cit. 1, pp. 865–66.

101　UCSCA, op. cit. 1, p. 47. Zheng Liang Shu, op. cit., vol. 4, p. 170.

102　UCSTA, op. cit. 1, pp. 492–93; Sim Mow Yu, *Sim Mow Yu Yan Lun Ji*, vol. 1 (Kuala Lumpur, 1998), pp. 250–52; UCSCA, op. cit. 1, pp. 48–50.

103　Zheng Liang Shu, op. cit., vol. 4, p. 181.

104　UCSCA, op. cit. 1, p. 57; Zheng Liang Shu, op. cit., vol. 4, p. 185.

105　Kua Kia Soong, *May 13* (Selangor, 2007), pp. 30–31 (hereafter Kua Kia Soong, op. cit. 2); Cheah Boon Kheng, op. cit., p. 105.

106　Kua Kia Soong, op. cit. 2, pp. 35–38; Harold Crouch, op. cit., p. 213.

107　Zakaria Hj Ahmad, *Government and Politics*, vol. 2 (Kuala Lumpur, 2007), pp. 54–55; Kua Kia Soong, op. cit. 2, pp. 42–51.

108　Cheah Boon Kheng, op. cit., pp. 106–08.

4

ONE-MEDIUM EDUCATION UNDER RUKUN NEGARA AND THE NEW ECONOMIC POLICY

After the general election and the racial riots of 1969, with Abdul Razak replacing Tunku Abdul Rahman as the leader of the nation, things took a radical turn in the country as observed. The Malays found Tunku Abdul Rahman to be too compromising with the Chinese, and his successor adopted a more pro-Malay attitude than him. Yet, at the same time, Abdul Razak did not seek to squeeze out the non-Malay communities altogether. In fact, he sought and worked out a better understanding with them.

On the pro-Malay side, Abdul Razak took measures to ensure the political dominance of the Malays in the country could and would not be challenged again. He had a national ideology, called the "Rukun Negara" or "Articles of Faith of the State", promulgated which defined the political orientation of the country for years to come. Next he made parliament, when it was reconvened, to pass legislation to bar all sensitive issues, that is, issues pertaining mainly to the special position of the Malays, from public discussion. He also initiated a New Economic Policy which sought to improve the economic lot of the Malays *vis-à-vis* the other communities radically.

As for forging a more workable *modus vivendi* especially with the non-Malay races, he enlarged the Alliance Party into a Barisan Nasional to include some of the opposition parties, which eroded the voter support of the MCA in the general election. He also extended a friendly hand to the PAS, which ate into the base of UMNO itself.

In line with the grim determination to put beyond the pale any questioning of the political dominance and intensified efforts to better the economic position of the Malays, an even more decisive thrust was made in the education field to realize the ultimate objective of a one-medium schooling. On this occasion, English-medium schools were to bear the brunt of the offensive.

On 31 August 1970, National Day, the Rukun Negara was promulgated. It read:[1]

> Our nation, Malaysia, being dedicated to achieving a greater unity of all her peoples; to maintaining a democratic way of life; to creating a just society in which the wealth of the nation shall be equitably shared; to ensuring a liberal approach to her rich and diverse cultural traditions; to building a progressive society which shall be orientated to modern science and technology.
>
> We, her people, pledge our united efforts to attain these ends guided by these principles:
>
> Belief in God
> Loyalty to King and Country
> Sanctity of the Constitution
> Rule of Law
> Good Behaviour and Morality

It was a definitive statement.

These articles of faith were to be taught to all children in all schools.[2]

Parliament was reconvened in February 1971 and a bill, the Sensitive Issues Bill, to amend the constitution so as to prohibit public discussion of sensitive issues, was debated. It was passed with an overwhelming majority and became the Sedition Act.[3]

The New Economic Policy, in general terms, aimed to enable the Malay community to acquire a 30 per cent share of the wealth of the country, to be realized over a period of twenty years from 1970 to 1990. The Chinese and Indians together were to own 40 per cent, and foreigners 30 per cent. This called for measures to be taken not only to increase the economic production of the country but to end the compartmentalization of economic activities along racial lines. This was because all along, most Malays were confined to the less productive, traditional agricultural sector of the country's economy, and the non-Malays were active in the more productive, modern industrial and commercial sector. The Malays were to be inducted into advanced economic activities.

In line with this, it is to be noted that in the education field, Malay students were to be given preference over non-Malay students in admission to public universities. The purpose of this was to increase the number of Malays in the various professions.[4]

On 1 June 1974, the Alliance was enlarged to become the Barisan Nasional (National Front). What is significant, for interracial relations in Peninsular Malaysia, was that Gerakan and the PPP were included in the new alignment. While the PAS, a party to the right of UMNO, was also included, the DAP, a party to the left not only of the MCA but also of Gerakan and the PPP, however, was not. It was considered too radical an organization. The Barisan Nasional rules the country even today. Along with this widening of the united front, Abdul Razak established diplomatic relations with mainland China and paid an official visit to the country. The move uplifted the spirits of the Chinese in Malaysia.[5]

The Conversion of English-stream Institutions to Malay

It has been noted in Chapter 3 that, after the passing of the National Language Act in 1967 and during the years between 1968 and 1982, steps were taken by the government to convert all English-medium National-Type Primary Schools, as well as National-Type Secondary Schools, into Malay-medium National Primary Schools, and National-Type Secondary Schools which use Malay as the main medium of instruction.[6] From 1983, English-medium tertiary institutions also started to be changed into Malay-medium institutions.

The following lists the years in which the conversions took place:[7]

1970

(1) All subjects in Standard One in English-medium National-Type Primary Schools no longer taught in English, but in Malay.

(2) Geography and history in Standard Four in English-medium National-Type Primary Schools no longer taught in English, but in Malay.

(3) In English-medium Secondary Technical Schools, Malay-medium classes were set up.

1973

All arts subjects in Form One in English-medium National-Type Secondary Schools no longer taught in English, but in Malay.

1975

All English-medium National-Type Primary Schools converted into Malay-medium National Primary Schools.

1976

(1) No more English-medium "remove classes" in English-medium National-Type Secondary Schools as they were no longer necessary.
(2) Not only all arts, but also all science and technical subjects in Form One in English-medium National-Type Secondary Schools no longer taught in English, but in Malay.
(3) All arts subjects in Form Four in English-medium National-Type Secondary Schools no longer taught in English, but in Malay.

1978

Arts streams in Form Six (Lower) in English-medium National-Type Secondary Schools no longer taught in English, but in Malay.

1980

The first year in arts and allied courses in English-medium universities no longer taught in English, but in Malay.

1981

Not only arts streams, but also science and technical streams in Form Six (Lower) in English-medium National-Type Secondary Schools no longer taught in English, but in Malay.

1982

All English-medium National-Type Secondary Schools fully converted to Malay.

1983

The first year, not only in arts and allied courses in English-medium universities, but also in other disciplines such as science, engineering, medicine, and so on, was no longer taught in English, but in Malay.

In conjunction with the above measures, the authorities also took steps to replace English with Malay as the medium of public secondary school examinations. These steps were:[8]

1978

The English-medium Lower Certificate of Education (LCE) examination replaced with the Malay-medium Sijil Rendah Pelajaran (SRP) examination.

1980

The English-medium Malaysian Certificate of Education (MCE) examination replaced with the Malay-medium Sijil Pelajaran Malaysia (SPM) examination.

1982

The English-medium Higher School Certificate (HSC) examination replaced with the Malay-medium Sijil Tinggi Persekolahan (STP) examination.

Admission Preference for Malay Students to Public Universities

In 1971, a Majid Report recommended that Malay students be given special considerations during admissions to public universities. This gave rise to what became known as the quota system, and scholarships being first given to Malay students, then to non-Malay students.

On these points, the report bears quoting:

> First ... the University should decide and state clearly that it is the university policy to ensure as far as possible that the racial composition of the student population, not only in the university as a whole but on a faculty by faculty basis, should reflect the racial composition in the country.

There were more Malays than non-Malays in the country.

Secondly, the University authorities should ensure that faculties with poor Malay representation ... should make every conscious effort to obtain the admission of Malay students. It is clear to us that there were more Malay students who had the required qualifications than were admitted. They could have, therefore, been admitted if the University authorities had been clearly directed to provide for a proper racial balance in the different faculties.

Thirdly, in each faculty, students, who come from rural areas where the facilities for the study of science are limited, should be given special assistance and tuition ... It is a fact that those living and educated in the rural areas are educationally under-privileged. Their full potential cannot be known on the basis of the HSC [Higher School Certificate] results alone.

Students from the rural areas were mostly Malay students.

Fourthly, we therefore recommend that the criteria for admission should include other factors besides the HSC results and that the University authorities should give weightage to those from the rural areas.

Fifthly, we recommend that the scholarship awarding authorities should award more scholarships in the sciences to Malay students in order to rectify the present racial imbalance in these faculties.

So the quota system was born. Some statistics which are available will enable us to see the picture of student representation of the various races in the various universities after the Majid Report was accepted and implemented.[9]

Table 4.1
Percentages of Students of Various Races Attending
Degree Courses in Various Public Universities

Year	Malay	Chinese	Indian	Others
1970	40.2	48.8	7.3	3.7
1980	66.7	26.2	6.0	1.0

Source: See note 9.

The dramatic change in fortune among the various races over a decade is unmistakable.

Efforts of the MCA to Win Back Chinese Support and Reverse Its Fortunes

Because of the loss of Chinese support and the reverses it suffered during the general election in 1969, during the decade that followed, that is, during the 1970s, the MCA made great efforts to try to regain that support and improve its position. Another compulsion was that, on one occasion, the deputy prime minister, Dr Ismail, remarked that if the MCA continued to lose support, UMNO might stop cooperating with it.[10] The movement was led by its president, Tan Siew Sin, and after 1974 by Lee San Choon who replaced Tan as the leader. The attempts by Tan did not seem to have led to results except in one area. The struggle by Lee also did not seem to have fared better.

The MCA had all along been identified as a party of rich men, known in Chinese as *tou jia*. This was considered to be one of the reasons the party was unable to arouse the thorough enthusiasm of ordinary Chinese. Rich men were generally looked upon as fending more for themselves than for the whole Chinese community. So the first move Tan Siew Sin made was to induct professionals into the party to become members and even leaders. As professionals were not as high up as the *tou jia* in the scales of wealth, they were thought of as more responsive to the aspirations of the masses. So prominent names such as Lim Keng Yaik, a physician, Alex Lee, a lawyer, and Tan Tiong Hong, another physician, joined the MCA. These were followed by many others, and the group of them became a force in the party.[11]

Lim Keng Yaik was made much of by Tan Siew Sin initially. He was appointed head of the MCA in the state of Perak as well as recommended to the cabinet to become a special functions minister.[12] Unfortunately, the two soon fell apart. Lim was bent on introducing drastic reforms to the party to clean it up. The breaking point was when Lim haboured the intention to usurp Tan's presidency in the party. Consequently, Tan got Lim expelled from the MCA and pressurized him to resign from his ministerial post. A number of the professionals came to the support of Lim, and spoke to Tan to try to get Lim rehabilitated. Tan not only refused to accept the request, but also expelled nearly 200 of the group from the party, including Alex Lee.[13]

After Lim was expelled from the MCA, he joined Lim Chong Eu's Gerakan. He prospered in that party thereafter.

Tan Siew Sin's dream and effort of working with professionals was, therefore, not a success. The outcome probably impacted adversely on the MCA.

A second enterprise undertaken by Tan Siew Sin to rebuild the fortunes of the MCA was to initiate a Malaysian Chinese National Unity Movement. This was done at the suggestion of the young professionals and various Chinese organizations. The first meeting towards the purpose was held on 7 February 1971 in Kuala Lumpur[14] and the second one eleven days later in Ipoh.[15] At the first meeting, Tan for the first time admitted that the MCA had made mistakes and declared that he was prepared to retire if he was considered to be an obstacle to Chinese unity. The second meeting was attended by a huge number of people, and Chinese educationists and others such as Sim Mow Yu and Guang Gu Xing participated. The movement was later to adopt a constitution which defined its purposes. This document deserved some attention:[16]

> The aims and objects of the Movement shall be:
> 1. To safeguard and uphold the constitution of Malaysia.
> 2. To strive for the unity of all Malaysian Chinese to make an effective contribution to consolidate the unity [of the people] of Malaysia.
> 3. To strive for the unity of all Malaysians of whatever origin for the stability, well-being and progress of Malaysia.
> 4. To uphold and safeguard the equal and inalienable rights and fundamental liberties of every Malaysian.
> 5. To strive for the upliftment of the "have-nots" of all races in sharing the growing prosperity of Malaysia.
> 6. To co-operate with other Malaysians in the spirit of the national ideology – Rukun Negara.
> 7. To strive for the furtherance of equal opportunities in the economic, social and political advancement of all Malaysians in a democratic and just society.
> 8. To use all lawful, political, social and economic means for the attainment of the aims and objects of the Movement and to do such other things as may be deemed incidental or conducive to the attainment of the above objects or any of them.

It seemed to be a well thought out philosophy.

Incidental to the meeting was that Sim Mow Yu and Gu Guang Xing were considered to have made seditious speeches at the meeting by the authorities.

Consequently, they were arrested and charged under the Sedition Act in court. The two went through many hearings in court, but finally the charge against them was annulled.[17]

The Malaysian Chinese National Unity Movement eventually came to a sorry end. It folded up. Two factors accounted for this. One was the UMNO exerting pressure on it to desist. The other was that the MCA developed differences with the various Chinese public organizations, the nature of which was not disclosed to the public.[18]

A third step taken by Tan Siew Sin to rebuild the MCA was to renew the party's former alliance with UCSCA and UCSTA. As seen previously, that alliance was forged in 1953, but unfortunately terminated in 1958.[19] On 4 December 1971, an all-nation conference of representatives from UCSCA, UCSTA and the MCA was convened to effect the renewed alliance. On that occasion, Tan Siew Sin declared that the meeting would strive to forge a common stand and struggle for a common goal for all.[20] The conference issued a manifesto of five demands to protect and further the cause of Chinese education. The five demands, in essence, were:[21]

(1) That organization and powers of committees of Chinese schools should be preserved so as to show respect for the tradition of the Chinese in running their schools.
(2) That the Chinese language, in both its written and spoken forms, be maintained as the main medium of instruction as well as of examinations in Chinese primary schools so that such schools would never changed in their character.
(3) That the proposals of the Aziz Report (which was first released to the public for discussion in 1969 and finalized in 1972) be implemented to revive the Senior Middle Three public examination so that there would be a supply of teachers for Chinese primary schools.
(4) That the degrees of Chinese-medium universities be recognized so that the graduates of such institutions could make use of their talents and fufil their responsibility as citizens of the nation.
(5) That other issues such as the ideal number of hours for teaching the Chinese language in National-Type Secondary Schools, training for temporary teachers and the correct salaries for teachers, were regarded as valid and legitimate, and should be met in a just and fair manner.

These aspirations, if met, would go a long way to promote the welfare of Chinese education indeed.

The renewed alliance started off with great promise.

However, it soon fell apart again. In 1975, the cabinet appointed a committee to review the education system in the country. The MCA on the one hand, and UCSCA and UCSTA on the other, could not agree on a common memorandum on Chinese education to be sent to that committee. Finally, each side presented its own memorandum. The alliance among the three organizations once more came to a naught. However, in 1975, it was no longer Tan Siew Sin who precipitated the break, but his successor, Lee San Choon. This parting of ways did no good to the image of the MCA in the Chinese mind.[22]

In 1974, there was a general election. In the past, the MCA was given thirty-three constituencies by the Alliance Party to contest. However, on this occasion, it was given only twenty-three by the Barisan Nasional which had replaced the Alliance Party. The stars of the MCA could not be dimmer.[23]

On the eve of the election, Tan Siew Sin resigned from his presidency in the MCA on grounds of ill health and was succeeded by Lee San Choon. On assuming the leadership of the party, Lee straightaway, following in the footsteps of his predecessor, took a deep plunge to change the fate of the party.[24]

The first thing Lee did was to affirm Tan Siew Sin's policy of changing the image of the MCA as an organization of rich men or *tou jia*. He also made it a point of bringing in professionals to join the party. He went to the extent of opening the party's doors even to leftists. The whole group became Lee's think-tank, and congregated frequently in his house to devise policies and plans. In befriending the professionals, unlike Tan Siew Sin, Lee never did a thing so disadvantageous to the party as breaking relationship with any one of them. This stood the party in good stead.[25]

After many discussions with the professionals, Lee San Choon came out with a five-point plan to win mass support for the MCA. The plan would benefit not only his party but the also the whole Chinese community. The five points were:[26]

(1) Turn the MCA into a mass party. Recruit as many people as possible to its membership.
(2) Expand the party's Rahman College to provide more opportunities to Chinese students to study at the tertiary level.

(3) Get the Chinese community to participate in big businesses so as to ease the difficulties they faced due to the working of the government's New Economic Policy.

(4) Establish Chinese cultural associations so as to develop Chinese culture.

(5) Erect prestigious premises to house the party so as to uplift its image.

It was an impressive plan.

While on the one hand, Lee San Choon put in his best efforts to save his party, on the other, he did something which soured its relationship with the Chinese community. And that was failing to work out a common memorandum on Chinese education with UCSCA and UCSTA to present to the Cabinet Committee reviewing the education system in the country. He even severed the MCA's alliance with them.

Boards of Managers and Boards of Governors to Wind Up, and Lower Qualified Teachers to Lose Status

In mid-July 1961, a Unified Teaching Service Salary Scheme was implemented in the country for the benefit of all teachers. This was later found to be deficient and was replaced in 1972 by an Aziz Salary Scheme as recommended by the Aziz Report. The effect of the new scheme was to have boards of managers in primary schools and boards of governors in secondary schools, hereafter school boards, wound up, and teachers with qualifications lower than a designated level to lose status. Both these developments were unwelcome in Chinese educational circles.

The Unified Teaching Service Salary Scheme made school boards employers of teachers and other staff in all assisted schools. This was different from the previous practice, which, in the case of government Malay and English schools, the government was the employer.[27]

It is to be observed that the change was not so advantageous for teachers in government institutions. So a number of them did not join the scheme. When they were employees of the government, they were entitled to government medical care, pensions on retirement, and other privileges. Under the Unified Teaching Service Salary Scheme, they would lose these benefits. To provide for retirement, they would have to contribute part of their salaries to an Employees' Provident Fund, as well as a Teachers' Provident Fund. However, many teachers who were not employees or servants of the government had no choice but to join the Unified Teaching Service Salary Scheme.[28]

Because so many teachers preferred to be employees of the government rather than of school boards, and due to some other considerations, in April 1967, the government appointed a committee led by Justice Abdul Aziz to look into the whole matter of renumeration for teachers.[29] In September 1971, Aziz finalized his findings and issued a report which embodied his recommendations.[30]

One recommendation made by Aziz was that school boards from henceforth should be wound up and transformed into organs performing the function of helping in school development. This recommendation came about because of the other recommendation which was that teachers in the Unified Teaching Service Salary Scheme who opted to join the proposed new Aziz Salary Scheme would henceforth no longer be employees of such school boards, but of the government instead. So such school boards were no longer necessary and should be transformed.

It was ironical that while the Aziz Report on the one hand made recommendations to benefit the teachers, on the other, it made recommendations which harmed the welfare of many of them. The latter came about because of the following stipulations. The report said that teachers who wished to join the new scheme must possess the Malaysian Certificate of Education (MCE) or its equivalent, as well as, simultaneously, recognized professional diplomas or certificates. Those who did not have the MCE, but who wished to join the new scheme must, within a stipulated period, take and pass the MCE examination with credits in three subjects. Teachers who were in this group were those who only had a Lower Certificate of Education (LCE) or a Junior Middle Three pass. Otherwise, they would be treated as B class teachers, that is, underqualified teachers. According to estimates, there were 25,000 people in this group. Along with the above two provisions, the Aziz Report also required that new recruits into the teaching service must not only possess the MCE, but must also have scored a credit in the Malay language.

The proposal to wound up school boards agitated Chinese educational circles very much. The requirement that teachers must have the minimal qualification of the MCE or its equivalent, however, was accepted as something inevitable. On the two recommendations, it is perhaps interesting to read the words of the Aziz Report itself:[31]

> We have recommended ... that all UTS [Unified Teaching Service] teachers should be given the option to become Government servants ... that a Central Pay System should be introduced whereby teachers' salaries will be administered directly by the Ministry. If these recommendations

are accepted, the Boards will no longer be required to exercise the powers of appointment and dismissal of teachers and other employees and payment of their salaries.

UCSCA and UCSTA first met on 26 October 1971, and then both met with the MCA on 4 December 1971, to voice protest against the proposal to have school boards wound up. Resolutions were passed to the effect.[32] A day after the second meeting, a delegation of 200 went to see the minister for education, Hussein Onn, about their case. The minister assured them that their school boards would not be dissolved, but only reorganized. (What this amounted to in the end was that the boards were allowed to retain their names, but their power of employing and dismissing teachers and other staff had to be given up. What would remain for them was to help in school development. They could also continue to run the canteens and textbook sales departments in their schools.)[33]

Regardless of the protests and actions taken by the Chinese educationists, the government went ahead with making changes to the school boards. The 1961 Education Act was amended to become an Akta Pelajaran (Pindaan) [Education Act (Amended)], 1972, to authorize the changes. On 7 February 1972, the senate of parliament passed the new law. Clause 26A of the new law stated:[34]

> On the date to be determined by the Minister, every board of managers and governors in any fully assisted school or fully assisted educational institution shall be wound up in such manner as the Minister may determine; and thereupon it shall cease to employ and to be the employers of teachers and other employees and every instrument of management or government pertaining to such school or educational institution shall cease to have effect.

The dice, although the names of the school boards were not to be changed, was cast.

According to Clause 116A of the amended act, the minister for education was also empowered to establish parent-teacher associations for schools. Such organizations were supposed to help the schools look after the welfare of both students and teachers, as well as to render financial assistance for school development so as to enable them to function more efficiently.[35]

In spite of the fact that the *de facto* dissolution of school boards had already been effected, Chinese educational circles were still not satisfied with what had happened. On 6 March 1977, they called a representatives' meeting in which they demanded that Clause 26A and another clause in the amended act be annulled. However, on 25 October the same year, the then minister for education, Dr Mahathir Mohamad, declared in parliament that in the future new schools would have no school boards, but only bodies which would raise funds to help in school development. Parent-teacher associations would help to look after the welfare of pupils and teachers to enable the schools to function more efficiently.[36]

People Ignorant of Chinese Deployed to be Headmasters and School Clerks in National-Type Chinese Primary Schools

In April 1973, the headmaster of a National-Type Chinese Primary School in a new village called Bercham in the state of Perak retired. Two months later, the state education authority sent a man to fill the vacancy. However, this man was ignorant of the Chinese language. How could a man ignorant of Chinese be the headmaster of a Chinese school? The move, therefore, evoked a storm of protest in the Chinese educational circles.[37]

Earlier on, when the government took the measure to remove the power of school management committees/boards to hire and fire school staff, including headmasters and other employees, due to pleas from such committees/ boards, it had verbally agreed that, when a new headmaster was to be appointed to a Chinese school, two months before the appointment took effect, it would send the name of the proposed new officer, together with his particulars, to the school management committee/board concerned for consideration. If the said school management committee/board was not satisfied with the proposed person, a new candidate could be chosen. On this occasion, when the Perak education authorities sent the new principal to Bercham, this agreement was ignored and flouted.[38]

The first to lodge a protest was the management committee of the Bercham school itself. However, this drew the response from the Perak education authority that the new man would be put on probation for two months. If found unsatisfactory, then something would be done.[39]

The next to follow was the local council in the new village. It sent a letter to the Perak education authorities, demanding that it rescind its order sending the new man. Otherwise, the council would get all parents of pupils and villagers to sign a petition to exert pressure.[40]

The above steps were followed first by UCSCA president Yang Cheng Cai who called on the Perak education authorities to desist from making its move.[41]

Then UCSCA, UCSTA and the MCA all joined hands to request the minister for education to intervene in the case and to punish the Perak education authorities.[42] Some time later, the three organizations petitioned the minister for education again.[43]

Eventually, because of all the pressures, the Perak education authorities succumbed. It sent another man to Bercham instead of the proposed original man. The new man was conversant with Chinese.[44]

Admidst all the hue and cry caused by the proposed misdeed of the Perak education authorities, the chairman and the secretary of a "Quan Guo Wei Hu Hua Jiao Xing Dong Lian Luo Xiao Zu" (All-Nation Protect Chinese Education Action Liaison Group), Chen Guo Jie and Chen Qing Jia, from the opposition party DAP, disclosed to the press that there had been other misdeeds on the part of the various state education authorities. It was revealed that in Selangor, persons who had no knowledge of Chinese had been sent to at least ten Chinese schools to be school clerks. And in Kedah as well as Perak, such persons were similarly deployed in several Chinese schools. The revelation was disturbing.[45]

Quite obviously, these moves of appointing persons ignorant of Chinese to be headmasters or school clerks in National-Type Chinese Primary Schools were to subvert them. While the Bercham case was rectified, what happened after the disclosure by the DAP in the other cases concerning school clerks, was unknown, however.

The Plight of National-Type Chinese Primary Schools in the 1970s

During the 1970s, the National-Type Chinese Primary Schools in the country were plagued with a number of problems. These was insufficient funding, insufficient qualified staffing, insufficient places for students, and a high rate of failure among students who had gone on from primary to secondary schooling.

The National-Type Chinese Primary Schools were either fully or partially aided by the government. Moreover, their students were exempt from paying fees. Yet the money given by the government was always found to be inadequate, and funds had frequently to be raised from the public for development purposes. Table 4.2 shows the finances for development given by the government to the various language streams of education during the 1970s:[46]

Table 4.2
Funds for Development Given by the Ministry of Education
to Schools of the Different Language Streams,
1971–78

Year	National Primary $	National-Type Chinese Primary $	National-Type Tamil Primary $
1971	2,401,156	—	—
1972	15,833,276	578,400	243,400
1973	24,856,230	746,500	139,450
1974	36,947,345	1,016,300	420,000
1975	28,790,308	2,309,900	1,569,000
1976	37,015,313	5,212,600	518,200
1977	30,427,850	1,892,800	880,600
1978	63,248,005	6,340,880	2,122,010
Total	239,519,483	18,097,380	5,892,660
%	91%	7%	2%

Source: See note 46.

The lion's share of the funds went to National Primary Schools which were Malay-medium schools. The amounts given to the Chinese and Tamil streams trailed far behind.

A second problem that stared the National-Type Chinese Primary Schools in the face in the 1970s was an insufficient supply of trained teachers. At the same time, the number of students in these schools increased greatly. This came about primarily because during those years, National-Type English Primary Schools were gradually being converted into National Primary Schools. The Chinese students in those schools flocked to National-Type Chinese Primary Schools rather than join the National Primary Schools. On the other hand, the government just could not or did not train enough teachers for the National-Type Chinese Primary Schools to cope with the increase. Table 4.3 shows the increase in the number of students in National-Type Chinese Primary Schools due to influxes from former National-Type English Primary Schools.[47]

Table 4.3
Numbers of Chinese Students in the National-Type Chinese Primary
Schools and Numbers of Chinese Students in the Former
National-Type English Primary Schools, 1971–78

Year	National-Type Chinese Primary Schools: Number of Chinese Students	Former National-Type English Primary Schools: Number of Chinese Students
1971	409,980	113,843
1972	431,018	103,675
1973	445,406	95,219
1974	458,788	84,273
1975	472,980	75,346
1976	478,849	70,065
1977	484,198	66,854
1978	486,710	64,916

Source: See note 47.

The figures in the last column are telling.

Because professionally trained teachers were in short supply, the government resorted to hiring non-professionally trained teachers to fill the need. Such teachers were looked upon as temporary teachers. Table 4.4 shows the number of temporary teachers employed each year from 1973 to 1980.[48]

Table 4.4
Numbers of Temporary Teachers in National-Type
Chinese Primary Schools, 1973–80

Year	Number of Temporary Teachers
1973	1,588
1974	3,188
1975	3,000
1976	1,600
1977	1,600
1978	1,346
1979	1,300
1980	1,630

Source: See note 48.

The figures for 1974 and 1975 ballooned because of the conversion of National-Type English Primary Schools to National Primary Schools during those years.

Because of the shortage of professionally trained teachers for the National-Type Chinese Primary Schools, the government had undertaken to train some of the temporary teachers to become fully qualified teachers from as early as 1969. This was done in holiday training classes, called "Kursus Perguruan Dalam Masa Cuti Sekolah Rendah Cina" [Chinese Primary School School Holiday Teacher Training Classes]. Table 4.5 portrays the number of such teachers trained between 1969 and 1979.[49]

Table 4.5
Number of Temporary Teachers Trained in
Kursus Perguruan Dalam Masa Cuti Sekolah
Rendah Cina, 1969–79

Year	Number
1969	206
1970	20
1971	Unavailable
1972	250
1973	255
1974	99
1975	285
1976	561
1977	973
1978	446
1979	437
Total	3,532

Source: See note 49.

The number of temporary teachers employed each year numbered much more than 1,000, and, out of these, so few were recruited to be trained each year that the problem was hardly solved.

It is to be observed that the various teacher training colleges in the country also turned out professionally trained ethnic Chinese teachers every year. But the number produced averaged only 600, and this number included not only ethnic Chinese teachers trained in the Chinese stream, but also ethnic Chinese teachers trained in the English stream. So, even with teacher training colleges put into the equation, the shortfall was not met.[50]

A third ill that plagued National-Type Chinese Primary Schools was that there were insufficient classrooms to accommodate the ever increasing number of students in the 1970s. According to records, from 1957, the year the country achieved independence, to the 1970s, the government built only one Chinese-medium primary school in Kepong Desa Jaya. Because of this, the classrooms in National-Type Chinese Primary Schools, particularly those in the urban areas, were crammed with students and became overcrowded. To solve this problem, many schools resorted to opening afternoon sessions besides the morning sessions. This affected the efficiency of teaching.[51]

A fourth malaise that hit National-Type Chinese Primary Schools hurt the graduates of these schools grievously. After 1961, because National-Type Chinese Secondary Schools were converted into National-Type English Secondary Schools, students graduating from those primary schools had to attend a "remove" or preparatory class for one year to study and improve their command of the English language before they could be promoted. In spite of the one-year special training, many students, however, were unable to cope with the English language. This led to their failing their Lower Certificate of Education (LCE) examination and the Malaysian Certificate of Education (MCE) examination in their secondary schooling and their future being affected. In the 1970s, as we noted before, the National-Type English Secondary Schools were converted into National-Type Secondary Schools which used Malay as the main medium of instruction. Graduates from the National-Type Chinese Primary Schools who wished to further their studies now had to attend a one-year "remove" or preparatory class not so much as to improve their command of the English language, but to improve their Malay language skills. Many students failed to make the grade and consequently failed the LCE and MCE examinations now conducted in Malay, and had to face dimmer prospects in life.[52]

The situations in the National-Type Chinese Primary Schools in the 1970s were in a sorry state.

The Independent Chinese Secondary Schools: Their Sorry State and the Initiation of a Movement to Revive Them

Table 3.1 in Chapter 3 shows the general trend of decline in the number of independent Chinese secondary schools and their students during the years between 1962 and 1969. It was also noted that the decline caused alarm in

Chinese educational circles. A movement, therefore, was initiated to save them during the 1970s. The movement was a success.

The main problem which independent Chinese secondary schools suffered from was that they did not have sufficient finance, which led to other problems. So the revival movement focused on raising funds to rehabilitate these schools.

At the time when many original Chinese-medium secondary schools were converted to National-Type English Secondary Schools, their premises or buildings and equipment were only partially appropriated by their new incarnations if these premises and buildings were large and there was plenty of equipment. The appropriation was total when such premises or buildings were small and equipment limited. In the first case, independent Chinese secondary schools could quite comfortably be accommodated along with their new incarnations. In the latter case, however, this could not be done. So what happened to the less fortunate category was that they had to get their students to attend schools only in the afternoon. Moreover, they had to borrow equipment from their new incarnations for use. And in the case of one independent Chinese secondary school, it was even evicted by the educational authorities for living as a parasite on its new incarnation after some time.[53]

There were other kinds of harm and humiliation suffered by the independent Chinese secondary schools. And this was true even in the case of those independent Chinese secondary schools which could comfortably share everything with their new incarnations. One problem was that they had no curricula and textbooks of their own, but had to follow and use those of their new incarnations. And these were all in English and not in Chinese except in the case of the Chinese language and literature. As a result of this, their students had to sit for the English-medium Lower Certificate of Education and Malaysian Certificate of Education public examinations instead of the Chinese-medium examinations. Later, when these public examinations in English were abolished, they had to sit for the Malay-medium equivalents, the Sijil Rendah Pelajaran (SRP) and the Sijil Pelajaran Malayisa (SPM). Therefore, as a further consequence of this, their teachers had to come often from their new incarnations to teach lessons. Because the independent Chinese secondary schools were using so much English, in the end, they deteriorated to the extent of being regarded as tuition institutions that enabled their students to improve their command of English.[54]

So the way to save the independent Chinese secondary schools was to raise money to finance them so that they could stand on their own feet. With enough money, these schools would have their own premises or buildings and equipment. They could devise their own curricula and compile their own textbooks in Chinese. And following this, they could hold their own examinations in Chinese. They could even hire or train their own Chinese-medium teachers. In short, they could become self-sufficient and a system of their own. It is to be noted that as the years passed, they worked so hard to have a really good standard of pedagogy that the certificates they awarded their students became recognized by tertiary institutions even in such countries as the United Kingdom, the United States, Australia, Canada, New Zealand, Japan, Taiwan and Singapore, for admission.[55]

It was expected that once the independent Chinese secondary schools were put on a sound footing such as this, they would attract not just overage students and those who had failed, but normal students as well. It could be observed that many parents, given a choice, would want their children to be educated in the mother tongue rather than in any other language. This was especially so when the National-Type English Secondary Schools were later converted into National-Type Secondary Schools, using Malay as the main medium of instruction. The expectation was later fulfilled as we shall soon see.

The decline in the number of students in the 1960s also led to the schools collecting less fees. With already insufficient finance and now falling revenues from students, the teachers in the schools were poorly paid. This led to teachers and even principals not having the intention to stay for long in their jobs. This had an adverse effect on the efficiency of teaching in schools.[56] However, when the revival movement came, first there were funds from the movement to cover the deficits. Then the increased intake of students into the schools raised the financial profile of the schools further. And with more income, the teachers in the schools were better paid. Better paid teachers had better morale and this improved the academic standard of the schools.

The revival movement began in Perak. It then spread to the whole country. In 1973, acting on the suggestion of a Chinese educationist, Shen Ting, a rich tin miner in Perak, Foo Wan Thot, launched the movement. The target was to raise a million dollars to save the nine independent Chinese secondary schools in the state.[57] Towards the end of the year, UCSCA and UCSTA, whose headquarters were in Kuala Lumpur, joined Foo to extend the movement to rescue all independent Chinese secondary schools in the whole country. A conference of interested quarters was convened which adopted a Hua Wen Du Li Zhong Xue Jian Yi Shu (Proposals for Independent Chinese Secondary Schools). This document enunciated a mission of four items and a set of six guiding principles to direct the revival and future development of these schools. It also suggested solutions for problems concerning such things as finance, sources of student intake, school curricula, examinations, teaching staff, and the future of graduates.[58]

It might be a matter of some interest to note that Foo Wan Thot was one of the student leaders in the Zhong Ling High School in Penang who, in 1957, led in the protest against the conversion of Chinese-medium secondary schools into National-Type English Secondary Schools. For his part in this, he was arrested and expelled from Zhong Ling.[59]

The Hua Wen Du Li Zhong Xue Jian Yi Shu was so significant and important that it is worthwhile looking closely at what its mission of four items and the six guiding principles were. First, the mission of four items:

(1) Twelve years of primary and secondary education would be basic education [for children]. The independent Chinese secondary schools were mother tongue education which would complete this basic education.

(2) The independent Chinese secondary schools, on the one hand, would continue from the Chinese-medium primary schools, and, on the other, would dovetail into tertiary educational institutions. They were a necessary bridge between the two sides.

(3) Six years of Chinese-medium primary education would be insufficient to preserve and propagate the expansive and deep Chinese culture. Only the independent Chinese secondary schools could be bulwarks and fulfill these purposes.

(4) The independent Chinese secondary schools would teach the three languages of Chinese, English and Malay. As such, they would be able to absorb the essence of cultures within as well as outside the country. They would be able to meld such essence and would be a main furnace to foster a Malaysian culture.

The six guiding principles were:

(1) Persist firmly in using Chinese as the main medium of instruction so as to transmit and propagate Chinese culture and make a contribution towards creating a new culture for our nation in a multi-racial society.

(2) Under the principle of not obstructing education in the mother tongue, strengthen the teaching of the National Language [Malay]

and English to fit the needs of objective conditions both within and outside the country.

(3) Uphold firmly the superiority all along of the subjects of mathematics and science in the independent Chinese secondary schools.

(4) Curricula must include the common interests of our nation's various races and must also embrace modern knowledge.

(5) Independent Chinese secondary schools must not regard schooling their students to take government's public examinations as their main objective. But if some students wished voluntarily to sit for such examinations, the schools could establish tuition classes to help them.

(6) Technical and vocational courses could be established according to the needs of individual schools, but independent Chinese secondary schools must never become technical and vocational schools.

The Hua Wen Du Li Zhong Xue Jian Yi Shu was earnestly put into execution. One result of its determined thrust was that, in 1975, independent Chinese secondary schools were able to conduct their own examinations for their own Junior Middle Three and Senior Middle Three graduates. The Junior Middle Three examination was equivalent to the English-medium Lower Certificate of Education and the Malay-medium Sijil Rendah Pelajaran examinations, and the Senior Middle Three examination was higher than the English-medium Malaysian Certificate of Education and the Malay-medium Sijil Pelajaran Malaysia examinations, and was equivalent to Lower 6 or University Matriculation examinations. This particular step was significant because it showed that independent Chinese secondary schools could now rely on their own certification of their students and not on any external agency. The move was so important that the then minister for education, Mahathir Mohamad, told Chinese educationists that such examinations would not be recognized by the government and warned them to desist. However, the Chinese educationists disregarded him and went on with their plans.[60]

The movement was a success. It inspired parents to send their children to enrol in independent Chinese secondary schools. Each year the enrolment increased. The increase in student population was a vital indication of the movement's triumph. Table 4.6 shows the student enrolment increases between the years 1976 and 1980.[61]

Table 4.6
Student Enrolment in Independent Chinese Secondary Schools, 1976–80

Year	Total Student Enrolment in All Independent Chinese Secondary Schools
1976	33,395
1977	35,094
1978	35,930
1979	38,284
1980	41,356

Source: See note 61.

The Chinese educationists were happy.

Meanwhile a liaison committee, consisting of representatives from UCSCA and UCSTA, was set up to enable the two organizations to take common and unified action on matters pertaining to Chinese education. This liaison committee was named the Dong Jiao Zong.

The Universities and University Colleges Act, and A Renewed Attempt to Found the Merdeka University

In 1971, to secure greater control over the establishment of universities and university colleges in the country, the government enacted a law known as the Universities and University Colleges Act. The Act required that the establishment of such institutions must have the approval of the *Yang di-Pertuan Agong* or be on pain of a fine or imprisonment, or both. The intention of the law was severe, yet Chinese educationists, who in the 1960s had initiated a movement to found a Chinese-medium Merdeka University which was suspended because of the racial clashes in 1969, now in the 1970s, made an attempt to revive the movement.

The story of the movement in the 1960s was related in Chapter 3. The renewed effort in the 1970s failed to get the nod from the government to get the university established.

It is instructive to see what the Universities and University Colleges Act was about. We shall quote here its relevant parts:[62]

> 5. No higher educational institution with the status of a University shall be established except in accordance with the provisions of this Act.

6. (1) If the Yang di-Pertuan Agong is satisfied that it is expedient in the national interest that a University should be established, he may by order:

      (a) declare that there shall be established a higher educational institution having the status of a University, which shall be a body corporate, for the purpose of providing, promoting and developing higher education in all such branches of learning as shall be specified in the order;

      (b) assign a name and style to that University; and

      (c) specify the location of the site which shall be the seat of the University.

23. (1) No person shall establish, form or promote or do anything or carry out any activities for the purpose of establishing or forming or promoting the establishment or formation of a University or University College otherwise than in accordance with the provisions of this Act.

  (2) Any person who contravenes subsection 23(1) shall be guilty of an offence and shall on conviction be liable to a fine of ten thousand dollars or to imprisonment for a term of five years or both.

The provisions were clear.

In August 1977, the Merdeka University Limited Company took the decision to submit within a few months a petition to the *Yang di-Pertuan Agong* to seek his approval to set up a Merdeka University.[63]

In October, the company got the required petition drawn up and mobilized 4,328 Chinese organizations and political parties to approve it. The petition was handed to the *Yang di-Pertuan Agong* in January the following year. Copies were also presented to the prime minister, Hussein Onn, and the minister for education, Musa Hitam.[64]

There were three reasons or considerations which led Chinese educationists to revive the campaign to found the Merdeka University. The first reason or consideration was that there were just not enough places in all the existing universities and university colleges to absorb all the graduates graduating from the secondary schools every year. Table 4.7 portrays the situation.[65] The picture was disheartening.

The second reason or consideration was that, while on the one hand, places were already insufficient, on the other, most of the places were reserved for Malays. The Chinese, Indians, and others were admitted only after them. This was the quota system. We have already mentioned the quota system earlier in the present chapter. It had arisen out of the Majid Report.

Table 4.7
Number of Applicants Applying for Admission to Universities,
Number Accepted and Number Rejected, 1973–78

Year	Number of Applicants	Number Accepted	Number Rejected
1973/74	10,000	4,400	5,600
1974/75	22,434	6,095	16,339
1975/76	13,000	4,800	8,200
1976/77	10,850	3,844	7,006
1977/78	25,998	5,953	20,045

Source: See note 65.

A third reason or consideration was the following. Many of the graduates of Chinese secondary schools in Malaysia had been going to the Nanyang University in Singapore among other places to further their studies. To gain admission to the Nanyang, such students had to sit for and pass a matriculation examination which the Nanyang specially held for them. In 1974, the education authorities in Singapore stopped this practice. Then, to make matters worse, it was announced the next year that the Nanyang University would convert from being a Chinese-medium institution into an English-medium one. Nanyang was, therefore, no longer a place for Chinese secondary school graduates from Malaysia to go to.[66]

In September 1978, the minister for education, Musa Hitam, made it known that he was rejecting Merdeka University Limited Company's application to establish the proposed Merdeka University. He gave three reasons for his rejection. These were, firstly, the institution was to be set up by a private body; secondly, that it would use the Chinese language as its medium of instruction; and, thirdly, that it would admit only students from independent Chinese secondary schools.[67]

In February 1979, the company obtained a response to its application from the *Yang di-Pertuan Agong*. The response was negative.[68]

In September the following year, the company took the case up against the government in the High Court in Kuala Lumpur.[69] A queen's counsel from the United Kingdom, Michael Beloff, was engaged to fight on its behalf. Beloff was met by the Malaysian attorney general, Abu Talib.[70]

Beloff argued that, in rejecting the Merdeka University Limited Company's application to establish a Chinese-medium university, the government acted contrary to the provisions of Clause 152 of the constitution of the country. That clause had stipulated that non-Malay languages, including Chinese, had the right to be used, to be taught and to be learnt by the people. They could not only be used for official purposes, that is, used as official languages.[71] Abu Talib countered Beloff by saying that if the proposed university was established, according to the terms of the 1971 Universities and University Colleges Act, it would be a "public organization". If the Chinese language was used as its medium of instruction, then that language would be used for official purposes. And that would be against the constitution of the country.[72]

In November 1981, the High Court passed sentence on the case. It pronounced the Merdeka University Limited Company the loser, and the government the winner.[73]

The Merdeka University Limited Company then filed an appeal with the Federal Court which adjudicated the case in 1982. The court consisted of five judges. The final outcome of the hearing was that, while one of the judges ruled in favour of the company, the other four judges ruled against it. So the company's appeal was rejected.[74]

After the dust had settled, the Merdeka University Limited Company announced to the press that it would look into the possibility of starting a Chinese language and Chinese cultural college or a research institute, including a Higher Studies Counselling Centre, to continue to fight for the interests of Chinese education.[75]

It may be a point of interest to note that, right from the beginning, the president of the MCA, Lee San Choon, was not optimistic about the prospect of setting up a Chinese-medium university. He thought the proposal a non-starter. Then in November, at a national meeting of party representatives, he announced that the MCA would not support the founding of the proposed institution.[76]

So the campaign to found a Chinese-medium university for graduates of independent Chinese secondary schools came to naught.

The Cabinet Report, 1979, and Its Recommendations for Chinese Education

In September 1974, the government appointed a committee to review the education situation in the country. The committee was to ensure that the education system would produce sufficient manpower for the needs of the country. It was also to take care that the system would bring about a society in which the people would be united, disciplined and skilled. The committee was headed by the then minister for education, Mahathir Mohamad, and made up of another eight ministers.[77]

The committee took five years to complete its task and produced a report in 1979. Meanwhile, UCSCA and UCSTA leading old boys associations and Chinese registered organizations, like many other organizations in this move, submitted a memorandum to the committee to give their views on how Chinese education should be treated. The MCA, on its part, also submitted a memorandum. The two memoranda were different in approach.

We shall first list here the salient points of the first memorandum. The points were grouped in three parts.[78]

The first part was called "The Basic Demands of Education". Listed under this were the following items:

(1) Schools of any language stream should be treated as a component of the whole educational system.

(2) Schools of any language stream should use their mother tongue and mother script as their medium of instruction.

(3) The language of public examinations for schools of any language stream should be the same as the medium of instruction of those schools.

(4) The National Language [Malay] should be a compulsory subject in schools of any stream, but it should not be at the expense of the mother tongue and mother script being used as the main medium of instruction as well as the medium of examinations in those schools.

(5) Budgets and allocation of resources for schools of all streams should be balanced.

(6) Salaries for teachers and other staff in schools of all streams should be equal.

(7) The training of teachers should meet the needs of schools of any stream.

(8) The erection of buildings and the supply of equipment should be the same for schools of all streams.

(9) The establishment of individual schools and the opportunity for development should meet the needs of the residents of any locality concerned.

(10) The opportunity to acquire an education and the opportunity to obtain government scholarships or bursaries for students of schools of all language streams should be the same.

(11) The establishment of elementary as well as advance vocational education should meet the needs of schools of all language streams. Moreover, the main medium of instruction as well as the medium of examinations should be the mother tongue and mother script.

(12) The government should encourage the people to set up institutions of higher learning of all language streams, using their own resources, so as to cultivate more talents for the country.

(13) Opportunities of employment should be the same for all youths. Students from all language streams who have passed public examinations should have the same opportunities of employment.

(14) The government should recognize the degrees of the Nanyang University, the Ngee Ann College [in Singapore] and the various Chinese-medium universities and colleges in Taiwan, and accord these institutions the same status as other institutions of higher learning.

(15) The government should set up a Chinese education advisory committee whose members should come from representative Chinese educational organizations to help it resolve problems regarding Chinese education.

The second set of points were listed as "The Powers and Privileges of School Management Committees". There were only two items on this list, *viz*:

(1) The government should in an enlightened manner declare the restoration of the original duties and powers of school boards, and their original constitutions. This was to enable them to fulfil the long-standing wish of the government in emphasizing and encouraging the people to be interested and to participate in promoting the welfare of education in the country.

(2) Or perhaps even to augment the duties and powers of the school boards so that they would be enabled to participate in the drafting of and consultation about the Ministry of Education's education rules and regulations, and the education of citizens.

The third section of the requests was entitled "Primary, Secondary and Higher Education". Included in this section were the following:

(1) Recognize the Senior Middle Three certificate of the Chinese secondary schools (private or otherwise) and treat it as equal to the School Certificate (SC), the Federation of Malaya Certificate (FMC), the Malaysian Certificate of Education (MCE), and the Sijil Pelajaran Malaysia (SPM), and accord the same entitlement

to its holders as to the holders of the other certificates to proceed to higher education.

(2) Senior Middle Three graduates of Chinese secondary schools should be given opportunities equal to those given to graduates with the other kinds of certificates to work in official and semi-official organizations.

(3) Senior Middle Three graduates of Chinese secondary schools should have the same opportunities as the others to apply for and receive various scholarships and bursaries awarded within or outside the country.

(4) Recruit Senior Middle Three graduates of Chinese secondary schools for teacher training to enable them to become qualified Chinese primary school teachers.

(5) Senior Middle Three graduates of Chinese secondary schools should be able to apply to become temporary teachers or Chinese school clerks. Their emoluments should be equal to temporary teachers and school clerks from other language streams.

(6) Junior Middle Three graduates of Chinese secondary schools should be regarded as having equivalent qualifications and be given equal opportunities as graduates with the Lower Certificate of Education.

(7) Abolish the quota system of recruiting students in the universities and colleges in the country, and go completely by academic criteria in such recruitment.

(8) Replace the present scholarship system with a study loan system.

(9) Treat equally graduates of universities of different language streams.

(10) Recognize the degrees of the Nanyang University, the Ngee Ann College [in Singapore], and the various universities and colleges in Taiwan.

It is apparent that the basic thrust of the memorandum was to fight for Chinese education to be treated equally with education of the other language streams, mainly, the Malay stream.

The MCA memorandum made six main requests regarding Chinese education. These were:[79]

(1) Propose that the medium of instruction used in the primary schools should obtain approval to be extended to the secondary stage so as to afford greater opportunities to the various races

to protect and encourage the development of their languages and cultures.

(2) Propose that in secondary schools which used Chinese as the main medium of instruction, Malay should be made a compulsory subject for study as well as a subject for examinations. In secondary schools which used other languages as the medium of instruction, then Chinese should become a subject of study among ethnic Chinese students. English should become the third language to be learnt.

(3) Restore the Senior Middle Three public examination so as to enable graduates of the Chinese independent secondary schools to have the opportunity to further their education and to return to the mainstream education system in the country.

(4) Accelerate teacher training so that there would be better and more qualified teachers. Because teachers joining teacher training already possessed a credit in the Malay language, mother tongue teachers should be trained through their mother tongue so that their standard of the mother tongue could be elevated.

(5) Recognize degrees obtained by students from abroad so that what they learnt could be made use of.

(6) Based on these objectives of the nation [sic], very clearly Malay should become the main medium of instruction in education because it could unify the various races. ... To promote unity in the country, that Malay was extensively used from primary school to university in the teaching of subjects concerning Malaysian society was correct and appropriate.

The MCA also spoke up for Chinese education, but not in the same way and in such a fundamental tone as the other group.

The Cabinet Report, released in 1979, was very comprehensive in nature and covered all aspects of the education system in the country and sought their improvement. However, on Chinese education, it said very little and had only a few statements about it. The memorandum of UCSCA's group was ignored. That of the MCA also seemed to have received scant attention. We shall narrate here what the report said about Chinese education.[80]

Concerning primary education, it stated that at the present moment, the three different kinds of primary schools used three different languages as their medium of instruction. The National Schools and the National Primary

Schools [when the National-Type English Primary Schools were converted from using English to using Malay as their main medium of instruction, they were called by this new name] used Malay, the National-Type Chinese Primary Schools used Chinese, and the National-Type Tamil Primary Schools used Tamil. Based on present circumstances, this system of primary schooling should continue.

For the National-Type Chinese Primary Schools, the purport of the recommendation was that the government should not seek to disallow the Chinese language to be used. The status quo regarding this should be respected. However, this was only "based on present circumstances".

Then on private schools and colleges, the report recommended three measures:

(a) The School Registrar should be empowered to immediately close any private school or college which had not been registered or which had contravened regulations concerning registration.

(b) The School Registrar should also be empowered to supervise the curricula pursued, fees collected, the medium of instruction used and examinations conducted in private schools and colleges.

(c) The School Registrar should be empowered as well to refuse to register any private school or college without giving any reason.

This second recommendation had, in the case of Chinese education, to do with private Chinese primary schools and the independent Chinese secondary schools. Registration meant control.

The third recommendation had to do with curricula and examinations. It was stipulated that all private schools must follow curricula adopted by the Ministry of Education at every stage until Form Five. At the same time, their students must sit for public examinations conducted by the Examination Syndicate. After Form Five, a private school could get its students to sit for its own examinations, but the Director of the Examination Syndicate, not infringing the powers of the Malaysia Examination Council in this matter, had the power to stop those examinations. However, prohibiting such examinations should be on the basis that those examinations would cause harm to the interests of the country. [The Malaysia Examination Council was responsible for the Sijil Tinggi Persekolahan Malaysia, formerly known as the Higher School Certificate examination.]

This recommendation also impinged on the interests of independent Chinese secondary schools.

The Cabinet Report raised a storm of protest from the group led by UCSCA. They issued a communique to express their dissatisfaction. The points listed in the communique were:[81]

(1) Protest against the Mahathir committee's ignoring the wishes of the Chinese people which were set forth in the memorandum presented by the more than three thousand Chinese organizations.

(2) Not happy with the fact that the Cabinet Report, in view of present circumstances, would allow the National-Type Chinese Primary Schools to continue as they were but did not propose annulling subsection (2) of section 21 of the Education Act of 1961. That subsection empowered the minister for education to convert the National-Type Chinese Primary Schools and the National-Type Tamil Primary Schools into National Primary Schools [that is, Malay-medium schools] at any time the minister for education deemed fit.

(3) The report recommended that private secondary schools should follow curricula adopted by the Ministry of Education and sit for public examinations conducted by the Examination Syndicate. This implied that the independent Chinese secondary schools had to become National Secondary Schools [that is, Malay-medium schools].

(4) The recommendation that the School Registrar should supervise the curricula pursued, fees collected, medium of instruction used and examinations conducted in private schools also carried the implication that the way would be prepared to change the nature and disestablish the independent Chinese secondary schools.

(5) To set up a committee to study the report in depth and prepare later a more comprehensive set of criticisms.

The protest was disregarded by the government.

While, on the one hand, the UCSCA group reacted unfavourably towards the Cabinet Report, on the other, the MCA manifested a different attitude. Its president, Lee San Choon, stated that his party was satisfied with the report. He also expressed the hope that the report's proposed limitations on private schools would not be exploited by interested quarters for attacking the MCA.[82]

So, for the time being, the system of Chinese education in the country, consisting of National-Type Chinese Primary Schools and independent Chinese secondary schools, could continue. The status quo would not change.

The 1970s was not a bed of roses for Chinese-medium schools in the country, but it was fortunate that they were able to continue to exist.

The thrust on the part of the government to realize the "ultimate objective" of putting into effect a one-medium education saw the English-medium schools being converted to Malay. The relevance of this to the Chinese-medium schools was that while in the 1960s, many of their secondary schools were converted to English, now these underwent another metamorphosis to convert to Malay. The establishment of the quota system for admission into tertiary institutions also worked to the disadvantage of Chinese secondary school graduates. Then there was the measure to abolish the power of school boards to hire and dismiss teaching and other school staff, which diminished their role in protecting and promoting Chinese education. Next, people ignorant of the Chinese language were sent to Chinese-medium schools to assume senior administrative positions which could lead to these schools becoming Chinese schools no more. It was noticed that the plight of National-Type Chinese Primary Schools during these years was severe. Independent Chinese secondary schools did not fare well either, but, in this case, fortunately, a campaign to have them revived turned out to be a success. Because of the quota system for student admission into tertiary institutions, and for other reasons, Chinese educationists initiated a movement to establish a Chinese-medium university. Unfortunately, the effort proved a failure. Finally, there was a Cabinet Report which reviewed and made suggestions for the improvement of the whole education system in the country. This report paid scant attention to Chinese-medium education. It allowed the status quo to continue, but there was fear among Chinese educationists that Chinese-medium education would be discontinued. We note too that during the decade, there was an effort made on the part of the MCA to regain support among the Chinese community. Generally speaking, however, the effort was not successful.

Notes

[1]   Zakaria Hj. Ahmad, ed., *Government and Politics*, vol. 2 (Kuala Lumpur, 2007), p. 57; Ruslan Zainuddin, et al., *Kenegaraan Malaysia* (Petaling Jaya, 2005), pp. 14–15.

[2]   Ruslan Zainuddin, et al., op. cit., pp. 14–15.

[3]   Cheah Boon Kheng, *Malaysia: The Making of a Nation* (Singapore, 2004), pp. 138–39.

4   Cheah Boon Kheng, op. cit., pp. 139–43; Tan Teong Jin, et al., *The Chinese Malaysian Contribution* (Kuala Lumpur, 2005), pp. 56–65; Zakaria Hj. Ahmad, op. cit., p. 58.

5   Cheah Boon Kheng, op. cit., pp. 147–48.

6   See Chapter 3.

7   UCSTA, *Jiao Zong 33 Nian* (Kuala Lumpur, 1985) (hereafter UCSTA, op. cit. 1), pp. 864–66; Alis Puteh, *Language and Nation Building* (Petaling Jaya, 2006), pp. 115–16.

8   UCSTA, op. cit. 1, p. 865; Mok Soon Sang, *Pendidikan di Malaysia* (Subang Jaya, 2000), pp. 302–05.

9   Malaysia, *Fourth Malaysia Plan* (Kuala Lumpur, 1981), pp. 351–52, Table 21.3.

10   Zheng Liang Shu, *Ma Lai Xi Ya Hua Wen Jiao Yu Fa Zan Shi* (Kuala Lumpur, 2003), vol. 4, p. 213.

11   UCSTA, *Hua Wen Jiao Yu Shi Liao* (Kuala Lumpur, 1984) (hereafter UCSTA, op. cit. 2), last vol., p. 7.

12   *Nanyang Siang Pau*, 3 April 2007: Min Zhen Xing, *Jing Yi Zhuan Qi.*

13   Ibid.

14   UCSTA, op. cit. 2, p. 7.

15   Sim Mow Yu, *Shi Zai Huo Bu Mie* (Kuala Lumpur, 1996), p. 208.

16   Sim Mow Yu, op. cit., pp. 225–26.

17   Sim Mow Yu, op. cit., pp. 232–34 and 236–51.

18   Liao Wen Hui, *Hua Xiao Jiao Zong Ji Qi Ren Wu* (Kajang, 2006), pp. 128–29.

19   See Chapter 3.

20   UCSTA, op. cit. 2, p. 3; Zheng Liang Shu, op. cit., vol. 4, pp. 216–17.

21   Various major Chinese newspapers of 5 December 1971; Zheng Liang Shu, op. cit., vol. 4, pp. 218–19; UCSTA, op. cit. 2, p. 4.

22   UCSTA, op. cit. 2, pp. 34–48.

23   Cheah Boon Kheng, op. cit., p. 147; Harold Crouch, *Government & Society in Malaysia* (Singapore, 1998) pp. 74–75; *Nanyang Siang Pau*, 10 November 2006: Zhu Ke Li, *Hua She Yan Yi.*

24   *Nanyang Siang Pau*, 11 November 2006: Zhu Ke Li, *Hua She Yan Yi.*

25   Ibid.

26   *Nanyang Siang Pau*, 14 November 2006: Zhu Ke Li, *Hua She Yan Yi.*

27   Mok Soon Sang, *Ma Lai Xi Ya Jiao Yu Shi, 1400–1999* (Kuala Lumpur, 2000) (hereafter Mok Soon Sang, op. cit. 1), p. 107.

28   Wong Hoy Kee and Ee Tiang Hong, *Education in Malaysia* (Kuala Lumpur, 1975), pp. 143–44; Mok Soon Sang, op. cit. 1, pp. 107–08.

29   Zheng Liang Shu, op. cit., vol. 4, p. 193.

30   Zheng Liang Shu, op. cit., vol. 4, pp. 201–03.

31   UCSTA, op. cit. 1, pp. 866–68.

32   Various major Chinese newspapers, 5 December 1971; Zheng Liang Shu, op. cit., vol. 4, pp. 210 and 218–19.

33 UCSCA, *Feng Yun Ji Dang Yi Bai Ba Shi Nian* (hereafter UCSCA, op. cit. 1) (Kajang, 2001), p. 61.

34 Ibid; Kuang Qi Fang, *Ma Lai Xi Ya Hua Wen Xiao Xue Jia Jiao Xie Hui de Zhu Zhi yu Gong Neng*, in UCSCA, *Ma Lai Xi Ya Hua Wen Jiao Yu*, 2007, No. 7 (Kajang, 2007), pp. 1–9.

35 Kuang Qi Fang, op. cit.; UCSTA, op. cit. 2, pp. 9 and 14.

36 UCSCA, op. cit. 1, pp. 88–91.

37 UCSTA, op. cit. 2, p. 15.

38 Ibid.; *Sin Chew Daily*, 10 June 1973.

39 Ibid.

40 *Sin Chew Daily*, 5 July 1973; UCSTA, op. cit. 2, p. 16.

41 *Sin Chew Daily*, 30 June 1973; UCSTA, op. cit. 2, p. 15.

42 *Sin Chew Daily*, 9 July 1973; UCSTA, op. cit. 2, pp. 18–19.

43 Ibid.

44 *Sin Chew Daily*, 12 September 1973; UCSTA, op. cit. 2, p. 20.

45 *Sin Chew Daily*, 4 July 1973; UCSTA, op. cit. 2, pp. 15–16.

46 Loh Kok Wah, *The Socio-Economic Basis of Ethnic Consciousness: The Chinese in the 1970's* as cited in Mok Soon Sang, op. cit., p. 140; S. Husin Ali, ed., *Kaum, Kelas dan Pembangunan, Malaysia* (Kuala Lumpur, 1984), p. 101.

47 Kementerian Pelajaran Malaysia, *Laporan Jawatankuasa Kabinet Mengkaji Pelaksanaan Dasar Pelajaran* (Kuala Lumpur, 1979), Table 5A.

48 UCSTA, op. cit. 1, p. 805.

49 UCSTA, op. cit. 1, p. 804.

50 Ibid.

51 Mok Soon Sang, op. cit. 1, p. 143.

52 Authors' personal experiences and observations.

53 Zheng Liang Shu, op. cit., vol. 4, pp. 107–08.

54 Shen Ting, *Wo Yu Pi Li Dong Lian Hui* (author's memoir) (Perak, no date), pp. 51–52; Zheng Liang Shu, op. cit., vol. 4, pp. 159–60.

55 Mok Soon Sang, op. cit. 1, pp. 193 and 259.

56 Zheng Liang Shu, op. cit., vol. 4. pp. 108–12.

57 Shen Ting, op. cit., p. 52; Foo Wan Thot, *Foo Wan Thot Hui Yi Lu* (manuscript), p. 29; Zheng Liang Shu, op. cit., vol. 4, pp. 162–65.

58 Mok Soon Sang, op. cit. 1, p. 144; Zheng Liang Shu, op. cit., vol. 4, pp. 166–67.

59 Foo Wan Thot, op. cit., p. 20; Tan Teong Jin, et al., op. cit., p. 141.

60 UCSCA, op. cit. 1, p. 79.

61 UCSCA, *Hua Guang Yong Yao* (hereafter UCSCA, op. cit. 2) (Kuala Lumpur, 1993), p. 32

62 UCSTA, op. cit. 1, p. 875.

63 UCSTA, op. cit. 2, p. 78; UCSCA, op. cit. 1, p. 99.

64 UCSTA, op. cit. 2, p. 78; UCSCA, op. cit. 1, pp. 102–03.

65 UCSTA, op. cit. 2, p. 79.

66 *Nanyang Siang Pau*, 16 January 2007: Zhu Ke Li, op. cit.; *Nanyang Siang Pau*, 21 March 1974; Liao Wen Hui, op. cit., pp. 109–10; UCSCA, op. cit. 1, pp. 132–37.

67 Kua Kia Soong, *A Protean Saga: The Chinese Schools of Malaysia* (Kuala Lumpur, 1985), p. 155; UCSCA, op. cit. 1, p. 121; Liao Wen Hui, op. cit., p. 114.

68 UCSCA, op. cit. 1, pp. 127 and 140; UCSTA, op. cit. 2, p. 88.

69 *Nanyang Siang Pau*, 17 September 1980; UCSCA, op. cit. 1, p. 144.

70 *Nanyang Siang Pau*, 27 April 2007: Zhu Ke Li, op. cit.; Kua Kia Soong, op. cit., pp. 157–58.

71 Kua Kia Soong, op. cit., pp. 158–163; UCSCA, op. cit. 2, pp. 89–90.

72 *Nanyang Siang Pau*, 27 April 2007: Zhu Ke Li, op. cit.

73 UCSTA, op. cit. 2, p. 91; UCSCA, op. cit. 1, pp. 148–52.

74 Ibid.

75 *Sin Chew Daily*, 20 November 1982; UCSCA, op. cit. 1, p. 153.

76 *Nanyang Siang Pau*, 20 April 1978; UCSTA, op. cit. 2, p. 84; UCSCA, op. cit. 1, p. 125; Kua Kia Soong, op. cit., pp. 156–57.

77 Kementerian Pelajaran Malaysia, *Laporan Jawatankuasa Kabinet Mengkaji Pelaksanaan Dasar Pelajaran* (Kuala Lumpur, 1979), pp. 1, 16, 56–57 and 113; Mok Soon Sang, op. cit. 1, pp. 147–48.

78 UCSTA, op. cit. 2, pp. 35–39.

79 *Nanyang Siang Pau*, 14 February 1975; UCSTA, op. cit. 2, pp. 39–41.

80 Kementerian Pelajaran Malaysia, *Laporan Jawatankuasa Kabinet Mengkaji Pelaksanaan Dasar Pelajaran* (Kuala Lumpur, 1979), pp. 16, 46–57 and 113–14.

81 *Sin Chew Daily*, 23 December 1979; UCSTA, op. cit. 2, p. 30.

82 *Sin Chew Daily*, 17 December 1979; UCSTA, op. cit. 2, pp. 29–30.

5

THE 1980s
A Decade of Continuing Challenges
for the Chinese Schools

The 1980s saw the rule of two men, Hussein Onn and Dr Mahathir Mohamad. The former vacated his office as prime minister of the country on 16 July 1981 due to poor health and was succeeded by the latter.[1] Under the rule of these two men, Chinese-medium schools in the country had to face continuing challenges.

The Society Amendment Act

In March 1981, Hussein Onn's government presented to parliament a bill to have the Society Act amended. The amendment proposed to have all registered societies divided into two kinds, *viz* social and political organizations. The former would not have the right to level criticisms against the government or its policies. Only the latter would be so empowered. Although political entities would be so privileged, they must not enter into any liaison with any foreign organizations or receive external aid. The minister of home affairs and the registrar of societies would have the authority to deregister any society contravening these rules or to refuse any society registration. Affected organizations would not be allowed to appeal to a court of law against any such decision, but only to the minister for home affairs himself.[2]

This proposed amendment to the Society Act would emasculate UCSCA, UCSTA, and other similar public organizations. How could UCSCA and UCSTA, which were educational bodies and could be classified as social organizations, defend and promote the interests of Chinese education when they would have their hands and feet tied? Hence in April, these two bodies, together with other Chinese organizations in Selangor, convened a meeting to voice their dissatisfaction with the government's move. The gathering passed four resolutions:[3]

(1) Protest strongly against the proposal to have societies divided into social and political ones;

(2) Protest strongly against conferring power upon the registrar of societies to solely make decisions;

(3) Protest strongly against depriving the right of societies to appeal to the courts; and

(4) Appeal earnestly to the government to widely consult public opinion in the framing of any law which would impinge upon the vital interests of the people in order to keep to the spirit of democracy.

The meeting followed this up by submitting a memorandum on the matter to the prime minister.

In spite of the protest of UCSCA, UCSTA and other Chinese organizations, parliament passed the amendment in the same month. And the revised act would take effect as from 15 May 1981.[4]

Following this, UCSCA, under its president Lim Fong Seng, and UCSTA, under its vice-president Loot Ting Yee, together with other leaders of the two bodies, organized a press conference whereby they called upon all Chinese organizations in the country to revise their constitutions appropriately and apply to the government to have themselves registered as political entities.[5] In May 1982, UCSTA itself made such an application to the authorities which was approved the following month.

Then a somewhat strange thing happened. An UMNO leader, Anwar Ibrahim, tried to persuade the government to review the recently passed Society Amendment Act and have the clauses pertaining to the matter of political organizations removed. He succeeded. Thereafter, UCSCA, UCSTA, and other Chinese organizations were liberated from their burdens.[6]

Originally, Anwar Ibrahim was not in UMNO, but in the wilderness. He was leader of an Angkatan Belia Islam Malaysia (ABIM) [Islamic Youth Movement, Malaysia], which was often critical of the government. In 1978, he had helped PAS, the Malay party opposed to UMNO, in electioneering. When the Society Amendment Bill came on the scene, he was elected head of a coordinating committee of various organizations which were against the bill. The committee submitted a memorandum on the bill to the government, which bore as many as 70,000 signatures. In September 1981, Dr Mahathir

Mohamad, the prime minister, invited him to join UMNO, telling him that he could more easily realize his dreams for Islam inside UMNO than outside. Hence, Anwar Ibrahim became a member of UMNO, and he effected the revision of the Society Amendment Act.[7]

The 3-M Issue

The so-called 3 Ms stood for the Malay words "Membaca", "Menulis", and "Mengira", which meant "read", "write", and "calculate" in English. It was found that pupils in primary schools of all language streams in the country were unable to read, write, and calculate proficiently enough. So the proposal was made to revise the curricula to improve the skills of the pupils in these three areas. The fact to note is that, when the proposal was made, it caused anxiety in the Chinese community. It was thought that the government would take the opportunity of amending the school curricula to dilute the "Chinese-ness" of the Chinese schools and assimilate them into the Malay schools. They were unhappy. It was only after the government took steps to show that it was not out to do away with the Chinese schools that the unrest died down.

The deficiency of primary school pupils in reading, writing, and calculating was discovered and noted by the Cabinet Report on education, a document which was mentioned in the previous chapter of this book.[8] Based on that report, between 1979 and 1980, the Ministry of Education conducted an investigation in government primary schools to ascertain specifically how bad the situation was.

It was found that 45 per cent of the pupils could not read, more than 50 per cent could not write, and 70 per cent of the pupils could not calculate. In December 1980, the minister for education, Musa Hitam, announced that reforms would be introduced which would take effect countrywide from 1983 onward. Under the proposed new scheme, the six-year primary schooling would be divided into two stages. Primary 1 to Primary 3 would be the first stage, and Primary 4 to Primary 6 would be the second stage. During the first stage, there would only be two kinds of textbooks, one for reading, and the other for calculation. In the second stage, about 65 per cent of the learning time would be devoted to continuing upgrade pupils capabilities in the three Ms, and the rest of the time would be devoted to other subjects.[9]

The compiling of the new curricula was undertaken in great secrecy so much so that even the deputy-minister for education, a Chinese from the MCA named Chan Siang Sun, was ignorant of what was going on. Hence, the exercise worried the Chinese community a great deal. Meetings were held, memoranda and proposals drawn up and submitted to the government, the essence of which was to plead with it not to dilute the "Chinese-ness" or the nature of the Chinese schools. UCSCA and UCSTA convened a large gathering of Chinese educational and cultural bodies, and sent a memorandum to the Ministry of Education. When this failed to receive a response, they followed it up by sending a set of proposals. UCSTA by itself called a meeting of seven educational organizations which also prepared a memorandum. The MCA, on its part, also posted a set of proposals.[10]

In spite of all the pleas and implorations of the Chinese, the government went ahead, as suspected, with trying to assimilate the Chinese schools. In December 1981, the new minister for education, Dr Sulaiman Daud, made an announcement to the effect that:[11]

(1) Other than languages, all school subjects would be compiled in the National Language, that is, Malay.
(2) The subjects of man and environment, moral education, and music would all be compiled based on the National Language versions.
(3) In music, 50 per cent of the content would be songs in the National Language and the rest would be Chinese translations of National Language songs.

If such a programme were implemented, indeed very little "Chinese-ness" would be left in the Chinese schools. There would also be a change of language medium for examinations in these schools from Chinese to Malay.

The Chinese contemplated getting their schools to go on strike. UCSCA, UCSTA, and the MCA released a common statement to the press in which they declared that:[12]

(1) All teaching and reference materials in Chinese primary schools, other than those for the Malay and English languages, must be compiled in Chinese.
(2) Other than for Malay and English, all subjects must use Chinese as the medium of instruction as well as for examinations.
(3) The subjects of man and environment, moral education, and music must reflect the cultural characteristics of the Chinese.
(4) Increase the time allotted for the learning of English.

This answered the minister for education "needle point by needle point".

The statement also called on all other Chinese organizations in the whole country such as the various assembly halls, business bodies, and political parties to rise up and mobilize their members to take action so that all Chinese would be united to defend Chinese education and Chinese culture, and to uphold the racial dignity of the Chinese and basic human rights .

Besides taking common action with the MCA, UCSCA and UCSTA also joined hands with Gerakan and the DAP to issue a common statement in which they requested the prime minister and the minister for education to take immediate action to terminate the threat to Chinese primary schools. The statement also asked for the annulment of section 21(2) of the 1961 Education Act which, the reader will remember, empowered the minister for education to convert any Chinese or Tamil primary school to Malay whenever he deemed fit.[13]

In spite of all these actions, the minister for education continued with his forward march. He came out with another announcement to the effect that all reference materials used by the teachers in their work, other than those for language subjects such as Chinese, Tamil, and English, would be written in Malay. Such materials would include, for instance, curricula and syllabuses, and general teacher guide books. He pointed out that the training of Chinese and Tamil primary school teachers was conducted in Malay, so such teachers would have no problems handling such materials. Also, since 1970, such materials had been prepared in Malay. Therefore, the teachers were already accustomed to using materials of this kind. The quality of teaching would not be affected.[14]

This further announcement aroused great anger in UCSCA and UCSTA, which published long articles to rebut Dr Sulaiman Daud's views. The MCA, through its president Lee San Choon, also voiced opposition to the minister for education.[15] When, in 1982, the new scheme was tried out in a limited number of schools on a pilot basis, the parents of the pupils of two schools, one in Kajang and the other in Semenyih, got their children not to attend school as an act of protest. It was only after the government warned them to desist in this on pain of punishment that they began to cooperate.[16]

In January 1982, a change came in the attitude of the government. That month, Prime Minister Dr Mahathir Mohamad made an announcement that his administration had definitely no intention of altering the medium of instruction in Chinese and Tamil primary schools. These schools could continue to use Chinese and Tamil to teach.[17] Two months later, the deputy minister for education, Chan Siang Sun, made it known to the public that the prime minister had given instructions to his ministry to amend the 3-M scheme for Chinese and Tamil primary schools. The following would now be allowed:[18]

(1)   All primary schools would use syllabuses common to all. But schools of different language streams would use textbooks and other learning materials compiled in their respective different languages.
(2)   For the subject of music, songs to be taught to pupils could be freely chosen by the schools themselves.
(3)   Chinese primary schools could teach their pupils Chinese poetry instead of Malay *pantuns* (poems).

The government indeed conceded to the Chinese. Anxiety, fear, and anger began to fade away.

In 1982, 302 primary schools were selected to try out the new 3-M scheme on a pilot basis in their Primary 1 classes. Of this number, sixty-two were Chinese schools. The next year, the new scheme was implemented in Primary 1 classes in all schools in the country. In 1984, Primary 2 classes became involved. By 1988, all classes from Primary 1 to Primary 6 followed the new scheme.[19]

After all the disputes and debates, it is perhaps now useful to take a look at what the pupils were learning under the 3-M scheme. Table 5.1 shows the curricula which they had to follow:[20]

Table 5.1
The 3-M Curricula for Primary Schools

Subjects			
Area	Component	**1st Stage:** **School's Medium of Instruction (Malay/Chinese/ Tamil)**	**2nd Stage:** **School's Medium of Instruction (Malay/Chinese/ Tamil)**
Communication (3 M)	Basic skills	School's Medium of Instruction, Malay, English, Mathematics	School's Medium of Instruction, Malay, English, Mathematics
Man & Environment	Religious Knowledge & Moral Values, Attitudes	Islamic Education, Moral Education	Islamic Education, Moral Education
	Man & Environment	—	Man & Environment
Development of the individual	Arts & Recreation	Music, Art, Physical Education	Music, Art, Physical Education

Source: See note 20.

Amending the Universities and University Colleges Act, and the Founding of the Universiti Islam Antarabangsa (International Islamic University)

It was related in the previous chapter that, in 1971, the Malaysian government enacted a Universities and University Colleges Act to achieve control over the founding of tertiary institutions of learning. By the provisions of this act, such institutions could not be easily established, especially institutions using a foreign language as its medium of instruction. However, in the 1980s, the government felt a need to set up an international university which would use the English language to teach, and it amended the 1971 Act for the purpose. The development gave hope to the Chinese community to try to revive the project of founding a Chinese-medium university. But the authorities disappointed them in this hope.

It was in December 1982 that the government submitted a bill to parliament to have the 1971 Act amended. In March the following year, parliament passed the bill.[21] The new university founded, which used English as its medium of instruction, was called the Universiti Islam Antarabangsa (International Islamic University). It was the implementation of one of the resolutions from a first meeting of Islamic countries in Mecca in 1977, and became a member of the League of Islamic Universities. After initiation, it entered into an alliance with an Institute of Islamic Thought and Civilization to develop Islamic studies commonly. All its students must study Islam as a compulsory subject. Optional subjects were disciplines in humanities, economics, management, as well as, law. By the 1989/1990 session, it had 2,188 students who hailed from forty-three countries.[22]

During the process when the bill to amend the 1971 Act was debated in parliament, the president of UCSTA, Sim Mow Yu, made a public statement to the effect that an academic institution should be set up, which would not be classified as a public body, so that it could use a non-Malay language to teach. This was harking back to the project of founding a Chinese–medium university in the country. That project failed, it will be remembered, because the attorney general then argued in a court of law that the purported university, if established, would be a public body, and as such must use Malay and not Chinese to teach. That argument was what brought about the failure of the project.[23]

The vice-president of the same organization, Loot Ting Yee, also made a similar call. He stated that an enlightened government should, based on the needs of the country, amend the 1971 Act such that an independent university could be set up. He further said that the government was at the time calling on the people to "Look East" so that they would become disciplined and diligent, just like the Japanese and the South Koreans. In line with this idea, Loot argued, tertiary education should be made more readily available so that the country would have more educated talents to fulfil its needs. Besides setting up tertiary institutions itself, the government should encourage the private sector to do so. This policy would reduce the number of students going overseas to study.[24]

Michael Chen, a MCA member of parliament, when debating the amendment bill, also appealed to the government not just to allow an International Islamic University to be set up, but to also give room to a local private university to be established.[25]

Lim Kit Siang of the DAP called on the government to set up not just a sixth university — there were already five in the country — but another five more as well. The reason was that at the time a great number of students studied overseas. If they were to do so back home, the money they spent in other countries could be used to establish these five additional universities. Presumably Lim had in mind the previously projected Chinese-medium university among the five for he was an ardent champion of Chinese rights.[26]

In spite of all these calls for latitude to be given to the founding of a private Chinese-medium university, the minister for education, Dr Sulaiman Daud, responded in a negative manner. He said that permitting an international university to be established was a different matter from allowing a private university to be set up. The two could not be put together for discussion. Any local university to be put up must abide by the provisions of the 1971 Act, as well as the policy governing national education.[27]

The Chinese had to face up to reality.

The 3-in-1 Strategy

As they did not achieve any significant success in their fight for equality of Chinese education with Malay education from the earliest days and in the 1980s, UCSCA and UCSTA conjured up a strategy that came to be known as the 3-in-1 strategy to change their fortunes. Their lack of success was clear from the government's announcement of the 3-M curriculum and its refusal to permit the Chinese community to establish a Chinese-medium university even when the 1971 Universities and University Colleges Act was amended and the Universiti Islam Antarabangsa was set up. The 3-in-1 strategy meant that UCSCA and UCSTA would cooperate with Chinese-based political parties within the government, such as the MCA and Gerakan on the one hand, as well as those outside the government such as the DAP on the other, to get things done. The cooperation would take the form of members of UCSCA and UCSTA joining these parties as their members, with those joining the MCA and Gerakan fighting to improve the fate of Chinese education within the ambit of government.[28]

UCSCA and UCSTA began by making an approach first to the MCA. They requested the MCA, in the event that some of their members joined that party, field these people as candidates in the country's elections and for one of those who got voted to be selected to become deputy minister for education. The president of the MCA, Lee San Choon, welcomed the two organizations' members to join the MCA, but could not accept any condition for cooperation. So the deal could not be sealed.[29]

UCSCA and UCSTA next turned to Gerakan. The leader of that party, Lim Keng Yaik, could accept all their conditions for cooperation but one. That was that one of those who won in an election be made a deputy minister for education. Lim proposed instead that this person be made only a deputy minister. The post of deputy minister for education was a special preserve of the MCA. UCSCA and UCSTA did not reject the counter condition.[30] Consequently, in March 1982, eight prominent Chinese educationists from Perak joined Gerakan and, in the following month, ten from Penang also joined.[31]

UCSCA and UCSTA then talked to the DAP. Lim Kit Siang, the leader of that party, was hostile in his reaction. He told the two organizations that, by collaborating with Gerakan, they had already compromised the interests of Chinese education. More than that, by their act, they had also injured the DAP's sixteen years of effort, both within and outside parliament, to fight for the rights of Chinese education and culture.[32]

Because of the refusal of the DAP to join hands with UCSCA and UCSTA, the latter's strategy was reduced from 3-in-1 to 2-in-1. Worse, in the countrywide election which soon followed, two members of UCSCA and UCSTA who had joined the Gerakan were pitted against DAP candidates in that contest. Lim Kit Siang described the event as UCSCA's and UCSTA's actual strategy of 3-hit-1, the three being the MCA, Gerakan, and the Dong Jiao Zong of UCSCA and UCSTA, and the one being the DAP.[33]

What then took place in the electioneering was that:[34]

(1) In the Kepong constituency in the Federal Territory, UCSCA's and UCSTA's Kerk Choo Ting who had joined Gerakan stood against Tan Seng Kiaw of the DAP. The former lost.

(2) In the Tanjong constituency in Penang state, UCSCA's and UCSTA's
     Dr Koh Tsu Koon who had joined Gerakan stood against Chen
     Qing Jia of the DAP. Koh won.

In this 1982 general election, the DAP lost massively. Out of a total of
sixty-three candidates who fought in the contest, only nine won. Even its
chairman, Dr Chan Man Hing, who stood in Seremban, lost to the MCA's
president, Lee San Choon. Lim Kit Siang attributed his party's failure to
the confusion caused among the electorate by the mischief of UCSCA and
UCSTA.[35]

The sadder result of the 3-in-1 strategy was not so much the defeat of the
DAP which was the most ardent supporter and vocal champion of Chinese
interests, but was that those UCSCA and UCSTA members who had got
into the Gerakan were unable to do much to improve the lot of Chinese
education from within the government. Throughout the 1980s, they achieved
little.

The situation was so disappointing that Loot Ting Yee, vice-president of
UCSTA, ruled that henceforth any member of his organization who wished
to join a political party to participate in elections should resign from any
post held in UCSTA and join that party on his own. Hereafter, UCSTA
would simply support any political party that would fight for the interests
of Chinese education. In 1990, when there was a general election in the
country again, the president of UCSTA, Sim Mow Yu, declared that his
organization would not deploy any of its members in any political party to
fight in the contest.[36]

The 3-in-1 strategy turned out to be a failure.

Culture and Education

Since achieving independence in 1957, there had been frequent discussions
and debates on how the culture of the country, which included education,
should be defined. Should it consist of Muslim-Malay culture as its core,
with the cultures of the Chinese, Indians, and the others, as the periphery, or
should it be made up of all the different cultures on an equal basis. Generally
speaking, the Malays voted for the first view, whereas the Chinese and the
others voiced support for the second.

In February 1982, the Ministry of Culture, Youth and Sports sent out
letters to various cultural and educational bodies of all races in the country,
informing them that it intended to review the implementation of cultural
policies in the country for the decade between 1971 and 1981, and inviting their

comments. Memoranda would be welcome. The closing date for submission was 10 May 1982, but was extended to 1983 on the recommendation of the deputy minister of the ministry, an MCA member, so that the Chinese community could more readily respond.[37]

On receiving the ministry's letters, the Malaysian Chinese Cultural Society, an organization sponsored by the MCA, the Selangor Chinese Assembly Hall, UCSCA, and UCSTA met and made the decision not to write a separate memorandum each for the government, but to prepare a common one among themselves so as to demonstrate a united stand. However, when they met again and deliberated on the details of what they should present as their views, the Malaysian Chinese Cultural Society found that it had differences with the other three organizations. So eventually, it split from the three and prepared a separate memorandum by itself. After the split, the other three bodies got into contact with twelve other organizations in the country and wrote a common memorandum together with them. This they duly submitted to the government after it had been endorsed by a Chinese cultural conference in Penang in March 1983.[38]

The memorandum submitted by the Malaysian Chinese Cultural Society did not have anything specifically on education, so we should not tarry with it here. That done up by the other fifteen organizations, however, did have, so we shall give it our attention. What the organizations said on education was as follows:[39]

1. The government should do away with section 21(2) of the 1961 Education Act so that the survival of Chinese primary schools would not be threatened. It should guarantee that the implementation of the 3-M Curriculum would not change the character of these schools. At the same time, it should treat schools of all the different language streams on a basis of equality in the allocation of funds, construction of premises, teacher training and the provision of equipment.

2. The government should recognize the contributions made to national education by the independent Chinese secondary schools and the significance of their existence. It should help these schools to develop by helping them in the matters of finance, teacher training, construction of premises and providing equipment. It should allow new schools to be established and existing ones to start branch schools. It should open the doors of the various tertiary institutions to their graduates.

3. The government should allow the people to set up private universities so as to ease the shortage of places for students in the existing universities and to nurture more talents for the country.

4. It should let graduates of the independent Chinese secondary schools join the Chinese Department in the University of Malaya to further their studies. It should treat the development of that department, scholarships to be given to its students, half-pay leave for its staff to go for further training and job openings for its graduates on the same basis as for departments of other languages.

5. It should make the mother tongue a compulsory subject for students to study. It should provide the subject with unified textbooks, sufficient teaching materials and qualified teachers.

6. It should in all fields allow the different races to exercise their constitutional rights to freely learn, use and develop their languages except in official contexts. It should not through legal means or administrative measures put limits on them.

7. Admission of students into the various universities should not be based on the quota system but should be based on the academic merit and financial circumstances of the families of the students. The appointment and promotion of teaching staff should be based on the basis of academic achievement, qualifications and work performance but not on the basis of race.

This was indeed a very exhaustive list of grievances from the Chinese community over the matter of education.

The minister for youth, culture and sports, Anwar Ibrahim, categorically rejected the memorandum of the fifteen organizations, including their pleas over Chinese education. He did this on several occasions. He did this twice in parliament, once in a dialogue with their representatives, and once more over television.[40]

This was not surprising as earlier on in October 1982, the *Yang di-Pertuan Agong*, had already in an address to parliament declared that the country would have only one race, one language, and one culture. Two months later, in a national cultural conference of the Malays, which met in Malacca, the prime minister reiterated the policy. Muslim-Malay culture and education would continue to dominate other cultures and education.[41]

Which Language to Use in School Assemblies and in Extra-curricular Activities

In October 1984, the Education Department in the Kuala Lumpur Federal Territory issued an instruction to the National-Type Chinese Primary Schools in the district to replace Chinese with the National Language, that is Malay, in all their assemblies and extra-curricular activities.[42]

The act aroused at once the ire of the whole Chinese community. First, it was UCSCA and UCSTA which lodged a protest with a memorandum on the issue sent to the Ministry of Education. The vice-president of UCSTA, Loot Ting Yee, even went to the ministry to stage a sit-in demonstration.[43] Next, it was political parties and old boys' associations issuing statements to show their displeasure. Then it was the management committees of the various Chinese primary schools in the district meeting up and demanding that the Department of Education rescind its order.[44]

The result of it all was that in the face of all the pressures, the authorities caved in. The director of education, Hj Murad bin Mohd Noor, finally gave orders to have the original instruction withdrawn. The Chinese community scored a victory.[45]

The Integrated School Plan and the School Pupils Integration Plan

It was an observed fact that the various races in Malaysia were polarized. The question was how to overcome the problem. Many people tried to come up with solutions.

In August 1984, at a seminar to find ways to promote integration among the various races, Professor Noramly Muslim, the acting vice-chancellor of the University Kebangsaan, struck on a bright idea. He said that racial polarization among adults actually originated from the time when they were still in school. The children of the different races attended different schools. The way to break down polarization among adults, therefore, lay in first breaking down polarization among school children. He proposed, then, that schools of the different language streams, Malay, Chinese, and Tamil, should all be housed in one common building and should not have separate campuses. That way, the children would socialize, and polarization would not arise. UCSCA and UCSTA, however, did not find the professor's arguments convincing. They did not feel that children beginning their school life with a mother tongue education was the cause of adult life racial polarization, and to put a finger on that as the cause was not looking for a real solution to the problem. MCA Youth also found Noramly Muslim unconvincing. It felt that what really gave rise to the social ill of racial polarization was the government dividing the populace into *bumiputra* (sons of the soil) and non-*bumiputra* (non-sons of the soil) and its bias in implementing policies relating to this.[46]

A year later, Noramly Muslim's idea was picked up by the then minister for education, Abdullah Badawi, who announced that, for a start, his ministry would in 1986 put into effect an Integrated School Plan to try to break down polarization among school children. The plan would consist of getting a Malay, Chinese, and Tamil primary school each to be housed together in one common building. Altogether eighteen primary schools would initially be chosen to try out the plan on a pilot basis. Following the announcement, the first such integrated school was started in Teluk Sengat in the state of Johor.[47]

Not surprising, the plan did not find favour with the Chinese community. UCSCA and UCSTA, besides having a different understanding of the problem of racial polarization to that of Noramly Muslim, found, as did Chinese organizations in the locality, that all procedures followed, equipment installed, etc., in the school building catered first to the needs of the Malay component of the school rather than the other two components. They felt that although the aim of this integrated school plan was to unify the different races, in effect the plan would in the end spell the demise of Chinese and Tamil schools.[48]

Soon representatives of UCSCA, UCSTA and the Tamil primary schools met the deputy minister for education, Dr Ling Liong Sik, to discuss the matter. Ling thought that they had misunderstood the whole plan. He proposed changing the name of the plan to ease their fear and suspicion. The new name should be: "The School Pupils Integration Plan". He requested them to hold meetings among themselves as soon as possible and come up with proposals by which the plan could be smoothly pushed forward.[49]

Consequently, UCSCA and UCSTA convened a large gathering of educational representatives to deliberate the issue. Chinese educationists from the eighteen designated pilot schools, as well as from other schools in the country and people from old boys' associations attended this gathering. The meeting resolved to oppose the plan[50] and delegated UCSCA and UCSTA, on the basis of the proceedings of the gathering, to prepare a memorandum for submission to the minister for education. The most important part of the memorandum was a proposal made at the meeting on what could be done to bring students closer together, instead of the government's scheme.[51]

The proposal was that, besides the regular curricula and extra-curricular activities followed in the schools, they could be encouraged, on a voluntary basis, to organize interschool programmes to promote interaction among students of the various races. Such programmes could be athletic and sporting events, cultural performances, children's festivals, teachers' festivals, and so on.[52]

Because of the widespread dissatisfaction among Chinese educationists and the Chinese public, after receiving the memorandum, the minister for education, Abdullah Badawi, called for a meeting with delegates from UCSCA and UCSTA. At the meeting, the minister for education stuck to his plan, but was willing to accept proposed revisions to his plan from the Chinese educationists. The two sides were able to reach a compromise in the end. The next day, the deputy minister for education released the good news to the press.[53]

So the Teluk Sengat School continued and the School Pupils' Integration Plan was effected. However, the plan was short-lived and lasted for only a while. It was then aborted. Why that happened was not known.

Educationists Lacking in Chinese Qualifications Appointed to High Positions in National-Type Chinese Primary Schools and Operation Lalang

We have seen in the last chapter that in the early 1970s, there had been attempts by the educational authorities to deploy educationists who lacked qualifications in the Chinese language to assume senior positions in the National-Type Chinese Primary Schools. In September 1987, it was learnt that a similar thing had happened again. The positions assumed were those of first senior assistant, second senior assistant, supervisor of afternoon sessions, and supervisor of extra-curricular activities. On this occasion, more than forty schools, involving about a hundred educationists, in the states of Penang, Perlis, Selangor, and Malacca, were affected.

In Penang alone, out of a total of ninety schools, at least twenty-nine were given sixty-seven such teachers.[54]

Such a move on the part of the government was clearly an attempt to change the character of the affected schools. Such schools conducted their businesses in Chinese. How could people who did not know that language be appointed to high positions in them? The event, as expected, triggered off widespread protests in the Chinese community. Even the deputy minister for education, Woon See Chin, from the MCA, was taken aback by the development and at once issued instructions to the various departments of education in the affected states to rectify the situation.[55]

On the same day Woon sent out his instructions, however, his superior, the minister for education, Anwar Ibrahim, disclosed to the press that what had been done could not be undone. Furthermore, two days later, at a meeting of UMNO, he stated that although the policy of deploying educationists who lacked qualifications in the Chinese language to Chinese schools to take up senior positions was unwelcome to the Chinese community, his ministry would persist in that policy. Another two days later, the *Berita Harian*, a Malay newspaper, levied criticism against the MCA by saying that there were elements in that party who might endanger the administration of the affected schools and the interests of the students. The editorial of the newspaper at the same time praised Anwar Ibrahim for upholding the government's principles and policies.[56]

The Chinese formed a joint-action committee of public organizations and political parties to spearhead their protest. The fifteen public organizations noted earlier, the MCA, Gerakan, and the DAP, were all included. In October, the committee organized a mammoth protest against the government attended by more than four thousand people. The meeting made five resolutions, the third of which called on the Ministry of Education and the departments of education of Penang, Perlis, Selangor, and Malacca to resolve the matter by the fourteenth of the month. Otherwise, it would get all the Chinese primary schools throughout the country to go on strike between the fifteenth and seventeenth.[57]

Because of the seriousness of the situation, the government set up a five-minister committee to handle the matter.

The chairman of the committee was the minister for education, Anwar Ibrahim, and the other members were the minister for youth, sports and culture, Najib, the labour minister, Lee Kim Sai, the minister for primary industry, Lim Keng Yaik, and the minister for public works, Samy Vellu.[58]

On the same day this committee was formed, the Chinese joint-action committee also met. Lee Kim Sai and Lim Keng Yaik assured the joint-action committee that the government was sincere in trying to resolve the problem and that this would be done before the last day of the year. On this understanding, the joint-action committee called on all Chinese primary schools to postpone the projected strike until further notice.[59]

However, fifty-seven schools, involving more than 30,000 pupils in the affected states, went on strike on the fifteenth. This was because some of the parents did not receive the notice or they did not agree with the postponement.[60]

On the thirteenth, Najib, after having chaired a meeting of UMNO Youth, told the press that on the seventeenth there would be a gathering of all the branches of UMNO Youth in the capital to demonstrate support for the policy of deploying educationists who lacked qualifications in the Chinese language to assume senior positions in Chinese primary schools. At the same time, he requested the government to dismiss Lee Kim Sai as a minister. The venue of the thirteenth meeting was flooded with slogans that provoked racial tension such as, "May 13 has begun!" May 13, the reader will remember, was the day in 1969 when there were racial riots in the country. On 25 October, Sanusi, the secretary general of UMNO, announced that on 1 November, there would be a gathering of 500,000 members of UMNO in the capital to celebrate the party's anniversary. All of a sudden, the atmosphere in the country was filled with the scent of gunpowder.[61]

Because of the possibility of racial riots breaking out, for several days beginning on 27 October, on the basis of the Internal Security Act, the government took action to round up what might be conceived as dangerous elements. The measure was called "Operation Lalang". Altogether 106 persons were detained, including members of political parties, leaders of public organizations and trade unions, environmentalists, religious personalities, and leading Chinese educationists. Among the last were such persons as Lim Fong Seng, president of UCSCA, Sim Mow Yu, president of UCSTA, Tuang Pik King, vice-president of UCSTA, and Kua Kia Soong, head of a Chinese research organization. Furthermore, the government banned the publication of three newspapers, *viz*, the Chinese paper, the *Sin Chew Daily*, the Malay paper, the *Watan*, and the English paper, the *Star*.[62] Next, on 26 October, the government announced that the scheduled UMNO meeting for 1 November to celebrate the party's anniversary would be cancelled. All meetings of any other kind were also prohibited.[63]

The dust did not settle until months later. On 23 March 1988, the government issued a white paper on "Operation Lalang". The government explained that the reason for the police action was the possibility of racial riots breaking out as in 1969. Following the publication of this document, the 106 persons detained were released from detention in batches. The last to be freed was on 19 April 1989. Meanwhile, on 26 March 1988, the three banned newspapers were allowed to resume publication.[64]

According to the government, the rationale for "Operation Lalang" was the preemption of another May 13 from happening. But according to some other quarters, the real reason was that the prime minister, Mahathir Mohamad, was facing an intraparty struggle within UMNO and had to create a national crisis to unify UMNO to fight a common enemy to save his position. For instance, Amnesty International's view was:[65]

> Informed observers argued that those arrested had done little or nothing to provoke racial or religious tension and that on a number of critical issues, government ministers and members of the ruling National Front coalition had played up and aggravated the perennial political

and communal tensions that underlie Malaysian society for purposes
of their own.

And Tunku Abdul Rahman, the first prime minister of the country, had
the following to say:[66]

> UMNO was facing a break up ... The Prime Minister, Dr Mahathir
> Mohamad's hold on the party appeared critical when election rigging was
> alleged to have given him a very narrow victory over Tengku Razaleigh.
> The case alleging irregularities brought by UMNO members was
> pending in court. If the judgment went against him, he would have
> no choice but to step down. So he had to find a way out of his
> predicament, a national crisis has to be created to bring UMNO together
> as a united force to fight a common enemy — and the imaginary
> enemy in this case was the Chinese community ... If there was indeed
> a security threat facing the country, why was action not taken much
> sooner?

So, there were different perspectives.

The story behind Tunku Abdul Rahman's analysis was the following.
On 24 April 1987, Tengku Razaleigh allied with Musa Hitam to form a
Team B in UMNO to fight against Mahathir Mohamad and Ghafar Baba
as Team A, for the respective positions of president and deputy president.
Team A won in the contest, but there was the allegation that some party
members who had cast votes had come from party branches which were
unregistered and, therefore, illegal. The case was brought to court. The
court ruled that UMNO under Mahathir and Baba was now an illegal
organization. Mahathir promptly called his party UMNO Baru, that is,
New UMNO, and applied straightaway to the registrar of societies to have
it registered. Mahathir was at the time, besides being prime minister, the
minister for home affairs. The registrar of societies was subordinate to him.
So UMNO Baru got registered. Tengku Razaleigh and Musa Hitam tried
to register as UMNO Malaysia. Their application was turned down, after
which they changed the name of their party to Semangat 46 which was then
registered in 1989.[67]

The police action did not resolve the issue of educationists not conversant
with the Chinese language being sent to Chinese primary schools to take
up senior positions. However, in April 1988, the newspapers reported that
the five-minister committee had found a solution. The way out was that
the positions of headmaster, first and second senior assistants as well as the
supervisor of afternoon sessions must only be filled by teachers who were

conversant with Chinese. Only the supervisor of extra-curricular activities could be a person without a Chinese qualification.[68]

An Educational Research Centre and the Situation of the National-Type Chinese Primary Schools in the Mid-1980s

Sometime in the 1980s, Chinese educationists in the country felt that if they were to solve the host of problems plaguing the Chinese schools, for instance, the 3-M issue, the status of the independent Chinese secondary schools, shortage of qualified teachers as well as finance and so on, they must have an understanding of the exact situation of those schools. It was crucial to come to grips with the following:[69]

(1) There must be a thorough understanding of the nature of the problems faced.
(2) There must be a complete collection of data.
(3) There must be an understanding of social trends and a comprehension of their historical background.
(4) There must be an organization, divided into different specialities or sections, to carry out research and planning systematically.

Consequently, in August 1983, at a national gathering of teachers, a research centre called the *Jiao Yu Yan Jiu Zhong Xin* [Educational Research Center] was established. It was housed in the premises of UCSTA and consisted of a secretariat and an archive. The functions of the two departments were to be as follows:

(1) The secretariat was to carry out duties assigned it by UCSTA, as well as coordinate research into and analysis of education problems, education developments, and education trends.
(2) The archive was to collect education data both within the country as well as from foreign sources, and to have such information analysed and classified systematically.

A substantial amount of funds was raised from the sale of key rings and public donations to finance its establishment and activities.

Two years later, in 1985, consequent on its founding, the *Jiao Yu Yan Jiu Zhong Xin* conducted a comprehensive survery of the National-Type Chinese Primary Schools, commonly known as Chinese primary schools, in the country. A report was accordingly compiled from the survey.[70] A brief summary of the findings is given below.

(I) School types and their numbers[71]

The first finding was about "school types" and their numbers. What type a particular primary school belonged to was classified according to the size of its pupil enrolment. Three types were found:

> Type A: Enrolment above 840
> Type B: Enrolment between 440 and 839
> Type C: Enrolment below 439

The numbers of the different types of primary school were found to be:

> Type A: 156 schools
> Type B: 194 schools
> Type C: 558 schools

The conclusion was that most of these schools were small.

It is interesting to note that the Ministry of Education also made a count of Chinese primary schools on its own. What it discovered was the following:

> Type A: 189 schools
> Type B: 244 schools
> Type C: 555 schools

The two sets of figures were different. But they both showed that there were fewer bigger schools than smaller ones.

(II) Ownership of school land[72]

There were three kinds of ownership of school land, *viz*:

(1)   Owned by a management committee
(2)   Owned by the government
(3)   Owned by private individuals or organizations

The numbers of the schools falling respectively into the three different categories were:

(1)   441 schools
(2)   321 schools
(3)   127 schools

In short, most of the schools were established through the common effort of the Chinese community itself.

The reader will notice that there is a difference between the total number of schools listed in (I) and that listed in (II) above. The discrepancy arose because different schools filled in the questionnaires sent out to them differently. Some answered some questions while others did not.

(III) Number of schools established during different times in history[73]

The report also looked into the question of how many Chinese primary schools were established during different times in the country's history. What was seen was the following:

> Before 1957: 636 schools
> 1957–69: 49 schools
> 1970–80: 2 schools
> 1980–85: 0 schools

1957 was the year when the country achieved independence from the British. 1969 was the year of racial riots, and 1970 was the year when the New Economic Policy was put into effect. This chapter started with 1980.

It will be noticed that most of the schools were set up before independence. This was so because of the effort of the Chinese community itself. During the years after independence, Chinese primary schools became the responsibility of the government. And the government built forty-nine schools during the time of one decade. After the racial riots in 1969 and the implementation of the New Economic Policy in 1970, the policy of the government towards Chinese education changed and so only two schools were started. Then the new attitude hardened and no new Chinese primary schools were set up from 1980 to 1985.

(IV) Number of Chinese Primary One school pupils in the 1980s[74]

Next, the report looked at the question of how many Primary One school pupils there were in the country over the years that it surveyed. It discovered the following.

The increase in number between 1982 and 1983 made the Chinese educationists happy, but the decrease between 1983 and 1984 caused alarm. What could have been the reason for the decline on the latter occasion? On investigation, it was found that the decrease was due to the fact that in the year 1977, fewer babies than usual were born. The discovery allayed the fear.

Table 5.2
Number of Chinese Primary One Pupils in the 1980s

Year	Number of Schools that Provided Information	Average Number of Primary One Pupils in Any One School	Estimated Number of Primary One Pupils in the Whole Country
1982	870	74	96,000
1983	878	81	100,000
1984	888	74	96,000
1985	895	75	97,000

Source: See note 74.

(V) Shortage of qualified teachers[75]

Chinese primary schools had always been plagued by a shortage of qualified teachers. Because of this, temporary teachers had to be engaged all the time to fill the gaps. Table 5.3 shows the situation in Peninsular Malaysia in 1984.[76]

Table 5.3
Teacher Situation in Chinese Primary Schools, 1984

State	Shortfall in Number of Qualified Teachers	Number of Temporary Teachers Hired
Negeri Sembilan	113	104
Johor	520	520
Kelantan	32	32
Penang	371	376
Perlis	7	6
Malacca	71	58
Kedah	140	120
Pahang	148	141
Selangor	306	282
Trengganu	Not available	6
Perak	Not available	121
Federal Territory	199	163
Total	2,137	1,979

Source: See note 76.

There were reasons for this situation, the first being the fact that the various teachers' training colleges failed to turn out enough qualified teachers. Table 5.4 gives the picture:[77]

Table 5.4
Number of Qualified Teachers Trained, 1980–84

Year	Number of Qualified Teachers Trained
1980	360
1981	800
1982	881
1983	455
1984	900

Source: See note 77.

Another reason for the shortage of qualified teachers in urban centres was that pupils from rural areas tended to migrate to urban centres to pursue their studies. This swelled the numbers of pupils in schools in these places, and so shortages arose.[78]

(VI) Shortage of finance and insufficient equipment[79]

Although the National-Type Chinese Primary Schools were a part of the national system of education, they were always inadequately financed by the government. They were given money only to pay staff salaries and cover daily expenditure, but were not given funds for development. One result of this was that they were frequently under-equipped, especially in the rural areas. For instance, audio-visual aids which were highly recommended by modern educationists were never found.

The Learning of Chinese in National-Type Secondary Schools and Progress in the Independent Chinese Secondary Schools

It is now useful to take a look at the learning of Chinese in the National-Type Secondary Schools in the 1980s. It is interesting too to see what progress the independent Chinese secondary schools made in the decade.

It will be remembered that in 1961, under the Education Act of that year, quite a number of Chinese secondary schools accepted government assistance and converted to become National-Type English Secondary Schools. They then replaced Chinese with English as their main medium of instruction. In the 1970s, they changed again and used Malay as their main medium of instruction.[80]

In 1961, when the first conversion came about, it was agreed that after conversion the schools concerned could still have one third of their teaching hours devoted to the teaching of Chinese. However, after the conversion, only five to seven periods a week were given to the teaching of Chinese.[81] This amounted to only around one-eighth of all teaching hours per week.

In 1989, the government put into effect a Secondary School Integrated Curriculum in the nation's government and government-assisted secondary schools to replace the old one. In the early 1980s, as seen, the government implemented a 3-M new curriculum in the primary schools. This new Secondary School Integrated Curriculum was a sequel to the 3-M Curriculum in the primary schools. Under the new Secondary School Integrated Curriculum, only three periods a week were alloted to the teaching of the Chinese language as an additional elective subject. In addition, only one of the three periods was included in the students' regular timetable. The other two periods of teaching could be conducted only after regular school hours.[82]

The National-Type Secondary School Board of Governors fought against the change in the teaching of Chinese brought about by the introduction of the Secondary School Integrated Curriculum. As a result, in June 1989, the deputy minister for education, Woon See Chin, announced in a circular that the Conforming National-Type (Chinese) Secondary Schools, commonly known as National-Type Secondary Schools, could have five periods of Chinese a week in their regular timetable.[83]

Because all the government or government-assisted secondary schools now used Malay as the main medium of instruction, a substantial number of graduates of the National-Type Chinese Primary Schools, commonly known as Chinese primary schools, chose not to go to these schools for their secondary education, but to the independent Chinese secondary schools instead. Such students were deficient in the Malay language. This helped the development of the independent Chinese secondary schools.

The 1980s saw a steady increase in the number of students attending independent Chinese secondary schools. Table 5.5 tells the story:[84]

Table 5.5
Number of Students in Independent Chinese
Secondary Schools

Year	Number of Students Attending
1980	41,356
1981	42,926
1982	44,486
1983	45,890
1984	48,246
1985	48,995
1986	49,099
1987	48,943
1988	49,567
1989	52,200

Source: See note 84.

The picture was encouraging.

It is also to be noted that most teachers who taught in these schools had university degrees. Table 5.6 shows the figures in 1983.[85]

Table 5.6
Qualifications of Teachers in Independent Chinese Secondary Schools, 1983

Qualifications	% of the Total Number of Teachers in All Independent Chinese Secondary Schools
Doctorate	0.2
Master's	2.4
Bachelor's	57.0
Professional certificate	6.3
Teachers' training	3.1
College graduate	3.6
Special certificate pre-university class	16.1
Malaysian educational certificate	7.7
Senior middle III	3.7

Source: See note 85.

The situation was very satisfactory.

In general, the independent Chinese secondary schools coached their students to take the Unified Examination which they themselves conducted in Chinese. However, there were some which also trained their students to sit for public examinations conducted by the government in Malay. Such examinations were the Sijil Rendah Pelajaran, the Sijil Pelajaran Malaysia, and the Sijil Tinggi Pelajaran Malaysia. Yet others even trained their students to take the 'O' level examination conducted by Cambridge University in English. Some of the schools did all of these so that employment as well as tertiary education opportunities for their graduates could be widened.[86]

The certificate awarded on the basis of the Unified Examination was, in the 1980s, a valuable document both within and outside Malaysia. When hiring personnel, business concerns within the country gave recognition to this certificate. When awarding scholarships or study loans, public organizations would also go by this certificate presented by applicants. Colleges and universities in many foreign countries, as already mentioned in the last chapter, would also give admission to students from Malaysia on the basis of this qualification. To repeat, the foreign countries concerned were Taiwan, the United Kingdom, the United States, Canada, Australia, and New Zealand.[87]

THE SOUTHERN COLLEGE

Like earlier on, in the 1980s, there was a shortage of places in the colleges and universities in the country, which led to many students being denied opportunities to further their studies, particularly Chinese students. This led to the founding of the Southern College, an institution which used Chinese as the main medium of instruction.

The figures in Table 5.7 show the shortage of places in the higher centres of learning in the country over the years:[88]

Table 5.7
Percentage of Applicants Accepted by Tertiary Institutions

Year	Number of Applicants	Number Accepted	% of the Number Accepted
1982/83	19,255	6,227	32.34
1983/84	28,858	6,890	23.9
1984/85	32,168	7,192	22.4
1985/86	32,209	8,213	25.5
1986/87	30,973	8,595	27.7
1987/88	27,658	9,289	33.6

Source: See note 88.

The picture, indeed, was less than rosy.

Among the numbers accepted for admission, the Chinese constituted only a minority. The following statistics in Table 5.8 reveal this:[89]

Table 5.8
Percentage of Chinese Students in Higher Institutes of Learning

Year	% of Chinese to Total Number of Students Studying for Professional Courses	% of Chinese to Total Number of Students Studying for Degrees
1980	3.5	31.2
1985	4.9	29.7

Source: See note 89.

The Chinese were disadvantaged.

In June 1986, the management committee of the Foon Yew independent Chinese secondary school in Johor Bharu applied to the Ministry of Education for permission to establish a Foon Yew College. In October the following year, the application was rejected. In December, Foon Yew followed up with an appeal, but in February the following year, the appeal was also rejected.[90]

In March 1988, on the eve of a parliamentary by-election in Johor Bahru, Prime Minister Dr Mahathir visited the town and met with Chinese community leaders, perhaps to canvass for votes. At the dinner given in his honour, the president of the Zhong Hua Gong Hui [Chinese Association] requested him to grant registration to the proposed Foon Yew College. The prime minister replied by saying that his government would consider the proposal, but the proposed college must abide by the policy on education of the nation and it must also admit non-Chinese students.[91]

In April, a delegation from the management committee of the Foon Yew visited the Ministry of Education to trash matters out. It proposed to change the name of the projected college from Foon Yew College to Southern College. At the same time, it proposed to transfer control of the college from the Foon Yew to the Zhong Hua Gong Hui.[92]

In August 1988, the deputy minister for education, Woon See Chin, handed over to the management committee of the proposed Southern College the permit from the government to set up the college. Some time later, the Southern College was also registered as a limited company with the registrar of societies.[93]

In December 1990, the college started teaching. The Malay and the Business Departments of the Foon Yew joined up with the college.[94]

The Lim Lian Geok Foundation and the Chinese Educational Festival

A specially significant development in Chinese education in Malaysia was the setting up of the Lim Lian Geok Foundation and the observation of his death anniversary as the Festival of Chinese Education. The steps were not only to commemorate Lim's contributions to Chinese education, but also, perhaps even more importantly, to propagate his spirit so as to continue to defend and advance the cause of Chinese education. The events took place in the late 1980s.

Lim Lian Geok, the former president of UCSTA and an ardent champion of Chinese education who lost, in 1961, his Malayan citizenship as well his registration to teach because of his stand, died on 18 December 1985.[95] Consequent upon this, UCSTA, leading fourteen other Chinese all-nation organizations, soon set up a Lim Lian Geok Foundation. The activities regularly conducted by the foundation to commemorate Lim and uphold his spirit ran into a long list. They included:

(1) Maintaining and repairing Lim's grave.
(2) Publishing Lim's works and works of others connected with him.
(3) Supporting the publication of educational journals and magazines as well as academic works pertaining to Chinese education.
(4) Celebrating the Chinese Educational Festival.

The Chinese Educational Festival was instituted in 1988, three years after Lim's death, and was celebrated in the following way:

(1) A public commemoration of Lim at his grave.
(2) Conferring "Lim Lian Geok Awards" on organizations and individuals that had made contributions to Chinese education.
(3) Holding "Lim Lian Geok Lectures", "Lim Lian Geok Forums", seminars, exchange meets, and so on.

Lim assumed an almost martyr status.

So the 1980s were very often a trying time for Chinese schools in the country. Some of the challenges they met with were successfully overcome.

Others were not. In one instance, during "Operation Lalang", some Chinese educationists were sent to jail. The primary schools continued to suffer from many limitations although there was progress at the secondary and tertiary levels. Of special significance to the future of Chinese education, perhaps, was the making of Lim Lian Geok into a model for all Chinese educationists to emulate.

Notes

[1]   Harold Crouch, *Government and Society in Malaysia* (NSW, Australia, 1996), p. 115.

[2]   *Nanyang Siang Pau*, 16 May 2007, Zhu Ke Li's article. Liao Wen Hui, *Hua Xiao Jiao Zong ji Qi Ren Wu* (Kajang, 2006), p. 136.

[3]   Ibid.; *Sin Chew Daily*, 27 April 1981.

[4]   Ibid.

[5]   Ibid.

[6]   *Nanyang Siang Pau*, 18 May 2007, Zhu Ke Li's article.

[7]   *Nanyang Siang Pau*, 17 May 2007 and 18 May 2007, Zhu Ke Li's articles.

[8]   Kementerian Pelajaran Malaysia, *Laporan Jawatankuasa Kabinet Mengkaji Pelaksanaan Dasar Pelajaran* (Kuala Lumpur, 1979), pp. 16–18, 100 and 229.

[9]   *Nanyang Siang Pau*, 9 December 1980; UCSTA, *Hua Wen Jiao Yu Shi Liao* (Kuala Lumpur, 1984) (hereafter UCSTA, op. cit. 1), last vol., pp. 50–55; Mok Soon Sang, *Ma Lai Xi Ya Jiao Yu Shi, 1400–1999* (Kuala Lumpur, 2000), pp. 152–56.

[10]   *Nanyang Siang Pau*, 12 April 1981, 14 April 1981 and 7 May 2007; *Sin Chew Daily*, 23 March 1981 and 16 June 1981; UCSTA, op. cit. 1, pp. 51–53; UCSTA, *Jiao Zong 33 Nian* (Kuala Lumpur, 1985) (hereafter UCSTA, op. cit. 2), pp. 588–92.

[11]   *Sin Chew Daily*, 31 December 1981; Mok Soon Sang, op. cit., p. 187.

[12]   *Sin Chew Daily*, 5 January 1982; UCSTA, op. cit. 1, last vol., p. 60.

[13]   *Sin Chew Daily*, 6 January 1982; Zheng Liang Shu, *Ma Lai Xi Ya Hua Wen Jiao Yu Fa Zan Shi* (Kuala Lumpur, 2003), vol. 4, pp. 285–86.

[14]   *Sin Chew Daily*, 8 January 1982; UCSTA, op. cit. 1, pp. 61–62.

[15]   *Sin Chew Daily*, 13 January 1982; Zheng Liang Shu, op. cit., vol. 4, p. 289; UCSTA, op. cit., 1, p. 64.

[16]   *Sin Chew Daily*, 30 January 1982; UCSCA, *Feng Yun Ji Dang Yi Bai Ba Shi Nian* (Kajang, 2001) (hereafter UCSCA, op. cit. 1), pp. 170–71.

[17]   *Sin Chew Daily*, 10–13 March 1982 as seen in UCSTA, op. cit. 1, p. 68; UCSCA, op. cit. 1, p. 169.

[18]   *Sin Chew Daily*, 14 March 1982; UCSTA, op. cit. 1, p. 68.

[19]   Tang Chee Yee and Mok Soon Sang, *3-M Xiao Xue Xin Ke Cheng: Jiao Xue Gai Lun* (Kuala Lumpur, 1983), p. 11; Mok Soon Sang, op. cit., p. 161.

20 Kementerian Pelajaran Malaysia, *Kurikulum Baru Sekolah Rendah* (Kuala Lumpur, 1981), pp. 5–20; Tang Chee Yee and Mok Soon Sang, op. cit., pp. 12–19; Mok Soon Sang, op. cit., p. 154.

21 *China Press*, 10 December 1982; UCSTA, op. cit. 1, pp. 95–98.

22 Mok Soon Sang, op. cit., pp. 182–83.

23 *Sin Chew Daily*, 10 December 1982; UCSTA, op. cit. 1, p. 97.

24 *Nanyang Siang Pau*, 1 December 1982; UCSTA, op. cit. 1, pp. 96–97.

25 *Sin Chew Daily*, 10 December 1982; UCSTA, op. cit. 1, p. 97.

26 *Sin Chew Daily*, 23 November 1982; UCSTA, op. cit. 1, p. 96.

27 *Sin Chew Daily*, 11 December 1982; UCSTA, op. cit. 1, p. 97.

28 *Nanyang Siang Pau*, 8 June 2007; Liao Wen Hui, op. cit., pp. 129–34; Zhen Gong, *Hua Jiao Chun Lei: Lim Fong Seng* (Kajang, 2006), p. 216.

29 *Nanyang Siang Pau*, 6 June 2007, Zhu Ke Li's article.

30 *Nanyang Siang Pau*, 7 June 2007, Zhu Ke Li's article.

31 Ibid.

32 *Nanyang Siang Pau*, 8 June 2007, Zhu Ke Li's article.

33 *Nanyang Siang Pau*, 11 June 2007 and 13 June 2007, Zhu Ke Li's articles; Zhen Gong, op. cit., p. 216; Liao Wen Hui, op. cit., p. 133.

34 *Nanyang Siang Pau*, 15 June 2007, Zhu Ke Li's article; Liao Wen Hui, op. cit., pp. 132–33.

35 *Nanyang Siang Pau*, 12 June 2007 and 15 June 2007, Zhu Ke Li's articles; Zakaria Hj. Ahmad, ed., *Government and Politics*, vol. 2 (Kuala Lumpur, 2007), p. 107.

36 *Tong Bao*, 8 June 1990; *Oriental News*, 25 August 2007; Liao Wen Hui, op. cit., pp. 133–34.

37 *Nanyang Siang Pau*, 29 June 2007, Zhu Ke Li's article.

38 *Nanyang Siang Pau*, 30 June 2007, Zhu Ke Li's article; UCSTA, op. cit. 2, p. 614; Liao Wen Hui, op. cit., pp. 136–38; Sharon A. Cartens, *History, Culture, Identities: Studies in Malaysian Chinese Worlds* (Singapore, 2006), pp. 153–54.

39 *Nanyang Siang Pau*, 2 July 2007, Zhu Ke Li's article; UCSTA, op. cit. 2, pp. 614–617 and 621; Yap Sin Tian, *The Chinese Schools of Malaysia: Towards the Year 2000* (Kuala Lumpur, 1992), pp. 111–46.

40 *Nanyang Siang Pau*, 2 July 2007 and 3 July 2007, Zhu Ke Li's articles; UCSCA, *Dong Zong 50 Nian* (Kajang, 2004) (hereafter UCSCA, op. cit. 2), pp. 938–45.

41 *Nanyang Siang Pau*, 19 June 2007 and 27 June 2007, Zhu Ke Li's articles.

42 UCSCA, op. cit. 1, pp. 177–82; Mok Soon Sang, op. cit., p. 188.

43 Ibid.; Liao Wen Hui, op. cit., p. 83; UCSCA, op. cit. 2, p. 245.

44 UCSCA, op. cit. 1, pp. 180–82; Liao Wen Hui, op. cit., p. 83.

45 *Nanyang Siang Pau*, 11 November 1984; UCSCA, op. cit. 2, p. 245; Liao Wen Hui, op. cit., pp. 83–84.

46 *Nanyang Siang Pau*, 8 August 1984, 10 August 1984 and 11 November 1984; UCSCA, op. cit. 1, pp. 185–88; UCSCA, op. cit. 2, p. 245.

47 Sia Keng Yek, *SRJK(C) dalam Sistem Pendidikan Kebangsaan: Delima dan Kontroversi* (Kuala Lumpur, 2005), pp. 108–13; UCSCA, op. cit. 2, pp. 249 and 964–68; Mok Soon Sang, op. cit., p. 188.

48 Ibid.

49 *China Press*, 2 December 1985; UCSCA, op. cit. 1, p. 193.

50 UCSCA, op. cit. 1, pp. 206–16; UCSCA, op. cit. 2, pp. 969–71.

51 UCSCA, op. cit. 2, p. 971.

52 Ibid.

53 UCSCA, op. cit. 1, pp. 216–19; Zheng Liang Shu, op. cit., vol. 4, pp. 334–35.

54 Sim Mow Yu, *Shi Zai Huo Bu Mie* (Kuala Lumpur, 1996), pp. 258–61; Liao Wen Hui, op. cit., p. 85; UCSCA, op. cit. 1, pp. 222–23.

55 UCSCA, op. cit. 1, p. 228; Zheng Liang Shu, op. cit., vol. 4, p. 338.

56 *Sin Chew Daily*, 30 October 1987; UCSCA, op. cit. 1, pp. 228 and 230–31; Lin Kai Zhong, *Jian Gou Zhong De Hua Ren Wen Hua* (Kuala Lumpur, 1999), p. 139.

57 UCSCA, op. cit. 1, p. 236; *Sin Chew Daily*, 8 October 1987.

58 UCSCA, op. cit. 1, p. 239; Sim Mow Yu, op. cit., p. 271.

59 UCSCA, op. cit. 1, p. 239.

60 UCSCA, op. cit. 1, pp. 240–44.

61 UCSCA, op. cit. 1, pp. 247–49; Kua Kia Soong, *The Chinese Schools of Malaysia: A Protean Saga* (Kajang, 1999), 3rd edition, p. 137.

62 UCSCA, op. cit. 1, pp. 250–51; Kua Kia Soong, op. cit., p. 138.

63 UCSCA, op. cit. 1, p. 251; Zheng Liang Shu, op. cit., vol. 4, p. 350.

64 UCSCA, *Feng Yun Ji Dang Yi Bai Ba Shi Nian* (Kajang, 2001), p. 256; Sim Mow Yu, op. cit., pp. 298–99.

65 Kua Kia Soong, op. cit., p. 138; Lin Kai Zhong, op. cit., p.140.

66 Ibid.

67 Cheah Boon Kheng, *Malaysia: The Making of a Nation* (Singapore, 2004), pp. 216–217; Khoo Boo Teik, *Beyond Mahathir* (New York, 2003), pp. 6–7; R.S. Milne and Diane K. Mauzy, *Malaysian Politics under Mahathir* (New York, 2006), pp. 39–44.

68 UCSCA, op. cit. 1, p. 257; Lin Kai Zhong, op. cit., pp. 139 and 141.

69 UCSTA, op. cit. 2, p. 636.

70 UCSTA, *1985 Nian Quan Guo Hua Wen Xiao Xue Diao Cha Bao Gao* (Kuala Lumpur, 1986).

71 Ibid., pp. 14–15.

72 Ibid., pp. 19–20.

73 Ibid., pp. 9–13.

74 Ibid., p. 50.

75 Ibid., pp. 23–35; Mok Soon Sang, op. cit., pp. 189–91.

76 UCSTA, op. cit. 2, p. 806; Mok Soon Sang, op. cit., p. 190.

77 UCSTA, op. cit. 2, p. 804; Mok Soon Sang, op. cit., p. 189.

[78] UCSTA, *1985 Nian Quan Guo Hua Wen Xiao Xue Diao Cha Bao Gao* (Kuala Lumpur, 1986), p. 96.

[79] Ibid., p. 95.

[80] See Chapters 3 and 4 of this book.

[81] Mok Soon Sang, *Pendidikan di Malaysia* (Kuala Lumpur, 2000), 7th edition, pp. 170 and 173.

[82]   Mok Soon Sang, *Ma Lai Xi Ya Jiao Yu Shi, 1400–1999* (Kuala Lumpur, 2000), pp. 163–65.

[83] Timbalan Menteri Pendidikan, Circular TMP 9.3/1 (38), 8 June 1989.

[84] *Oriental News*, 15 August 2007.

[85] Mok Soon Sang, *Ma Lai Xi Ya Jiao Yu Shi, 1400–1999* (Kuala Lumpur, 2000), p. 193.

[86] Ibid.

[87] UCSTA, op. cit. 2, pp. 635–36.

[88] Shahril et al., *Pendidikan di Malaysia* (Kuala Lumpur, 1993), p. 146.

[89] Mok Soon Sang, *Ma Lai Xi Ya Jiao Yu Shi, 1400–1999* (Kuala Lumpur, 2000), p. 184.

[90] UCSCA, op. cit. 1, pp. 270–71; Zheng Liang Shu, op. cit., vol. 4, pp. 385–89.

[91] Ibid.

[92] Ibid.

[93] Ibid.

[94] Ibid.

[95] UCSCA, *Hua Guang Yong Yao* (Kuala Lumpur, 1993), pp. 60–78; Liao Wen Hui, op. cit., pp. 187–88.

6

VISION 2020 AND
THE CHINESE SCHOOLS

The 1990s into the year 2003 saw the continued rule of Mahathir Mohamad as the prime minister of the country. Mahathir introduced a grand vision for the development of the country called Vision 2020. While the new regime brought blessings to the Chinese schools in certain ways, it also created difficulties for them in other respects. There were occasions of joy as well as occasions of disappointment.

Vision 2020, Smart Schools and Vision Schools

Under the inspiration of Vision 2020, the schools in the country, including Chinese schools, were to be converted into Smart Schools. They were also to become Vision Schools. While the Smart School scheme was of benefit indirectly to the Chinese schools, the Vision School plan would work to their disadvantage.

Vision 2020

On 28 February 1991, in an address to a business conference, Mahathir broached the idea of Vision 2020.[1] In his visualization, from 1991 to 2020, Malaysia should develop to become an advanced country. There were to be two dimensions to the plan, *viz*, economic and social. The economic target was to double the Gross Domestic Product of the country every ten years, and the social target was to do away with ethnicity in every aspect, and see the evolution of a unified society. He also mentioned that the nation must meet a series of challenges, economic or social in nature, to achieve these aims. The challenges, which could be considered to be economic in nature, were as follows:[2]

(1) To build a prosperous society which would be economically competitive and which would be spirited, alert, and resilient.

(2) To build a society which would be scientifically progressive, creative, and far-sighted. Its people would not only be consumers of modern science and technology, but also contributors to such science and technology in future.

(3) To build a society which would be free, peaceful, confident and proud of its achievements, and in possession of sufficient alertness to meet obstacles of all kinds. It should be a society which would have the attribute of pursuing outstanding achievements, understand its own full potential and not be fettered mentally by any bondage, and be respected by the peoples of other countries.

And the challenges which may be deemed to be social in nature were:

(1) To build a mature society which would be enlightened and tolerant, in which every citizen, regardless of his colour or creed, could follow freely his customs, culture, and religion and would not feel persecuted by any other race.

(2) To build a nation in which the various races would be united and share common objectives, and in which they would, on the basis of equality and justice, live together and render their loyalty.

(3) To ensure the building of a society in which there would be economic equality. This society would ensure the equal and reasonable distribution of the wealth of the country so as to enable the enjoyment of the fruit of economic development by every citizen. Such a society would not be realized if economic functions were assigned on the basis of race, and economic backwardness were concentrated on some particular racial groups.

(4) On the basis of mutual consultation, to build and develop a democratically mature society which would ultimately become a model of a developed nation.

(5) To build a society in which there would be a culture of morality and love, in which society would be more important than the individual, and in which the welfare of the people was not based

on the nation or the individual, but on a mature and stable family system.

(6) To build a society in which its nationals would embrace religious values, would be perfect in spirit and noble in behaviour, and which would be characterized by morality and ethics.

The economic challenges would be met by transforming schools in the country into Smart Schools, and the social challenges towards racial integration would be met by turning schools with different medium of instruction into Vision Schools.

Smart Schools

Smart Schools were to be schools which make extensive and intensive use of information technology and the computer. Such schools would keep their students abreast of the globalization of the modern world and would turn them into citizens who could fulfil the economic objectives of Vision 2020.

In 1995, in line with Vision 2020, Mahathir announced that the government would build a Multimedia Super Corridor in a region south of the capital Kuala Lumpur. The project was to turn the country into one which would be advanced in information technology and computer science. Smart schools were to be one of a number of items to be implemented to bring about the establishment of this corridor. Two years later, the corridor was initiated.[3]

For a start, the Ministry of Education would build two primary and two secondary Smart Schools in the corridor to serve as models for other schools in the country to emulate. Next to these, private sources would also build a multimedia university in the corridor.[4]

Other than the above, the Ministry of Education would build six Smart Schools in other parts of the country. And it would also select eighty existing primary and secondary schools to be gradually converted into Smart Schools. The exercise would begin in 1999. It was envisaged that by 2010, all schools in the country would be turned into Smart Schools.[5]

In the initial stages, among all subjects taught, only four subjects, *viz* Malay, English, mathematics, and science, would be taught using information technology.[6]

The MCA as a political party also played a part in the campaign to convert schools into Smart Schools by undertaking to convert Chinese schools. In 1997, the same year as the Multimedia Super Corridor was inaugurated, it prepared a plan for 114 National-Type Chinese Primary Schools to be gradually converted. The scheme was implemented methodically. It also appealed to institutions not in the 114 to follow in the footsteps.[7]

The Smart School idea was definitely of benefit to the Chinese schools as it lifted them to a higher level of competence. However, unlike the Malay-medium National Primary Schools, they did not obtain funding from the government. They had to find money to purchase equipment, among other things, themselves. In the end, they relied on a Hua Ren Jiao Yu Ji Jin [Hua Ren Education Foundation] and a certain company set up by the MCA as well as their own resources for funding.[8]

For the Chinese, the Smart School scheme was the bright side of Vision 2020.

Vision Schools

In December 1995, the Ministry of Education came out with a plan to create Vision Schools.[9]

According to the plan, what was involved was the following. A Vision School would be one in which there would be a National Primary School, that is, a Malay-medium school, a National-Type Chinese Primary School, and a National-Type Tamil Primary School. It would be a composite school. Each of the constituent school would have its own administration, headed by its own headmaster, and its own classrooms. One of the three headmasters would be selected to shoulder coordination work with his two colleagues. But the three schools would share the same school hall, library, canteen, and school field. They could also share their teachers. All extra-curricular activities, for instance sports-meet, award-conferring ceremonies, fund-raising schemes, open day, etc., would also all be planned and held in common. The language used outside the classroom would be Malay.[10]

Each of the constituent schools would not have an enrolment exceeding 840 pupils, and the whole school would consist of not more than 2,520 pupils.[11]

The Vision School was, in fact, a resurrection of the Integrated School tried out in Teluk Sengat in Johor in the late 1980s. We have given an account of the Integrated School Plan in the last chapter. Actually, in 1997, the minister for education, Najib, did announce that the Teluk Sengat School would be, in due course, renamed a Vision School.[12]

According to the Seventh Five-Year Plan of Malaysia, which spanned 1996 to 2000, the Ministry of Education would build twelve Vision Schools in different localities in the country. At the same time, the ministry would also try to bring together existing schools of the different language medium into one common school either by shifting them all into one existing campus, or by erecting new buildings in an existing campus to house all of them.[13]

After all these initial moves, suddenly for a while, there was no more talk about Vision Schools. This was partly because the scheme was opposed vehemently by UCSCA and UCSTA, as well as the Chinese community at large. The reason for Chinese opposition was the same as in the case of the Integrated School Plan. The Chinese felt that the Malay component in the Vision Schools would dominate the other two components, which would result in the other two components losing their identities in the end. The schools would become Malay-medium schools. Also in 1997, a number of other factors arose, more importantly, the country being stricken by the Asian financial crisis, which diverted the attention of the government to dealing with that development.[14]

However, in mid-2000 Mahathir revived the project. He announced that all the fourteen constituent members of the ruling Barisan Nasional, which included the MCA and MIC, agreed on creating Vision Schools. In the days that followed, UCSCA and UCSTA voiced opposition against Mahathir, publishing a pamphlet Jian Jue Fan Dui Hong Yuan Xiao Xue Ji Hua [Firmly Oppose the Vision Primary School Plan]. Other Chinese organizations threw in their support behind UCSCA and UCSTA. The management committees and parents of several Chinese schools involved also resisted their schools being moved to join Vision Schools. The opposition was so vocal that the president of the MCA, Dr Ling Liong Sik, finally announced that the government would respect the wishes of the Chinese community and would desist in trying to implement the Vision School scheme. Prior to that, the Barisan Nasional had just lost a by-election in Lunas in Kedah to a rival party.[15]

But Ling Liong Sik was to go back on his words. Early in 2002, in a locality called USJ District, a Vision School was created and began teaching half a year later. The school involved a Chinese school joining in as a component. It had 203 pupils in the Malay section and 99 in the Chinese section. UCSCA, through its president, Guo Quan Qiang, and UCSTA, also through its president, Wang Chao Qun, criticized the move vehemently.[16]

In October 2003, just before he resigned as prime minister, Mahathir voiced the desire that he would like to see parents sending their children to study either at National Schools or Vision Schools.[17]

It is an irony to note that while the Vision School scheme had the aim of eradicating ethnicity in Malaysian society, it resulted instead in precipitating a cleavage between the government, led by UMNO, a Malay party, and the Chinese community, led by UCSCA and UCSTA.

To the latter, the scheme would do immense damage to the cause of Chinese education because the "ultimate objective" of the 1956 Razak Report of making Malay the only main medium of instruction in the schools, an ambition of the Malay community as a whole, would be realized.

Education Bills and Education Acts

1996 saw the enactment of an Education Act which had the purpose of adjusting the education system in the country so that the twin aims of Vision 2020, that is, the economic advancement of the country and the eradication of ethnicity in society, could be more easily realized. This had its forerunners.

A Gesture from the Prime Minister

Actually, even before the announcement of Vision 2020 in 1991, Mahathir, several years earlier in 1986, in a speech to a Chinese school in Ipoh, the Shen Jai Independent High School, had said that he would review and amend subsection 21(2) of the 1961 Education Act. The subsection of the said act, the reader may remember, empowered the minister for education to convert National-Type Chinese Primary and National-Type Tamil Primary Schools into National Primary Schools, that is, Malay schools, any time he considered fit. That provision had always plagued Chinese educationists and the Chinese community. In his speech, Mahathir showed that this would be a new deal for the Chinese, and ethnicity in society would be done away. The Chinese primary schools could remain as they were and there would be no sacrifice of Chinese interest. A little later, the deputy minister for education reiterated Mahathir's message.[18]

What Mahathir and his deputy minister for education said was soon countered by others. One Awang Had Salleh, the vice-chancellor of the Northern University, expressed the opinion that, ultimately, National-Type Chinese and Tamil Primary Schools would eventually become National Primary Schools. UMNO Youth called on Mahathir not to forget to promote the overall interests of the Malays, and a member of parliament and the son of the deputy prime minister, Tamrin Baba, called on the government to have the Chinese and Tamil primary schools closed. Mahathir did not check these people and that caused Chinese educationists to cast doubt on the sincerity of his promise.[19]

The 1990 Education Bill

Nevertheless, in July 1990, the government initiated an Education Bill for deliberation with educationists and the public, with the intention of replacing the 1961 Education Act.[20] And in October, there was to be a general election in the country. Chinese educationists took the opportunity of the latter to press the point that the proposed bill should give fairer treatment to Chinese education by issuing demands, and joining and aligning themselves with political opposition parties. In the face of the challenge, the government became concerned, and eventually shelved the bill and did not get it enacted into an act. But it won the election.

The demands were issued in the name of fifteen Chinese organizations which called on any political party that was to take part in the coming election to show support, on the promise that votes in the election from the Chinese community would be given to it. The demands, in essence, ran as follows:[21]

(I)　General education demands of ethnic Chinese citizens:

    (1)　The mother tongue and original script should be the main medium of instruction in schools of the different language streams.

    (2)　The language medium used in examinations, in school administration, and in teacher training should be the same as the language medium used in teaching in Chinese schools.

    (3)　The National Language, that is Malay, should be a compulsory subject in all schools, but should not be upheld at the expense of the two principles above.

(II)　Schools of the different language streams should be treated equally.

    (1)　Schools of the different language streams should all be regarded as components of the education system in the country.

    (2)　Grants and assistance given to the schools of the different language streams should be based on the number of students in each school.

    (3)　Resolve the problem of shortage of teachers in the Chinese schools.

(4) Opportunities for training of primary and secondary school teachers should be fair to all.

(5) Finance given for erection of school buildings and purchasing equipment should be on a fair basis.

(6) Opportunities for development for schools of the different language streams should be given on a fair basis.

(7) Opportunities of education given to children and young people should be granted on a fair basis.

(8) Establish elementary and advanced technical and vocational schools for the different races, using their different languages and scripts as different medium of instruction.

(9) The government should encourage the people to promote education, build more schools, and start more classes depending on their own resources.

(10) Opportunities of employment for young people should be equal. Students of the different language streams who have passed their examinations should have equal opportunities of employment.

(III) The government should set up a Chinese educational advisory body whose members should come from representative Chinese educational organizations to help the government resolve problems pertaining to Chinese education.

(IV) All non-profit-making educational organizations and schools of the different races should be accorded the same treatment as that given to charitable organizations and should be exempt from having to pay taxes on donations from the public.

To give teeth to their demands, Lim Fong Seng, president of UCSCA, resigned from his post in the organization and led a group of educationists to join the DAP, a political party opposed to Mahathir's Barisan Nasional, as members. Lim in the 1980s, as seen in an earlier chapter, had created the idea of a "3-in-1" strategy to get educationists to take part in politics to advance the cause of Chinese education. That strategy had not worked as well as was hoped. Now he had come out with a new formula of "politicking, a 'two-line strategy'". This move would also enable Chinese educationists join opposition parties to further their cause.[22]

Mahathir had not only the DAP to face in the general election, as seen in an earlier chapter, but also Tengku Razaleigh, who had broken off from Mahathir's UMNO and was challenging Mahathir for leadership in the country through a new party, Semangat 46. Lim Fong Seng, along with others, now got the DAP, Semangat 46, as well as PAS, to form a united front to take on the Barisan Nasional.[23]

The Barisan Nasional won the election. However, the event caused so much concern to Mahathir that he shelved the proposed new Education Bill. His coalition won eventually because not all Chinese voters deserted it. Mahathir retained the support of them by making concessions to the Chinese community, for instance, by allowing them to go to China for tours or to do business, and giving money to some Chinese primary schools to help them put up school buildings.[24]

The proposed 1990 Education Bill and the general election of the same year did not do much to improve relations among the different races in the country.

The 1996 Education Act

In 1995 a new Education Bill was floated again. The next year, the bill was passed by parliament and became an act. This time a new act replaced the 1961 Education Act.[25]

This 1995 bill also had the twin aims of making the educational system in the country technologically more advanced and racially less divisive. However, in the present discussion, we shall not go into the first aspect of the bill as Chinese educationists did not take issue with it. We shall deal with only the second aspect as it was considered, contrary to its intention, harmful to Chinese interests and, therefore, resented.

The government had scheduled to present the bill to parliament for deliberation and voting in October 1995. In July, UCSCA and UCSTA submitted a memorandum to make known what they wished to see in the proposed legislation. Among the many items included were the following:[26]

(1) Abandon the "ultimate objective" of making Malay the main medium of instruction in all educational institutions.

(2) Abandon 26(A) of the 1972 Education Amendment Act which empowered the Ministry of Education to dissolve school boards of managers or school boards of governors and constitute new ones as it deemed necessary.

(3) Recognize the examinations, called Unified Examinations, conducted by the independent Chinese secondary schools themselves. Students who pass these examinations should be allowed to join tertiary institutions in the country to further their studies.

To allay the fears of the Chinese, the minister for education, Najib, made it known that the bill had no intention of doing harm to their schools. In December, on the second reading of the bill in parliament, he made the following points:[27]

(1) The status of the National-Type Chinese Primary as well as the National-Type Tamil Primary Schools would not be changed. Also, their management committees would be allowed to continue.

(2) The status of the independent Chinese secondary schools, as recognized by the 1961 Education Act, would remain the same. The same applies to the Unified Examinations. Their management committees would continue to exist. Also, presently, the schools had to renew their registration with the Ministry of Education each year. Henceforth, they would be allowed to register only once and for all.

(3) The Chinese and Tamil languages would from now no longer be taught outside regular school hours, but within regular school hours. Also, they would be taught in the National Primary Schools so that more students could learn them as second languages.

However, the anxiety of the Chinese was not to be allayed. A little earlier on, UCSCA and UCSTA, together with other Chinese organizations, had got together a team of lawyers to make a close study of the education bill. The findings of the team were negative, and it was concluded that the new bill had even more severe unfavourable implications for Chinese education than the 1961 Education Act. The following were what the lawyers discovered.[28]

Firstly, it was true that the new bill made no reference to an "ultimate objective" which was to be achieved in the country's education system, yet one of its provisions carried the implication that it was not abandoned. This provision was section 17. The section read:[29]

> And whereas the above policy is to be executed through a national system of education which provides for the national language [i.e. Malay] to be the main medium of instruction, a National Curriculum and common examinations; … (17).
>
> (1) The national language shall be the main medium of instruction in all educational institutions in the National Education System except a national-type school established under section 28 or any other educational institution exempted by the Minister from this subsection.

(2) Where the main medium of instruction in an educational institution
     is other than the national language, the national language shall be
     taught as a compulsory subject in the educational institution.

Judging from subsection (17)(1), the National-Type Chinese Primary as
well as the National-Type Tamil Primary Schools were not exempted from
having to use the national language as the main medium of instruction.
Similarly, independent Chinese secondary schools which were also educational
institutions were not exempted.

Actually, in an interview with a group of Chinese newspapers in March
2002, Mahathir admitted that the new education bill which became the 1996
Education Act still preserved the "ultimate objective". At the same time, he
expressed the view that the objective would never be abandoned.[30]

Secondly, although section 26(A) of the 1972 Education Amendment Act
which gave powers to the education authorities to dissolve school boards of
managers and school boards of governors or constitute such when necessary
no longer appeared in the new education bill, there were provisions in the new
bill which enabled them to do the same thing.[31] These provisions were:

(58) (1) If the Minister is satisfied that in an educational
           institution
           (a) the governors have been acting or are proposing to act
                unreasonably with respect to the exercise of any power
                conferred or the discharge of any duty imposed by or
                under this Act; or
           (b) the governors have failed to discharge any duty imposed
                upon them by or under this Act, the Minister may
           (aa) give such directions in writing as to the exercise of the
                power or the discharge of the duty as appear to him to
                be expedient, with which directions it shall be the duty
                of the governors to comply; or
           (bb) suspend or dismiss all or any of the governors and,
                notwithstanding the provisions of any instrument of
                government relating to the institution, appoint such
                persons or persons as he may think fit to have and
                to exercise all the functions of the governors for such
                period as he may direct.
      (2) If at any time, for an educational institution, there is no
           Board of Governors constituted under this Act the Minister
           may appoint such person or persons as he may think fit to
           exercise the functions of governors for the Institution for such
           period as he may direct.

(61) (1) Where the Minister dissolves a board ... the Minister shall at any time thereafter appoint a different board in accordance with the Act.

       (2) Where the Minister had not appointed a board under subsection (1), the powers, functions and duties of the board shall be exercised by the head teacher of the educational institution or by such other person as the Minister may nominate who shall be a member of the public service.

(62) (1) Every board of managers or board of governors of a government educational institution except –

          (a) a government national-type primary school; and

          (b) a government national primary school or government national secondary school to be determined by the Minister, established prior to the appointed date, shall be dissolved on that date in such manner as the Minister may determine, and thereupon it shall cease to employ and to be the employer of teachers and other employees, and every instrument of management or government pertaining to the educational institution shall cease to have effect.

(125) The Minister may suspend or cancel or cause to be suspended or cancelled the payment of any grant to an educational institution if the governors or any other person responsible for the management of the educational institution has failed to comply with any of the provisions of this Act or any regulations made under this Act.

The powers given to the minister for education were telling.

Thirdly, independent Chinese secondary schools had been conducting their own Unified Examinations for their students and had not as a general rule prepared them to sit for examinations conducted by the government. And the government, on its part, had not compelled such students to sit for its examinations. Now, the new educational bill contained provisions that might be interpreted as not permitting this state of affairs to continue any more. On the first issue, the relevant provision read:[32]

(69) (1) ... no person or educational institution shall conduct, permit or cause to be held or conducted, or be in any manner concerned in the holding or conducting of, any examination for any pupil of an educational institution or for any private candidate without the prior written approval of the Director of Examinations.

And even if approval were given, restrictions, etc. could be imposed:

(69)   (2)   In granting approval under subsection (1), the Director
             of Examinations may impose such restrictions, terms and
             conditions as he deems fit.

Any disobedience could be penalized:

(69)   (5)   A person who contravenes subsection (1) or fails to comply
             with any restriction, term or condition imposed under
             subsection (2) shall be guilty of an offence and shall, on
             conviction, be liable to a fine not exceeding ten thousand
             ringgit or to imprisonment for a term not exceeding one year
             or to both.

On the second issue of the government compelling students to sit for its
examinations, the relevant provisions were:

(19)   Every school shall prepare its pupils for examinations prescribed
       by or under this Act or any regulations made under this Act unless
       otherwise exempted by or under this Act.

(74)   A private educational institution providing primary education or
       secondary education or both shall comply with the requirements
       of the National Curriculum and shall prepare pupils for prescribed
       Examinations.

The compulsion could not be clearer.

As the new bill was so harmful to the interests of Chinese education,
it evoked strong protests from the Chinese community. On an occasion in
December, 2,000 delegates from 307 organizations met and through the
president of UCSCA and the chairman of the meeting, Guo Quan Qiang,
called upon the government not to rush the bill through parliament, but to
give time to the community to respond and submit proposals. However, the
plea fell on deaf ears. The bill was duly passed by parliament and became
the 1996 Education Act.[33]

By enacting the new education act, the government had the aim of trying
to please the Chinese by not repeating some of the provisions of previous
legislation which were injurious to their educational interests. However, the
effect of the act betrayed this good intention as Chinese educationists and the
Dong Jiao Zong, a liaison committee of UCSCA and UCSTA, did not see

the act in the same light as it did. The act, in fact, intensified the misgivings of the Chinese.

The 1999 General Election and the Educational Appeals of the Chinese Educationists

As noted earlier, Malaysia was stricken by a financial crisis in 1997. The effect on its economy was thoroughly upsetting. Prime Minister Mahathir combated it by imposing exchange control and other measures. His deputy, Anwar Ibrahim, disagreed with him on resorting to such measures and the difference resulted in a split between the two men. Mahathir dismissed Anwar from his post. Anwar retaliated by launching a movement called Reformasi against him. Mahathir followed this up by getting Anwar convicted on corruption charges and thrown into prison. Later on, Anwar was further convicted by the court for practising sodomy and was given a further imprisonment term.[34]

In 1999, there was a general election. Anwar's movement joined up with the opposition parties to form a Barisan Alternatif to take on Mahathir's Barisan Nasional. Mahathir's coalition won, but his UMNO, a constituent member of the coalition, lost a great number of Malay votes.[35] UCSCA and UCSTA took the opportunity of the cleavage between Mahathir and Anwar to try to advance the cause of Chinese education. They came out with a Mu Yu Jiao Yu Xuan Yan [Manifesto on Mother Tongue Education] which consisted of a number of demands and appealed to the various contending political parties to show support for it. They also presented a copy of it to Mahathir who said that he would give it consideration. The Mu Yu Jiao Yu Xuan Yan was actually a part of a larger document of demands or appeals presented by a host of Chinese organizations to exert pressure on the government to advance Chinese interests in general. This document was called the Hua Tuan Suqiu [Appeals of the Chinese Organizations], which, insofar as the part dealing with education was concerned, include the items of the Mu Yu Jiao Yu Xuan Yan (first draft), and it ran as follows in essence:[36]

(1) Amend the 1996 Education Act to reflect the education policy of the 1957 Education Ordinance so as to ensure that every racial group could use, teach, and develop its mother tongue.

(2) In places where there were concentrations of Chinese and Indian residents, on the basis of need, build more Chinese and Indian primary schools to ensure that the right of the children of these

two racial groups to a mother tongue education would not be deprived.

(3) Resolve the long-standing problem of shortage of teachers in the Chinese and Indian schools.

(4) The government should abandon the Vision School project. It should not send teachers who did not possess a Chinese qualification to take up senior posts in Chinese schools so as to ensure that such schools would not changed in character.

(5) Ensure that schools of the different language streams were given equal treatment in funding, teacher training, curriculum design, the compilation of teaching materials, basic equipment, and hardware installations. The Smart School project should be included in this provision.

(6) Provide teacher training and curriculum planning for the implementation of the educational system based on multi-lingualism or the various medium of instruction.

(7) In any school which had five or more students from any racial group, mother tongue class (POL) for these students should be included in the regular curriculum of the school.

(8) Increase educational funding.

(9) Improve and adjust the salaries of teachers.

(10) Implement bursary and loan schemes and give awards based on a means-tested sliding scale, regardless of the students' race.

(11) Give recognition to the Unified Examinations conducted by independent Chinese secondary schools.

(12) Permit more independent Chinese secondary schools to be established. Give grants to such schools to develop.

(13) On the basis of increases in population, build more primary and secondary schools, colleges, and universities.

(14) On the basis of international academic standards, give recognition to degrees conferred by various colleges and universities, including those of the former Nanyang University, of institutions in mainland China, and in Taiwan, and of institutions in countries which did not belong to the English-speaking world.

(15) Abolish the quota system for student admission to universities.

After the election, Mahathir had the Mu Yu Jiao Yu Xuan Yan as well as the Hua Tuan Suqiu shelved.[37] This step was not conducive to improving racial relations in the country.

National-Type Chinese Primary Schools during the Years 1990–2003

It is perhaps useful to take a look at the overall situation of the various grades of Chinese educational institutions from primary to college level during the years 1990 to 2003. We shall begin our account with the National-Type Chinese Primary Schools.

The Plight of National-Type Chinese Primary Schools

UCSCA and UCSTA did a survey of National-Type Chinese Primary Schools and in mid-1999 presented a memorandum to the Ministry of Education, listing the woes faced by such schools, and pleaded with the ministry to take measures to set things right. It was not reported if the ministry responded. The situation was not conducive to the improvement of racial relationships.[38]

Shortage of Schools

It was always found that there were not enough primary schools to accommodate the increases in the Chinese student population. According to statistics released by the Ministry of Education, between the years 1987 and 1998, the following was the scenario:[39]

Table 6.1
Number of Schools in Relation to Student Numbers, 1987–98

| | Year | | | | Increase/Decrease | |
| | 1987 | | 1998 | | | |
	No. of Students	No. of Schools	No. of Students	No. of Schools	No. of Students	No. of Schools
Chinese Primary	582,126	1,295	599,520	1,283	+17,394	−12
Malay Primary	1,604,408	4,856	2,175,831	5,283	+571,423	+427

Source: See note 39.

The figures show that, over the years, there were both increases in the Chinese student population as well as in the Malay student population. However, no new schools were built for the former whereas new schools were built for the latter. For Chinese students, the number of schools for them actually decreased by twelve. The number of schools for Malay students, however, increased by 427.

For the years between 1999 and 2004, there were no information on the changes in the school populations, but there were information on the numbers of new schools built for the Chinese and Malay students. For the Chinese, only three new schools were built whereas for the Malays, there were 400 new schools. Table 6.2 shows this.[40]

Table 6.2
Schools for Chinese and Malay Primary Students, 1999–2004

Medium	Year		Increase/Decrease
	1999	**2004**	
Chinese Primary	1,284 schools	1,287 schools	+3 schools
Malay Primary	5,313 schools	5,713 schools	+400 schools

Source: See note 40.

The contrast in the treatment of Chinese and Malay schools was surprising. The authorities were not even-handed in their dealings with the two types of schools.[41]

The shortage of Chinese primary schools was felt most keenly in places where the Chinese population was dense and in new housing estates. For instance, in the Klang Valley of Selangor, 103 new Chinese primary schools were needed and in Johor Bahru, twenty-one were needed. But these were not built.[42]

Disproportionate Grants

It was found that, in 1991, Chinese primary school students made up 23.07 per cent of the total primary school population in the country. But the grants given to their schools by the government constituted only 8.14 per cent of all grants given to schools. In 1996, the respective figures were 21.07 per cent and 2.44 per cent. The situation was not good.[43]

Shortage of Qualified Teachers

National-Type Chinese Primary Schools were short of 2,000 to 3,000 qualified teachers. This contrasted strongly with the situation in National Primary Schools which had a surplus of about 12,000 teachers. Chinese schools were afflicted because the authorities did not have a proper system to train enough qualified teachers for them. So UCSCA and UCSTA pleaded with the government to lower the requirements imposed on candidates wishing to join the various teachers' training colleges to become teachers. They requested particularly that the Unified Examinations of independent Chinese secondary schools be recognized, and persons who passed such examinations be admitted to the various teachers' training colleges.[44]

Unqualified Teachers Appointed to Assume Senior Positions in the National-Type Chinese Primary Schools

In 1988, it might be recalled that the Ministry of Education had laid down the ruling that teachers who did not possess an academic qualification in Chinese could be appointed to become supervisors of extra-curricular activities in National-Type Chinese Primary Schools. Ten years later, in 1998, in a move to improve the situation, the Ministry of Education directed that such teachers should attend short Chinese courses run by the Aminuddin Baki Institute and get qualified. The intention of the ministry was good. But UCSCA and UCSTA viewed the move in a different light. To them, the move would not only not improve things but would, in fact, make matters worse. They were of the opinion that the affected teachers would not be able to develop a good grasp of the Chinese language in courses of short duration. So they did not support such a move. They felt that such teachers should possess the Sijil Pelajaran Malaysia (SPM) certificate with a Chinese Language qualification before they were appointed to their posts. At the time, it was discovered that there were nine schools in Pahang, eight in Perak, five in Johor, five in Malacca, four in Selangor and one in Kuala Lumpur, which had supervisors of extra-curricular activities with insufficient qualifications.[45]

In addition to the above, UCSCA and UCSTA found that in recent years, in certain states, persons without proper Chinese qualifications were appointed to senior administrative positions in the schools. It was not a healthy state of affairs. The positions were those of first senior assistant and second senior assistant, and the states involved were Perak and Johor, each of which had one school with such unqualified officers.[46]

The SJK (C) Damansara Incident

SJK (C) Damansara referred to Sekolah Jenis Kebangsaan (Cina) Damansara, which, in English, meant Damansara National-Type Chinese Primary School. This school was located in the Damansara New Village near Kuala Lumpur. It was a well developed school, boasting three buildings which housed not only the school office and classrooms, but also a conference room, a hall, a music room, an educational resource centre, and so on. In 2001 it caught media attention because it got into a fracas with the authorities.[47]

In 1999, the board of managers of the school had applied to the Ministry of Education to allow it to build a branch school or to move to a new site. The ministry replied that it could move to Bandar Utama 3. Later, the ministry changed its mind and said that the Bandar Utama 3 site was already occupied by the Puay Chai Primary School and that it could move to Bandar Tropicana instead. The residents of Damansara New Village were keen to build a branch school, but were not willing to let the school relocate. The board of managers of the school had not consulted the residents about the second alternative. When news reached them that the school would move, they launched a protest movement, spearheaded by a committee.[48]

In 2001, when the new school term started, the students of the school were for the time being to go to Bandar Utama 3 to study and share premises with Puay Chai. However, on the day concerned, 145 students refused to go to Bandar Utama 3. Their parents insisted on them staying in their original school. If the children had no teachers to teach them there, the parents would get voluntary teachers.[49]

The Ministry of Education reacted by sealing off the school and getting policemen posted there to lock out the students. The students moved to a village temple nearby to attend classes. Later on, they changed their venue to containers installed in the vicinity.[50]

The ministry kept on warning them to desist. It threatened that punitive action would be taken against the voluntary teachers, the recalcitrant students would be dismissed from school and barred from taking examinations. However, the students continued to disallow their school being moved to a new site. The standoff between the ministry and the school continued into the 2000s, and was not settled until 2008.[51]

Why did this incident occur? The Legal Advisor of UCSCA and UCSTA, Kuang Qi Fang, expressed the opinion that it broke out because the government refused to build new schools easily for the Chinese. In this case, it was refusing to let any Sekolah Jenis Kebangsaan (Cina) (National-Type Chinese Primary School), have a branch school. It pursued the ultimate policy of having only one kind of schools in the country and that meant schools which used Malay as the main medium of instruction.[52]

Mathematics and Science to be Taught in English

In pursuit of the economic aims of Vision 2020 and to meet the challenges of globalization, the government announced in 2002 that, beginning the following year, schools were to use English as the medium of instruction for mathematics and science. This would began with Primary One in the National Primary Schools, and with Form One and Lower Six in the National Secondary Schools.[53]

The government also instructed the MCA and Gerakan to work out a plan by which mathematics and science could be taught in English in National-Type Chinese Primary Schools. After much deliberation, the two parties came out with the following suggestion. The proposal was to have four periods and three periods to teach the two subjects in English respectively. Along with this, two periods were to be allotted to teaching the English language only. Additionally, six periods and three periods respectively were to be allotted to have the two subjects taught in Chinese. So, in National-Type Chinese Primary Schools, students were to learn the two subjects in both English and Chinese. It was a compromise formula.[54]

The proposal of the two Chinese parties evoked a storm of protest from Chinese organizations, led by UCSCA and UCSTA. The first to sound a warning that such a scheme could lead to Chinese primary schools being changed to English, like in the case of Chinese secondary schools in the wake of the 1961 Education Act, was Loot Ting Yee, vice-president of UCSTA. A first group protest meeting against the new proposal was held in August and the second in November 2002. That was before the government's new policy was put into effect. Then in March 2003, another meeting was convened, this time after the new policy was implemented. The reasons for opposing were spelt out more fully in the last meeting and it is perhaps instructive to see what they were. They ran as follows:[55]

(1) Support the government's move to raise the standard of English in schools, but oppose this being done through teaching mathematics and science in English, as well as conducting examinations in the two subjects in English.

(2) The superiority of using the mother tongue, compared with using other languages, as the medium of instruction was upheld by the

United Nations and was an educational principle followed by all nations in the world. It was also a basic human right for people to learn through their mother tongues.

(3) Under the provisions of the education act, schools of the different language streams could use their respective mother tongues, except in the learning of languages of other races, as the main medium of instruction in teaching, as well as in conducting examinations. They would also be the languages used in school administration. To compel Chinese primary schools to use English to teach mathematics and science was a first step towards changing the character of these schools.

(4) According to a survey, in the three months that the Chinese primary schools had been forced to teach mathematics and science in English, the following shortcomings of the measure had already come to light:

(a) The level of mathematics taught had been drastically lowered.

(b) The government provided only mathematics and science textbooks published in English for loan to students, but not textbooks published in Chinese. Parents had to spend their own money to purchase the latter. The government also provided supplementary learning materials and computer software only in the English language. The teaching of mathematics and science in Chinese had been marginalized.

(c) Students had to learn mathematics and science through both English and Chinese. The same subject matter had to be studied twice. This increased the burden on the students.

(d) The original stipulation of the government was that the teaching of mathematics and science in English was to begin with Primary One in the present year. However, the Ministry of Education had already instructed Primary Six students in Chinese schools to choose sitting for their mathematics and science papers either in English or Chinese in their coming final examination. This implied that, eventually, the ministry would set such papers only in English so that all schools, no matter which language stream they belong, would use only English to teach the two subjects.

(5) It had been discovered that, in some states, teachers who did not possess a Chinese qualification had been sent to teach mathematics and science in English in certain schools.

(6) The Ministry of Education was giving a special allowance of 10 per cent of a teacher's salary to teachers who taught the English language and to teachers who taught mathematics and science in English. This was grossly unfair to teachers of other subjects and created conflict between teachers of the two kinds. This would also quicken the pace towards using only English to teach mathematics and science.

(7) Presently, officials from the Ministry of Education were closely monitoring the teaching, as well as the effect of such teaching, of mathematics and science in English in schools. However, they were not doing the same with the teaching of the two subjects in Chinese. This was marginalizing the latter and showed that the ministry was actively pursuing the final goal of using only English to teach the two subjects

It was not known if the authorities paid any heed to the protests.

A policy which had the aim of attempting to achieve the economic targets of Vision 2020 had the effect of compromising the social goals of the vision. The Chinese were made unhappy by it and ethnicity in Malaysian society was further entrenched.

Preserving the Last Vestiges of "Chinese-ness" in National-Type Secondary Schools

It might be recalled that in the early 1960s, after the Education Act of 1961 was enacted, many Chinese secondary schools were converted into National-Type Secondary Schools which used English and not Chinese as their medium of instruction. And in the 1970s and 1980s, such schools also dropped English as their main medium of instruction and substituted it with Malay.[56]

Although they were converted, the National-Type Secondary Schools retained many vestiges of their previous "Chinese-ness", such as continuing to teach the Chinese language as a subject. In the 1990s, there was the danger that even these vestiges might be eventually eliminated. So Chinese educationists addressed the problem by taking a stand with the government to request that the status quo be maintained.

In August 1997, the members of the boards of governors of fifty-four schools out of a total of seventy-eight from all over the country came together for the purpose. They decided to make representations to the government on the following issues:[57]

(1) Ensure that there would be sufficient time for students to learn the Chinese language and an adequate number of teachers to teach them. Encourage students to learn Chinese and sit for Chinese examinations.

(2) Allow boards of governors to continue and function, and not have them dissolved which might be done as stated in subsection 62(1) of the 1996 Education Act.

(3) Keep the name of the schools as National-Type Secondary Schools. Do not change them to National Secondary Schools (although the main medium of instruction was now Malay just like in the National Secondary Schools).

(4) Ensure that school principals have Chinese qualifications. Ensure the preservation of the campus practice of upholding Chinese culture and communicating in Chinese.

(5) Grants given by the government to National-Type Secondary Schools should be the same as those given to National Secondary Schools. The two kinds of schools should be treated alike.

The government responded positively to at least two of the requests. Eventually, the schools were notified by the deputy director for education that their boards of governors would not be dissolved, and by the deputy minister for education, Dr Fong Chan Onn, that the names of National-Type Secondary Schools need not be changed to National Secondary Schools.[58]

In this particular case, the social objective of Vision 2020 of improving racial ties in society was indeed enhanced.

Independent Chinese Secondary Schools

The period under review saw independent Chinese secondary schools, on the one hand, making progress and, on the other, meeting some reverses which, however, were arrested in the end.

Progress

The independent Chinese secondary schools' working committee of UCSCA and UCSTA worked diligently to improve the standard of the schools.

The first phase of an administrative centre of UCSCA and UCSTA, which would serve as a base to conduct all kinds of educational activities, was put up in Kajang in 1993.[59]

Next, the working committee at once initiated the following programmes to get things going. It started classes to train teachers for the independent secondary schools. It conducted education seminars and sometimes invited foreign experts to share their educational expertise with participants of these gatherings. It organized education work camps. It dispatched missions to Taiwan and China to learn from the education institutions there, and bring back knowledge and expertise. It published education journals. The crowning achievement was the opening of the New Era College in March 1998 which was a significant step towards creating opportunities for tertiary education not only for graduates of the independent Chinese secondary schools, but also for other students in the country.[60]

In the end, independent Chinese secondary schools did so well that the results of its Unified Examinations were recognized by the hundreds of private colleges in the country as well as colleges and universities overseas. The foreign countries which admitted graduates of these schools for higher studies included Singapore, Hong Kong, Taiwan, China, Japan, the United Kingdom, the United States of America, Australia, Canada, New Zealand, France, Germany, and the Philippines.

The performance of independent Chinese secondary schools finally impressed the government. All along, they had to renew their licence to operate with the Ministry of Education on a year-to-year basis. In 1998, however, probably because of their good peformance and in the spirit of Vision 2020, they were given the permission to register just once and for all.[61] And in September 1999, the minister for education, Najib, in a speech at one such school, the Zhong Hua in Kuala Lumpur, openly praised them for their academic efforts.[62]

With information technology, Chinese educationists discussed to find out what they should do to safeguard the future of the schools. In 1996, they convened a seminar for the purpose. The next year, the independent Chinese secondary schools' working committee set up an "Educational Reform Group". In 1999, another gathering to discuss matters was convened. Then in 2003, the "Educational Reform Group" produced an "Independent Chinese Secondary Schools' Reform Plan" (draft), which was finalized two years later and circulated to all independent Chinese secondary schools. The years that followed witnessed attempts to put the plan into effect.[63]

Reverses

Although great efforts were made through the years to improve the standard of the independent Chinese secondary schools, the enrolment in such schools kept on declining. The following figures showed the trend:[64]

Table 6.3
Enrolment in Independent Chinese Secondary Schools, 1993–98

Year	Enrolment in All Independent Chinese Secondary Schools
1993	59,383
1994	59,773
1995	58,948
1996	57,092
1997	55,143
1998	54,170

Source: See note 64.

From the very beginning, Chinese educationists were aware of this problem. Many meetings were held to discuss the matter. Finally, in 1995, the chairman of the Perak Council of Chinese School Committees, Foo Wan Thot, suggested changing the textbooks used to teach mathematics and science from Chinese to English. Examinations in the two subjects could be held in both Chinese and English. This, he thought, would attract more graduates of Chinese primary schools to join independent Chinese secondary schools and thus boost the student population of the latter. However, he was opposed by UCSCA, UCSTA, and some members of his own council. They felt that the proposal, if effected, would change the independent Chinese secondary schools into English-medium schools. Foo's announcement also caused ten of his school committee members, together with the school principal and vice-principal, and fifteen teachers, to resign.[65]

What turned the situation around in the end was an improvement in the quality of teachers in the independent Chinese secondary schools. Since 1998 the schools' working committees, together with the New Era College, stepped up programmes to train teachers for such schools. With better quality teachers came more students. The figures in Table 6.4 show the improvement:[66]

Table 6.4
Enrolment in Independent Chinese Secondary Schools, 2000–02

Year	Enrolment in All Independent Chinese Secondary Schools
2000	53,258
2001	53,635
2002	54,048

Source: See note 66.

The decline was arrested. In 2003, however, the figure dropped to 52,850. This was seen as only a temporary aberration and it was expected that the upward climb would continue in subsequent years.

Chinese Colleges

In consonance with the aims of Vision 2020 during the period under review, the government liberalized tertiary education in the country so as to create more opportunities for young people to pursue higher studies and for the nation to increase its pool of trained manpower. Many private tertiary institutions were allowed to start operation. In the congenial atmosphere, Chinese educationists availed themselves to the chance to expand existing institutions or to inaugurate fresh ones.

The Government Opened the Door Wider

In 1996, the government enacted four acts to open the doors of higher education wider. These acts were the Private Higher Education Institution Act, the Universities and University Colleges Amendment Act, the National Higher Education Council Act, and the National Accreditation Board (Lan) Act. The first measure was to give room to private sources to start up higher educational institutions in the country. The second was to pave the way for government tertiary institutions to be privatized so that their standards could be raised. The third was to enable the Ministry of Education to plan and make policies as well as to coordinate higher education. And the fourth was to ensure that the standards of all colleges and universities in the country were up to specifications.[67]

Close on the heels of the passing of these four pieces of legislation, private tertiary institutions mushroomed in the country. In 1995, there were only 280 private colleges, but in the following year the number increased to 576, a more than 100 per cent leap. In the latter year, there were 215,850 students and 7,330 lecturers in these colleges. And many colleges registered previously began degree courses by twinning programmes with foreign partners. Besides, between 1996 and 1999, private sources established nine universities. In spite of all this, however, there was still room for more institutions to be launched. Up to August 1999, the Ministry of Education received 193 applications to start up colleges or universities.[68]

It was in this kind of atmosphere that the Southern College obtained the opportunity to expand, and the New Era College and the Han Jiang International College of the Chinese to start.

The Southern College

It was seen in the last chapter that the Southern College was established in the late 1980s. The college registered progress as the years went by.

At the beginning, the college only had a Business Department and a Malay Department. Later on, it expanded by starting an English as well as a Computer Science Department. What is more significant to our present discussion is that in 1996, the government, in line with the goals of Vision 2020, granted it permission to establish a Chinese Department. The development certainly contributed to an improvement in the relations among the different races in the country.[69]

The college also registered progress by establishing relationships with sixty-nine universities in such countries as the United Kingdom, the United States of America, Australia, New Zealand, Indonesia, Taiwan, and China whereby academic credits acquired by students in the college would be recognized by these institutions, and its students could transfer to study in such universities for one or two years and then obtain their degrees.[70]

The college had plans to upgrade eventually to become a university. In 1999, it had an enrolment of more than a thousand students.[71]

The New Era College

In 1993, UCSCA and UCSTA, together with the Merdeka University Limited Company, decided to establish a college which was to be housed in the building in Kajang. The building had just been constructed by the independent Chinese secondary schools' working committee under the leadership of the Dong Jiao Zong. It was to be called the New Era College.[72]

In 1994, an application was submitted to the government to obtain permission to start the college. Three years later, the government granted it approval to begin teaching. In 1998, the college began functioning with the first batch of students.[73]

The college had four departments, *viz* a Chinese Language and Literature Department, a Business Department, an Information Technology Department, and a Social Studies Department.[74]

The college established relationships of cooperation with thirty foreign universities, of which twenty-three were in China, three in Taiwan, two in Australia, and one each in the United States of America and New Zealand. Those from Australia and New Zealand would recognize academic credits acquired by students in the college and allow them to transfer over to continue with degree studies. The college had the eventual plan of enabling its students to complete all courses of studies in the college itself and still obtain degrees from the cooperating foreign universities.[75]

Like the Southern College, the New Era College embraced the ambition of eventually becoming a university. In 2000, a Vintage Height Sdn. Bhd., belonging to the Hong Leong Group of companies, donated 100 acres of land in Pantai Sepang for the college to develop into a higher institution of learning. In 1999, it had only 264 students. A year later, the number of students increased to 540 and by 2003, to 1,400.[76]

The Han Jiang International College

In 1998, the Board of Governors of the Han Jiang High School in Penang applied to the government for approval to establish a college on the island. The next year, approval was granted. The deputy minister for education, Dr Foong Chan Onn, personally handed the document of approval to the board.[77]

The college started teaching with four departments. They were a Business Department, a Mass Communication Department, an Information Technology Department, and a Science and Technology Department. Later on, in cooperation with the Nanking University in China, it initiated a master degree course in Chinese studies.[78]

The Han Jiang International College also had plan to become a university eventually.

The main factor which influenced the development of events during the period under review in this chapter was Vision 2020. This brought both joy and disappointment to the Chinese community. The Smart Schools, which were transformed from existing schools, found favour with them, but not the Vision Schools. Then the 1996 Education Act was received by the Chinese community with deep misgivings. Their Hua Tuan Suqiu, including the Mu Yu Jiao Yu Xuan Yan in 1999, got nowhere. And their National-Type Chinese Primary Schools continued to be beset with problems, with the policy of having mathematics and science taught in English (besides Chinese) in these schools upsetting them. They found some consolation in the fact that the National-Type Secondary Schools were allowed to retain some vestiges of Chinese culture, and their independent Chinese secondary schools registered progress. But their greatest joy was that they were given the chance to expand existing or start new colleges, so that their children would have greater opportunities to pursue higher studies. This was an eventful period.

Notes

[1] Mok Soon Sang, *Ma Lai Xi Ya Jiao Yu Shi, 1400–1999* (Kuala Lumpur, 2000) (hereafter Mok Soon Sang, op. cit. 1), pp. 204–05; R.S. Milne and Diane K. Mauzy, *Malaysian Politics under Mahathir* (New York, 1999), p. 165.

[2] Mok Soon Sang, op. cit. 1, pp. 204–06; Dr Mahathir Mohamad, *Malaysia Melangkah Ke Hadapan* (Kuala Lumpur, 1991), pp. 2–4.

[3] Mok Soon Sang, op. cit. 1, pp. 231–35.

[4] Ibid., p. 234.

[5] Ibid., p. 236.

[6] Ibid., p. 235.

[7] UCSTA, *Tiao Zan Yu Hui Ying* (Kuala Lumpur, 2001), pp. 161–62.

[8] Ibid.

[9] Mok Soon Sang, op. cit. 1, pp. 228–29; UCSCA, *Dong Zong 50 Nian* (Kajang, 2004) (hereafter UCSCA, op. cit. 1), pp. 1119–20.

[10] Ibid.

[11] Ibid.

[12] Ibid.

[13] UCSCA, op. cit. 1, pp. 544 and 1118–22.

[14] Cheah Boon Kheng, *Malaysia: The Making of a Nation* (Singapore, 2004), pp. 226–28; Khoo Boo Teik, *Beyond Mahathir* (New York, 2003), pp. 8–9.

[15] UCSCA, *Jian Jue Fan Dui "Hong Yuan Xiao Xue Ji Hua"* (Kajang, 2000), pp. 4–6 and 9–10; UCSCA, op. cit. 1, pp. 309–10 and 546; *Nanyang Siang Pau*, 13 August 2000, 16 October 2000, 4 November 2000 and 8 November 2000,

[16] UCSTA, *2002 Nian Gong Zuo Bao Gao Shu* (Kajang, 2002), pp. 53–54 and 97–98.

[17] UCSCA, op. cit. 1, p. 553.

[18] UCSCA, *Feng Yun Ji Dang Yi Bai Ba Shi Nian* (Kajang, 2001) (hereafter UCSCA, op. cit. 2), pp. 259–60.

[19] Ibid., pp. 261 and 265.

[20] Ibid., p. 267.

[21] UCSCA, op. cit. 1, pp. 1018–19.

[22] Ibid., pp. 266 and 555–57; *Nanyang Siang Pau*, 15 January 2007: Zhu Ke Li, op. cit.

[23] *Oriental News*, 30 August 2007.

[24] *New Straits Times*, 14 November 1989, as cited in Harold Crouch, *Government and Society in Malaysia* (Singapore, 1996), pp. 124–25.

[25] UCSCA, op. cit. 2, p. 273; *Nanyang Siang Pau*, 21 December 1995.

[26] UCSCA, op. cit. 1, pp. 1054–58.

[27] Mok Soon Sang, op. cit. 1, p. 221.

[28] UCSCA, op. cit. 2, pp. 280–81.

29   Yang Pei Gen, *1996 Jiao Yu Fa Ling Hui Da Lu* (Kajang, 1998), pp. 20–35; UCSCA, op. cit. 1, p. 1067; Malaysia, *Education Bill* [1995] (Kuala Lumpur, 1995), pp. 12, 23 and 24.

30   UCSCA, op. cit. 1, p. 553.

31   *Oriental News*, 27 October 2007: article by Zhang Shu Jun; UCSCA, op. cit. 1, p. 1070.

32   Malaysia, *Education Bill* [1995] (Kuala Lumpur, 1995), pp. 24 and 41–44.

33   UCSCA, op. cit. 2, pp. 280–81.

34   Cheah Boon Kheng, op. cit., pp. 226–28; R.S. Milne and Diane K. Mauzy, op. cit., p. 156; Khoo Boon Teik, *Beyond Mahathir* (London, 2003), pp. 8–10.

35   Khoo Boon Teik, op. cit., pp. 9 and 11–12.

36   UCSCA, *1999 Nian Dong Jiao Zong Mu Yu Jiao Yu Xuan Yan* (1st draft) (Kajang, 1999), pp. 2–5; *Oriental News*, 26 December 2007; UCSCA, op. cit. 2, p. 289; UCSCA, op. cit. 1, pp. 303–04 and 1097–98.

37   *Oriental News*, 26 December 2007; UCSCA, op. cit. 1, pp. 401–06.

38   UCSCA, *1999 Nian Dong Jiao Zong Mu Yu Jiao Yu Xuan Yan* (final draft) (Kajang, 1999), pp. 6–24. (The final draft has 12 items.)

39   Mok Soon Sang, op. cit. 1, p. 278.

40   "*Ma Lai Xi Ya Jiao Yu Bu Ge Nian Tong Ji Bao Gao*" as cited in UCSCA, *Ma Lai Xi Ya Hua Wen Jiao Yu*, No. 2 (Kajang, 2004), p. 68.

41   Ibid.

42   Ibid., p. 70.

43   "*Ma Lai Xi Ya Jiao Yu Bu Ge Nian Tong Ji Bao Gao*" as cited in UCSCA, *Ma Lai Xi Ya Hua Wen Jiao Yu*, No. 2 (Kajang, 2004), p. 71; *China Press*, 6 November 1996.

44   UCSCA, *1999 Nian Dong Jiao Zong Mu Yu Jiao Yu Xuan Yan* (final draft) (Kajang, 1999), pp. 11–12 and 17–19.

45   Ibid., pp. 19–27.

46   Ibid., pp. 23–26.

47   UCSCA, op. cit. 1, pp. 313–14 and 1137–40.

48   Bai Xiao Bao Liu Yuan Xiao, Zeng Qu Fen Xiao Wei Yuan Hui, *Ba Gen Liu Zhu 500 Tian* (Kuala Lumpur, 2002), p. 73.

49   Ibid., p. 74.

50   Ibid., pp. 79–80.

51   UCSCA, *Huan Wo Bai Xiao* (Kajang, 2001), p. 8.

52   UCSCA, op. cit. 1, p. 1140.

53   Molly Lee N.N., *Educational Reforms* in Bridget Welsh, et al., *Reflections: The Mahathir Years* (Washington, 2004), p. 442; Liao Wen Hui, *Hua Xiao Jiao Zong Ji Qi Ren Wu* (Kajang, 2006), pp. 88–89.

54   Liao Wen Hui, op. cit., p. 89; Mok Soon Sang, *Nota Ulangkaji & Latihan PTK Bahagian II, Kompetensi Khusus (P&P)* (Puchong, 2008), p. 309.

55 *Sin Chew Daily*, 23 July 2002 and 12 November 2002; UCSCA, op. cit. 1,
    pp. 610–21, 1149 and 1153; UCSCA and UCSTA, *Zui Hou Fang Xian*
    (Kajang, 2003), p. 19.

56 See Chapters 3 and 4.

57 UCSCA, op. cit. 1, p. 1078.

58 Hua Zhong Xiao Zhang Li Shi Hui, *Ma Lai Xi Ya Guo Min Xing Hua Wen
    Zhong Xue Zhi Nan* (Kuala Lumpur, 2006), pp. 70–71.

59 UCSCA, *Hua Guang Yong Yao* (Kuala Lumpur, 1993), pp. 1–2 and 44–45;
    UCSCA, op. cit. 1, pp. 276–77.

60 *Sin Chew Daily*, 3 October 1997; *China Press*, 2 March 1998; UCSCA, op. cit. 2,
    pp. 285–87.

61 Mok Soon Sang, op. cit. 1, pp. 259–62; *China Press*, 17 November 1998.

62 Mok Soon Sang, op. cit. 1, p. 260; various Chinese newspapers of 5 September
    1999; UCSCA, op. cit. 1, p. 299.

63 UCSCA, *Jiao Yu Gai Ge Gang Ling* (Kajang, 2005), pp. 42–46.

64 Figures from Dong Jiao Zong Jiao Yu Zhong Xin as cited in Mok Soon Sang,
    op. cit. 1, p. 260.

65 Shen Zhai Independent High School in Ipoh and Chong Hua Independent
    High School in Kuala Kangsar, Perak, announced formally that, in 2000, English
    textbooks instead of Chinese books would be used to teach mathematics and
    science in Senior Middle classes. See Mok Soon Sang, op. cit. 1, p. 261; UCSCA,
    op. cit. 1, p. 286.

66 Figures were provided by the Education Department of the New Era College
    in 2007; *Oriental News*, 15 August 2007.

67 Mok Soon Sang, *Nota Ulangkaji dan Latihan PTK, Bahagian 1, Kompetensi
    Umum (Teras dan Profesional)* (Kuala Lumpur, 2007), pp. 181–82.

68 Mok Soon Sang, op. cit. 1, p. 264.

69 Ibid., p. 265.

70 Ibid.

71 Ibid.

72 UCSCA, op. cit. 2, p. 285; Liao Wen Hui, op. cit., pp. 118–19.

73 UCSCA, op. cit. 2, pp. 285–87; *Sin Chew Daily*, 3 October 1997; *China Press*,
    2 March 1998; UCSCA, op. cit. 1, p. 297.

74 Kua Kia Soong, *New Era Education* (Kajang, 2005), p. 6.

75 New Era College, *1998 Nian Gong Zuo Bao Gao* (Kajang, 1999), p. 19.

76 UCSCA and UCSTA, *Jian She Yu Fa Zan* (Kajang, 2000), p. 20; Kua Kia Soong,
    op. cit., pp. 8–9 and 11.

77 UCSCA, op. cit., 1, p. 302; UCSCA, op. cit., 2, p. 287.

78 Mok Soon Sang, op. cit. 1, p. 268.

7

CONCLUSION
Challenges and Responses

From the first day, when the first old-style school was founded in Penang in 1819, until 2007, Chinese schools in Malaysia have undergone a development of more than 180 years. According to statistics, in 2007, there were 1,289 Chinese primary schools with 643,679 pupils in the country;[1] in 2005, there were 78 National-Type Secondary Schools with 128,459 students;[2] and in 2007, there were 60 independent Chinese secondary schools with 55,818 students.[3] In the tertiary field of education, in 2007, there were the Southern College in Johor, the New Era College in Selangor, and the Han Jiang International College in Penang. Such results were achieved only after serious challenges were met and great sacrifices made in the course of struggle.

In this conclusion, we propose first to review briefly the salient points of what happened to these schools from 1786 to 2003, as accounted for in the last six chapters in this book, then to discuss briefly what took place from 2004 to early 2009, and finally to anticipate what these schools could expect in the near future.

1786–2003: UNITARIANISM OR PLURALISM

The British ruled Peninsular Malaysia from 1786 to 1957. After 1957, political power was transferred from the British to the local races, namely the Malays, Chinese, and Indians, with the Malays as the leading element, who then formed the government of the country. When the British were around, they gave full support to schools which used English as the main medium of instruction and some support to schools which used Malay as the main medium of instruction. They were less than forthcoming in giving assistance to schools which used Chinese or Tamil as the main medium of instruction. They could be said, by and large, to practise unitarianism. The Chinese and Tamil schools had hoped that they could be treated equally as the English and Malay schools, but they were to be disappointed. These schools believed in pluralism.

For the years before the Pacific War, the important things to note were the Schools Registration Ordinance/Enactment and their subsequent amendments. After 1919, Chinese schools were to indulge in a great deal of nationalistic political activities which disturbed the peace and economic life of the land. These laws were designed to curb such activities. The years after the war till the 1950s saw the British convening a number of committees, one after another, to review the education system in the country with a view to introducing reforms. The thrust of these committees was to effect unitarianism. The Chinese schools protested against the attempt, upholding pluralism. Out of the furore UCSTA and UCSCA were born and became the bulwarks of Chinese education.

After the Malays gained political power, they chose to follow unitarianism. However, in their case, naturally and as expected, instead of seeking to promote English, they sought to promote Malay. Not only did they give full support to schools which used Malay as the main medium of instruction and less assistance to schools which used other languages, they also looked for opportunities to convert these other schools to Malay. The Chinese-medium schools defended themselves and so they could continue to exist until today.

1956, the year after the British gave Peninsular Malaysia self-government, but a year before independence was granted, saw the appearance of the Razak Report which enunciated that the "ultimate objective" of a Malay-led government in the education field was to use Malay as the main medium of instruction in all schools. It was because of protests from UCSTA, UCSCA and the MCA that this objective was not written into the Education Ordinance, which was adopted the following year.

However, in 1960 came the Talib Report and the next year, a new Education Act. Two points are notable about the new act. One is that, by it, Chinese secondary schools which used Chinese as their main medium of instruction, if they wished to receive assistance from the government, had to convert to using English as their main medium of instruction and would henceforth be known as Chinese National-Type Secondary Schools. Those which did not mind not receiving assistance could remain as independent secondary schools. Replacing Chinese with English as the main medium of instruction was only a preparatory step towards realizing the "ultimate objective" in these schools. Later, English would be replaced by Malay as was what happened in the 1970s. A second important point about the 1961 Education Act was that it contained a subsection 21(2) which empowered the minister for education to convert any National-Type Primary School into National Primary School whenever he deemed fit. A National-Type Primary School, the reader will remember, did not use Malay as the main medium of instruction, but a National Primary School did. This subsection 21(2) also looked to further the cause of the "ultimate objective".

Lim Lian Geok, president of UCSTA, opposed the Talib Report and the conversion of Chinese-medium secondary schools to English. For this, he was first to lose his Malayan citizenship and then his registration as a teacher. Following this, the adviser of Lim's UCSTA, Dr Yan Yuan Zhang, was expelled from the country and was never allowed to return.

The action taken by the government against Lim and Yan did not, however, douse the enthusiasm of Chinese educationists for the cause of the Chinese language and Chinese education. In 1964, Sim Mow Yu, a new man to lead UCSTA, revived a campaign to get Chinese recognized as an official language of the country, which would work to the benefit of it being used as the main medium of instruction in Chinese schools. Two years later, Sim was able to draw up a memorandum on the issue with representatives from various registered Chinese organizations, endorsed by their signatures or seals, to be presented to the government.

Graduates of independent Chinese secondary schools had been going abroad or to the Nanyang University in Singapore to further their studies. In 1968, the minister for education announced that, unless such students possessed the Malayan Certificate of Education or the Overseas School Certificate conferred by Cambridge University, they would not be allowed to continue to do so after that year. Few students possessed such certificates as the examinations for them were conducted in Malay or English. The move was to deprive these students of opportunities for higher education and thus discontinued the independent Chinese secondary schools. The move catapulted the vice-president of UCSTA, Loot Ting Yee, into making a proposal to UCSTA and the Chinese community to establish a Chinese university, to be called the Merdeka University, in the country itself, to find a way out for the graduates of independent Chinese secondary schools. A Merdeka University Limited Company was formed for the purpose and it applied to the government for registration. In 1969, there was a general election in the country. In order to win Chinese votes, the government approved the application of the company. However, the election eventuated in a bloody showdown between the Malays and the Chinese after which the proposed university was prohibited from trying to raise funds for its establishment, and the attempt to start it was suspended.

The 1970s continued to be challenging times for Chinese schools. The first event to note was that in 1971, Sim Mow Yu was brought to court by the authorities under the 1969 Sedition Act. This happened because Sim fought too hard for Chinese education. Fortunately for him, the charge against him was dropped in the end.

In 1971, the government passed a Universities and University Colleges Act which required that any effort to establish a tertiary institution in the country must first have the approval of the *Yang di-Pertuan Agong*. This worked to the disadvantage of the Chinese attempt to found the Merdeka University. 1971 also saw the appearance of the Majid Report which proposed that admission of students to public universities should reflect the racial composition in the country rather than be based on academic merit. This proposal was made with the view to enable more Malay students as opposed to students of other races to join the universities. So the quota system for student admission was created.

In the following year came the Aziz Report. It recommended that school boards of fully-assisted schools, which had the power to hire and dismiss teachers and other school staff, be wound up. On the basis of this recommendation, the 1961 Education Act was amended to include a Clause 26A to provide for such dissolution. The report also recommended that parent-teacher associations for the schools be formed to look after the welfare of students and teachers. A Clause 116A in the amended act gave effect to this. The changes struck at a core element in the Chinese school system — the school boards. The Chinese protested strongly, but to no avail.

From the 1960s to the early 1970s, the number of students in independent Chinese secondary schools declined, leading to a reduction in the number of such schools. This happened because in 1964 the government allowed, which it did not do before, graduates from Chinese primary schools to be automatically promoted to the National-Type Secondary Schools. This drew most of the graduates of Chinese primary schools into such schools, thus reducing the intake of students into independent Chinese secondary schools. The decline of independent Chinese secondary schools also came about because such schools were usually deficient in finance, which led to problems of all kinds, resulting in parents shying away from sending their children to them. The phenomenon caused alarm among Chinese educationists. In 1973, led by Foo Wan Thot, they initiated a movement to revive these schools. The goal was to raise a million ringgit to finance the system which was eventually reached. A Hua Wen Du Li Zhong Xue Jian Yi Shu [Proposals for Independent Chinese Secondary Schools] was adopted to guide the effort. After a while, the schools were able to attract the interest of parents again and they revived. In the late 1970s, both the number of students and the number of schools kept rising. In 1975, the schools were able to conduct their own examinations for students, the Unified Examinations, the certificates of which later came to be recognized even by some foreign universities for student admission. This development was inspiring to Chinese educationists. It is noticeable that at about the time when independent Chinese secondary schools were reviving, a very important organization in Chinese education was founded. This was the Dong Jiao Zong which was a liaison committee between UCSCA and UCSTA, made up of representatives from the two bodies.

The period from the 1970s to 1982 also saw the government taking very bold steps to bring about the realization of the "ultimate objective". Beginning from 1970 until 1975, English-medium National-Type Primary Schools were required to give up using English as their main medium of instruction in favour of Malay. By 1975, they all became Malay-medium National Primary Schools. In the case of the English-medium National-Type Secondary Schools, a similar first step was taken in 1976 and the conversion process was completed by 1982. It is also to be noted that along with the conversion of English-medium institutions, the original Chinese secondary schools which substituted using Chinese as their main medium of instruction with English in accordance with the 1961 Education Act, had now to convert further by replacing English as their main medium of instruction with Malay.

Like the 1970s, the 1980s were also not a bed of roses for Chinese education. Towards the end of the 1970s, the Merdeka University Limited Company had submitted a petition to the *Yang di-Pertuan Agong* for approval to establish the university. However, it received a negative response. In 1980 the company took the case up to the High Court in Kuala Lumpur. But when the High Court ruled in favour of the government, it made an appeal for its case to the Federal Court. To its dismay, the Federal Court rejected its appeal too. Nevertheless, the company refused to give up its effort to try to find a way out for graduates of the independent Chinese secondary schools to pursue a tertiary education. It set up a Higher Studies Counselling Centre for the purpose.

The 1980s also witnessed the government doing a number of things that affected Chinese schools which made clear its intention of further realizing the "ultimate objective". In 1981, the minister for education announced that beginning from 1982, there would be a move to put into effect a 3-M curriculum in all schools. Under this scheme, the materials for all subjects used to teach students, except that for the Chinese language, would be compiled in Malay. Although after much protest from the Chinese community, the government finally decided that such materials could continue to be compiled in Chinese, the fears of the Chinese community were not allayed.

In 1982, the *Yang di-Pertuan Agong*, in an address to parliament, made a declaration that Malaysia would have as its core only one race, one language, and one culture, that is, the Malay race, the Malay language, and the Malay-Muslim culture. A little later, this policy was echoed by the prime minister at a national cultural conference of the Malays.

In 1984, the Education Department in the Kuala Lumpur Federal Territory notified Chinese National-Type Primary Schools in the district to substitute using Chinese with using Malay in all their assemblies and extra-curricular activities. The instruction evoked strong protests from the Chinese community, led by their various organizations. In the face of this, the authorities eventually rescinded the order, but the fears of the Chinese had already been aroused.

To solve the problem of racial polarization in the country, one proposal was to get students from the various races to socialize while they were still young. This was to be achieved by housing the primary schools of the different races in one common school building. The scheme would be called the Integrated School Plan. Eighteen schools would initially be chosen to pilot the scheme. The first such integrated school was started in 1986 in Teluk Sengat in Johor.

The scheme aroused the fear of Chinese educationists and the Chinese community. It was felt that the Malay component would in the end come to dominate the other two components which would then lose their character. They aired their misgivings to the educational authorities who got the scheme revised and the two sides were eventually able to reach a compromise. Meanwhile, the scheme had been renamed the School Pupils Integration Plan. Nevertheless, the incident had put the Chinese on their guard.

In 1987, it was discovered that the educational authorities had deployed a great number of teachers who did not possess qualifications in Chinese to be first senior assistants, second senior assistants, supervisors of afternoon school sessions, or supervisors of extra-curricular activities, in Chinese primary schools. This posed a threat to the "Chinese-ness" of these schools. The whole Chinese community in the country was roused to protest. The Malay community, on their part, from government ministers down, insisted on the policy and matched the anger of the Chinese with their own anger and there was the fear that racial riots would break out. To pre-empt a bloodbath, the government had leaders from both communities arrested and detained. Finally, it was decided that people without qualifications in Chinese could not be first senior assistants, second senior assistants, or supervisors of afternoon school sessions. They could only be supervisors of extra-curricular activities. The decision solved the disagreement between the two sides, but Chinese educationists were still not really happy with the solution.

UCSCA and UCSTA were the keenest in the Chinese community to feel the pressure from the Malays. Consequently, in the earlier 1980s, they devised a "3-in-1" strategy to try to defend Chinese educational interests. This strategy, however, did not produce the results hoped for. It was, therefore, replaced by a "two-line strategy" in the later 1980s. The second strategy proved to be so successful that it caused the government to shelve an education bill in 1990 which it had intended to adopt as a new education law.

Vision 2020 dominated the 1990s up to 2003. While the economic goals of the vision brought some benefit to Chinese education, its social goals of improving relations between the Malays, on the one hand, and the Chinese and Indians, on the other, could not be fully realized. This happened because of the persistent desire on the part of the former to keep furthering the realization of the "ultimate objective".

The benefit which the vision conferred on the Chinese schools was that it enabled them, along with Malay schools, to become Smart Schools. It also afforded the opportunity to the Chinese to expand their Southern College, and establish the New Era College and the Han Jiang International College.

The negative aspect of the vision for Chinese education was the proposal to establish Vision Schools, which was a reincarnation of the Integrated School Plan of the 1980s. The Chinese protested strongly against the proposal, but to no avail. Eventually the first of such a school was established in a locality called USJ District. A little later, the prime minister also pronounced that he would like to see parents sending their children to study in Vision Schools or National Schools.

1995 saw the appearance of a new Education Bill which became an Education Act the following year. The government hoped that the new legislation would help to bring about not only the realization of the economic, but also the social goals of Vision 2020. However, Chinese educationists viewed things from a different perspective. To them, what had plagued the Chinese schools in the past continued to do so, in fact, more severely, in spite of the innovation.

It was true that the new law did not mention the "ultimate objective". But it had a section 17 which made provision for Malay to be used as the main medium of instruction in educational institutions. Chinese and Tamil primary schools were not exempted from coverage by this section. Similarly, independent Chinese secondary schools were also not exempted. In 2002, in an interview with Chinese newspapers, the prime minister acknowledged that the new law still preserved the "ultimate objective" and he also said that the objective would never be abandoned.

Another point about the 1972 Education Amendment Act was that its section 26(A) had empowered the educational authorities to dissolve school boards or constitute new ones when necessary. Although such a section no longer appeared in the 1995 bill, yet sections 58, 61, 62, and 125 of the new bill enabled them to do exactly the same thing. School boards were the brains of the Chinese schools.

A third point was that independent Chinese secondary schools had been conducting their own Unified Examinations in Chinese for their students and had not, as a general rule, prepared them to sit for government examinations conducted in Malay. Now the new education law contained provisions which might be interpreted as not permitting this state of affairs to continue. Sections 19, 69, and 74 were the provisions. Independent Chinese secondary schools could be compelled to become Malay-medium schools.

In 1999, there was a general election which principally involved a contest between the prime minister, Mahathir, and his erstwhile deputy, Anwar Ibrahim. Chinese organizations took the opportunity of the cleavage to present a list of demands to the government to advance Chinese interests. Included in the list were items pertaining to Chinese education. The list was called Hua Tuan Suqiu [Appeals of the Chinese Organizations] and its educational section was called Mu Yu Jiao Yu Xuan Yan [Manifesto on Mother Tongue Education]. On receipt of the requests, the prime minister undertook to give them consideration. After the election which he won, however, he got them shelved.

In 2001, the government allowed the SJK (C) Damansara, that is, the Sekolah Jenis Kebangsaan (Cina) Damansara in Malay, or National-Type School (Chinese) Damansara in English, to move to a new site altogether, but not to build a branch school to augment the existing old school. And it closed down the existing old school. The incident led to a confrontation between the government and the parents of some of the students. It was observed that the SJK (C) Damansara was not permitted to build a branch school because the government's attitude was not to build new schools for the Chinese easily. It pursued an ultimate policy of having only one kind of schools in the country, that is, Malay-medium schools.

In pursuit of the economic goals of Vision 2020, the government in 2003 introduced the policy of having the subjects of mathematics and science taught in English. Although this was not the "ultimate objective" of having school subjects taught mainly in English, it aroused the fear of Chinese educationists who surmised that the move could end up converting Chinese-medium schools to English.

2004-EARLY 2009: UNITARIANISM OR PLURALISM CONTINUED

In 2003 Mahathir resigned as prime minister, and was succeeded by Abdullah Badawi. Badawi continued with the practice of unitarianism in educational matters.

The Issue of Teaching Mathematics and Science in English in Chinese Primary Schools

The formula worked out for teaching mathematics and science in Chinese primary schools could work only from Primary One to Three. It could not work for Primary Four to Six. This was because these higher classes were already loaded with school subjects. The problem vexed Chinese educationists, but the government was intent on having the two subjects taught in English all the way. Eventually, in 2006, the government came up with a solution. It was decided then to have six periods and two periods a week for mathematics to be taught in Chinese and English respectively, and three periods and two periods for science to be taught in Chinese and English respectively.[4]

Before the government had devised a solution, Chinese educationists were so worked up that in 2005 they organized a mammoth meeting to demonstrate against having the two subjects taught in English. The meeting was attended by 3,000 participants of various races, coming from more than 600 organizations. The meeting called on the government to abandon its policy and permit the schools to revert to teaching the two subjects only in the mother tongue.[5]

Related to the question of which language to use in teaching mathematics and science was the question of what language to use to set examinations in the two subjects for Primary Six. Since 2003, it had been the practice to set such examinations in both English and the mother tongue. But the practice was not the ultimate solution.[6] Then, in 2007, Badawi announced that for the following year the Chinese primary schools could continue with the standing practice, and, also, pupils could choose to answer questions in the examination papers in either English or Chinese.[7]

The president of UCSCA, Dr Yap Sin Tian, did not consider Badawi's announcement satisfactory. What Chinese educationists and educationists of other racial groups wanted was to have the two subjects taught in the mother tongue and examinations for them also to be conducted in the mother tongue only. Besides, the government scheme of loaning only textbooks for the two subjects written in English to students harboured the aim of forcing parents to have their children study the two subjects in English. Dr Yap revealed that UCSCA and nine other organizations from different racial groups had supporters of their appeals against the policy sign cards to request that the two subjects be taught again only in the mother tongue, and that he had already received more than 70,000 such cards. And he would in the near future convened a meeting of a coordinating committee made up of representatives from the various races to prepare a memorandum on the issue to present to the prime minister.[8]

The Issue of SJK (C) Damansara, and the Issues of Building More and Moving Chinese Schools

It was seen in the last chapter as well as earlier on in this chapter that the government refused to allow the SJK (C) Damansara, a National-Type Chinese Primary School, to build a branch school, but allowed it to move to a new site. And after the school had moved, the government closed down its original campus. This policy was followed because the government would permit schools to exchange only an original school campus for a new campus, but not have an additional campus. In 2007, UCSCA, UCSTA, and a number of other Chinese organizations called on the government to allow the original campus of the SJK (C) Damansara to reopen and be used again. They hoped that the government would be sympathetic.[9]

In connection with the SJK (C) Damansara issue, it is timely to a look at the whole question of the Chinese being permitted or not to build new schools as well as the issue of existing schools being allowed or disallowed to move to new sites during the years here under review, that is, from 2004 to early 2009.

According to the findings of UCSTA, between 1970 and 2007, the number of Chinese primary students increased by 203,998 on the one hand. However, the number of Chinese primary schools to accommodate them decreased from 1,346 to 1,289 on the other, with 57 schools closed down.[10] Student increase was particularly acute in urban centres. Schools in such places were over crammed with them. Again, according to a conservative estimate by UCSTA, in recent times, the Klang Valley and Johor Bahru were short of 121 Chinese primary schools.[11] And according to the president of UCSCA, Dr Yap Sin Tian, in 2000, the population in Petaling Jaya numbered 429,548 (no specification if the figure was for Chinese only or for all races) and they needed 57 Chinese primary schools for their children. However, by the end of 2007, there were only 18 schools in the place, a shortage of 39 schools.[12]

In 2008, again according to what UCSTA had discovered, the number of very small schools in the whole country, which had only thirty or fewer students, numbered 106. Such schools were located in sparsely populated areas and they needed to move to places where there were more residents. Such schools had applied to the government for approval to relocate, but so far only fifteen were successful. The applications of the rest were rejected, or were still under consideration. The Ministry of Education had laid down seven conditions for approval and those which were rejected could have failed to fulfil any one of such conditions. The seven conditions were:[13]

(1) The schools which desired to relocate must have obtained the written agreement of the parents of the students to do so and such agreement must be filed with the Ministry of Education.

(2) The boards of management and the parent-teacher associations of such schools were themselves to be responsible for finding the required land for the purpose, as well as responsible for erecting the new buildings.

(3) The proposed land must be at a place where the need for the new school was highly needed.

(4) The proposed land must not be land reserved for a government school.

(5) Data about the proposed land must be submitted to the Ministry of Education and approval obtained from the ministry for it to be used.

(6) The plan to build the new school must also be submitted to the Ministry of Education and be approved by it.

(7) After the school had moved, its original premises must be closed.

UCSCA and UCSTA expressed the view that the fact that such conditions were laid down by the Ministry of Education showed that the ministry did not really regard Chinese primary schools as part of the country's education system although they were classified as Chinese National-Type Primary Schools.[14] The restrictions imposed on the relocation of Chinese primary schools were a manifestation of the government's education policy of pursuing unitarianism and the fulfillment of the "ultimate objective" of making Malay the main medium of instruction in schools.[15]

Issues Relating to Teachers

From 1957, the year the country achieved independence, to 2007, there had been a shortage of qualified teachers in the Chinese primary schools each year. To fill the gap, temporary teachers were used. In recent times, 2,000 to 3,000 temporary teachers were hired every year. One reason there were not enough qualified teachers was, according to UCSTA, due to the following.[16]

Early in 2006, there were 264 degree students who were studying mainly in the Chinese sections in teacher training colleges. Then, one day, 171 of them were transferred to other sections which did not specialize in Chinese studies. Only 93 were left behind.

And in the case of the employment of temporary teachers, there were also problems. Again, according to the UCSTA, the following situations were seen in the early years of 2006:[17]

(1) The Ministry of Education limited the number of temporary teachers it would pay to employ. The shortfall would have to be made up by parent-teacher associations and boards of management of the schools paying out of their own pockets.

(2) The ministry would pay temporary teachers it hired up to only November 2006.

(3) 492 teachers who had the necessary qualifications applied to be trained in school holiday classes to become regular teachers. Their applications were rejected. Their appeals were also ignored.

UCSTA also discovered the following situation. Surplus teachers who did not have qualifications in Chinese from National Primary Schools were sent to the Chinese National-Type Primary Schools to teach. We have seen in the earlier chapters that this sort of situation had happened in the past.[18] In 2007, there were 158 such teachers deployed as counsellors in the various Chinese primary schools to help students cope with their learning problems. Their distribution in the various states in the country were as follows:[19]

Table 7.1
Counselling Teachers Without Chinese Qualifications
Posted to Chinese Primary Schools

State	Number of Counselling Teachers Who Did Not Possess Qualifications in Chinese Posted to Chinese Primary Schools
Perlis	3
Johor	38
Penang	12
Perak	9
Negeri Sembilan	23
Malacca	15
Kedah	23
Pahang	12
Trengganu	2
Sabah	21

Source: See note 19.

UCSCA and UCSTA protested strongly against the Ministry of Education ignoring the problem of the shortage of qualified teachers in Chinese primary schools. They also clamoured against teachers not possessing qualifications in Chinese being sent to teach in such schools. To their relief, the deputy minister for education announced on 11 June 2007 that teachers who did not possess Chinese qualifications would be withdrawn.[20]

The Question of Government Finance for Chinese Primary Schools

Money given by the government to Chinese primary schools were of two types, *viz* administrative grants and development grants. The former was for teachers' salaries and for other items such as utilities bills, telephone charges, and the purchase of teaching aids. The latter was for the expansion of the schools, repairs, and the purchase of hardware equipment. Development grants were given only to fully-aided Chinese primary schools, but not to partially-aided schools. Fully-aided Chinese primary schools were those whose land belonged to the government, and the partially-aided schools were those whose land belonged to the private sector.

Under the Seventh Malaysia Plan (1996–2000), Chinese primary schools obtained 2.44 per cent of the total amount of money given out by the government to primary schools of all languages. Under the Eighth Plan (2001–05), they obtained 2.73 per cent. And under the Ninth Plan (2006–10), they would obtain 3.6 per cent. During the time of the Ninth Plan, Chinese primary school students would make up 21.12 per cent of the total number of primary school students in the country. For that number of students to be given only such a small amount of money can be said to be meagre. This is even more so with the development grants, for which they were to be given only 0.59 per cent of the total amount of grants set aside for primary schools of all language streams.[21]

The current minister for education, Hishamuddin, declared that of all the ministers for education the country had ever had, he was the one who had given the greatest amount of money to Chinese primary schools. From 1999 to 2007, he had given the partially-aided Chinese primary schools 1,789 million ringgit.[22]

The National-Type Secondary Schools

It will be remembered that, by the 1961 Education Act, a number of Chinese-medium secondary schools in the country converted to become schools which used English as their main medium of instruction and came to be called the National-Type Secondary Schools. And beginning from 1976, they converted a second time to become institutions which used Malay as their main medium of instruction. In 1996, when a new education act was adopted, they had their names changed to National Secondary Schools, although subsequently, because they fought against the change of name, quite a number of them were allowed to retain their old names.

These secondary schools suffered from a shortage of Chinese language teachers. The deputy minister for education expressed the view that if the schools lacked such teachers, they could spend their own money to hire them. UCSTA was unhappy about this. It blamed the government for the shortfall. In its opinion, there was a shortage because the government followed the wrong policy, arising from unitarianism, for instance, in the deployment of Chinese language teachers. It was discovered that, in 2006, sixteen teachers who had degrees and who had majored in Chinese studies in the teacher training colleges were sent to full-board secondary schools to teach students who were Malays and who had never studied Chinese before. This was not only putting manpower to wrong use, but was also depriving the National-Type Secondary Schools of needed Chinese language teachers.[23]

Although the government pursued unitarianism in its handling of the National-Type Secondary Schools, these schools preserved quite a lot of the "Chinese-ness" which they had when they were the original Chinese-medium secondary schools. Firstly, nearly 90 per cent of their students came from Chinese primary schools. Next, their school songs were in Chinese. Then, the covers of their exercise books not only had the school names printed in Malay, but also in Chinese. Every week they were taught five periods (40 minutes per period) of Chinese lessons, which were included in their regular syllabus. In SMJK Chung Ling and one or two other schools, they were taught seven periods. Many of their Chinese language teachers were enthusiastic in promoting an interest in Malaysian-Chinese literature, and many students as well as Chinese-based cultural organizations among the students were keen to respond. Many students also sat for Chinese Language examinations although they knew that it was very difficult to score an A1 in that subject.[24]

In 2005, there were 78 National-Type Secondary Schools in the country with 128,459 students and 6,483 teachers.[25]

The Independent Chinese Secondary Schools

In 2007, there were sixty independent Chinese secondary schools in the country. The Chinese community had wanted to increase this number. Several years before 2007, they applied to the government for approval to reopen one such defunct school in Segamat, another in Kajang, and one in Kuantan. They also asked for permission to expand a functioning one in Petaling Jaya. The government did not respond to their requests. It seemed that the government's policy was not to allow the Chinese to have more than sixty such schools.[26]

The Malaysian federal government did not recognize independent Chinese secondary schools as part of the country's education system. Because of that, it did not give grants to them. However, some state governments had a different attitude. The Perak state government did extend a helping hand to the nine independent Chinese secondary schools in the state. In 2006, it gave each of them 27,000 ringgit and in the following year, 30,000 ringgit. Penang and Selangor also distributed money, and Kelantan gave land. This was the silver lining in a dark cloud.[27]

The federal government also refused to recognize the certificates of the Unified Examinations conducted in Chinese by independent Chinese secondary schools for their own students, although they were recognized by many private colleges in the country and by foreign universities abroad. However, on one occasion, the minister for education told them that their graduates could apply to be trained as teachers and, on completion of their studies, be deployed to teach in the National Primary Schools. This ought to be good news for these schools, but the president of the Lim Lian Geok Foundation, Loot Ting Yee, surmised that the implication of the offer could be that these graduates must first have the Malaysian Certificate of Education or the Malaysian Higher Certificate of Education — the examinations for which were conducted in Malay — before they could apply.[28]

In 2007, the Ministry of Education informed ten independent Chinese secondary schools that they had been selected to be model schools. This seemed to be good news for Chinese education. However, in the opinion of Wu Jian Cheng, a responsible official of the National Working Committee of Independent Chinese Secondary Schools, the meaning of this might not be that straightforward. The 2006–2010 Education Development Blueprint and the Ninth Malaysia Plan had no word on independent Chinese secondary schools. This did not bode well for them.[29]

A problem that plagued independent Chinese secondary schools was that a great number of their teachers were not professionally trained. This did not give parents of students much confidence in these schools. To solve the problem, the National Working Committee of the Independent Chinese Secondary Schools cooperated with the New Era College to run professional courses for the under-qualified teachers. The joint effort was successful, and, by 2007, there were five centres in the country which professionally trained teachers for independent Chinese secondary schools. Other than the New Era College, the other four centres were the Zhong Hua High School in Kuala Lumpur, the Perak Council of Chinese School Committees in Perak, the Han Jiang High School in Penang and the Jian Guo High School in Sabah. The enrolment of all the five centres was more than 200.[30]

The Dewan Bahasa dan Pustaka also had the intention of running professional training courses for independent Chinese secondary schools. This was to upgrade the teaching of the Malay language in these schools.[31]

In 2005, the National Working Committee of Independent Chinese Secondary Schools adopted a Ma Lai Xi Ya Hua Wen Du Zhong Jiao Yu Gai Ge Gang Ling [An Educational Reform Guideline for the Independent Chinese Secondary Schools of Malaysia] to overhaul the curriculum especially of these schools. The proposed reform would stand the schools in good stead in an age of information technology. They could become institutions of a superior quality in a few years' time.[32]

In 2007, there were 55,818 students and 3,215 teachers altogether in the various independent Chinese secondary schools.[33] It was reported that in January 2009, the student enrolment in all these schools had risen by about 700 from the previous year. About 5,000 applicants wishing to enrol as students were turned away because there was not enough room to accommodate them.[34]

The MCA Caught Between Pluralism and Unitarianism

The MCA was founded to protect and advance the interests of the Chinese community, including those of Chinese education. In fighting for the interests of Chinese education, it was caught between the pluralism embraced by the Chinese schools, and the unitarianism followed by the government. Therefore, it had to know how to balance the two. To date, the MCA has been able to achieve something for the Chinese schools.

From 1999 to 2006, according to information provided by the office of the deputy minister for education, who was a member of the executive committee of the MCA, the political party was able to get eight new Chinese primary schools built and thirty in the process of being built for the Chinese community. During the same period, it was able to help twenty-two existing schools move to new premises. In 2007, sixty-one existing schools obtained approval to relocate and nine existing schools obtained approval to expand. It was also made known that in the following year, six new schools would be built and thirteen existing schools would be allowed to move to new localities. The president of the MCA, Ong Ka Ting, announced that his party would, through the building of new schools, and the expansion or relocation of existing schools, help the Chinese primary schools to develop.[35]

The MCA also helped in the training of teachers for Chinese primary schools. Between 2000 and 2006, 10,715 teachers were trained. And every year, the party fought for the quota given to the training of temporary teachers in school holiday classes to be increased.[36]

Partially-aided Chinese primary schools did not qualify to obtain development grants from the government. However, recently, the MCA was able to help the Yu Hua High School and the Yu Hua Primary School in Kajang to obtain 300,000 and 50,000 ringgit respectively.[37]

In spite of the admirable efforts of the MCA, UCSCA and UCSTA considered that the assistance given to the Chinese primary schools needed to be put on a systematic basis before the problems of such schools could be fundamentally solved. They felt that there had to be legislation in parliament and plans drawn up for the purpose. But would the government concede this?

The 2006–2010 Education Development Blueprint

In 2007, the Ministry of Education made public a 2006–2010 Education Development Blueprint. The development of the education system in the country for the years mentioned was to follow this blueprint. The document was characterized by unitarianism.[38]

Chapter 4, paragraph 4.12, quoted from the 1956 Razak Report, reads as follows:

> ... the ultimate objective of educational policy in the country must be to bring together the children of all races under a national educational system in which the national language [i.e. the Malay language] is the main medium of instruction though we recognize that progress towards this goal cannot be rushed and must be gradual.

The commitment could not have been clearer.

Chapter 4, paragraph 4.26 mentioned that education was an important factor which came under consideration when a blueprint to foster integration and unity among the people of the country was drawn up. It said that the education system must provide the environment and convenience for young people to come together and socialize. It then proposed two courses of action to bring about the realization of this aspiration:

(1) Encourage the setting up of an education system for pre-school up to secondary level in which one medium of instruction [that is, the National Language or Malay] would be used for instruction, and the establishment of unified curricula as well as unified extra-curricular activities to be followed. There should also be an examination system and certificates issued which would both be recognized.

(2) At the primary and secondary levels, provide the convenience for students to learn the languages of the main races in the country. Such languages should be treated as selective subjects.

The thrust of the two items was also clear.

Chapter 6, paragraph 6.01 called for the strengthening of National Primary and National Secondary Schools which used Malay as the main medium of instruction. Right from the start, it reiterated an opinion on the cause of racial separation and division in the country that was found in a publication on schools in Peninsular Malaysia published by Aminuddin Baki, a Malay scholar, in 1953. The publication asserted that the flaw of the then educational structure was that it had a pluralistic system of schools which not only brought about, but also encouraged, separation and division among the various races. On the basis of this understanding, the strengthening of the National Primary and the National Secondary Schools was proposed. The blueprint also advocated the continued implementation of the Vision Schools plan.

The blueprint suggested that 1,296,850,000 ringgit be budgeted for the building of 178; 656,828,000 ringgit be budgeted for the expansion of 337; and 2,170,507,000 ringgit be budgeted for the rebuilding of 890 National Primary Schools. It also suggested that 229,870,111 ringgit be set aside for the completion of the construction of various types of schools which had not been completed under the Eighth Malaysia Plan. Chinese and Tamil primary schools had for a long time been plagued by the problems of a shortage of school accommodation, teachers, government funding, insufficient land, and so on. The blueprint did not have a single word on the solving of these problems. It did not have any concrete plan for the development of these schools.

So, the government was interested only in the National Schools, and was not concerned about the Chinese and Tamil schools.

UCSCA and UCSTA firmly argued that the government should keep to the social contract agreed among the various races at the time when the country gained independence from the British. This contract permitted all races and cultures in the country to coexist. The pluralistic system of education should be allowed to flourish. While UCSCA and UCSTA upheld this belief, the government accused them of being chauvinistic organizations.

The 2008 General Election and Its Effects on the Chinese Schools in the Country

On 8 March 2008, there was a general election in Malaysia. It is necessary and interesting to take a look at how the outcome of this event would affect the fate of Chinese schools in the country.

The various contesting parties made different appeals to voters to win their support. Included in these appeals were items which touched on the interests of Chinese schools. In its election manifesto, the Barisan Nasional, the then ruling party, declared that it would seek to strengthen the National Primary Schools, which were Malay-medium schools, to become schools of first choice among parents. But it would also expand the teaching of the Chinese language and maintain the status quo of the National-Type Primary Schools, which were Chinese-medium or Tamil-medium schools, and would not change their character. Prior to this, the MCA, under the Barisan Nasional, had actually made the promise that it would permit Chinese schools to increase their number, to expand, or to relocate to new sites.[39]

In this election, the MCA, which was a member of the Barisan Nasional, had a manifesto of nine items. Among these were three which dealt with education. The first one stated that it would commit the party "to rejuvenate education", the second "to strengthen Chinese education", and the third to promote a "life-long education movement". Simultaneously, it devised a "Great Education Blueprint" to cover education from pre-school to old age.[40]

Gerakan, which was also a member of the Barisan Nasional, put out an election propaganda pamphlet which recounted how much it and the MCA had done for Chinese education in the past eight years. The two parties had fought for the opportunity for the Chinese to build fifteen new Chinese primary schools and enabled seventy-four Chinese primary schools to move to new locations. It had also set up in Penang, where it formed the state government, a coordinating committee to develop Chinese primary schools, as well as another committee to develop independent Chinese secondary schools on the island.[41]

The DAP, which was an opposition party, campaigned for equitable financial assistance to be given to schools of all language streams by the government to protect mother tongue education.[42]

Chinese educationists had a great influence over the Chinese community in the country. Taking advantage of the fact that the various contending parties had to make promises to do something for Chinese education in order to win votes, six national organizations among them came out on 28 February with a set of five demands on Chinese education for the various contending parties to honour. Those that would show support would get the Chinese vote. The five demands were:[43]

(1) Restore the practice of teaching and conducting examinations in mathematics and science in the mother tongue.
(2) Systematize formally the building of new Chinese and Tamil primary schools. Treat equitably the development of schools of all language streams.

(3) Give recognition to the certificates of the Unified Examinations of independent Chinese secondary schools to solve the problem of the shortage of teachers in Chinese primary schools.

(4) Reopen the original campus of the SJK (C) Damansara, that is, the Damansara National-Type Chinese Primary School, to fulfil as soon as possible the need of Chinese pupils in the locality to have a mother tongue education. Give importance to mother tongue education.

(5) Elevate the New Era College and the Southern College to universities to fulfil the aspirations of the Chinese community so that tertiary institutions established by the Chinese themselves can take root in Malaysia.

The general election was duly held on 8 March. The ruling party, the Barisan Nasional, a coalition made up of UMNO, the MCA, Gerakan, the MIC, and others, was opposed by a united front of the PKR, the DAP, and the PAS, formalized into a Pakatan Rakyat or People's Alliance after the election. For decades, the Barisan Nasional had enjoyed a two-thirds majority in parliament and ruled all the states in the country, except Kelantan, as well as the Federal Territory. In this election, however, to its surprise and that of many others, it lost its dominance. It won parliament by only a simple majority, taking only 140 seats against the opposition's eighty-two, and, besides Kelantan, it lost four states to the opposition, *viz* Penang, Kedah, Perak, and Selangor. It was also defeated at the polls in the Federal Territory. The general feeling about these results of the election was that the race-based politics of the Barisan Nasional was now no longer favoured by a very sizeable segment of the electorate. The various promises made on Chinese education by the Barisan Nasional and two of its components, the MCA and Gerakan, during electioneering, made no impression on most of the Chinese voters. On the other hand, the appeal of the DAP was heard.[44]

The results of the general election and the new political configuration in the country are likely to have an effect on the future of Chinese schools. Will the Barisan Nasional-led government now become more moderate in its attitude towards Chinese schools? How will the opposition from now onwards behave towards these schools? We shall try to answer these questions.

Some events which took place soon after the general election was over indicated that the Barisan Nasional-led government would likely become more concessionary towards Chinese schools. Firstly, one may note that soon after the election, Dr Wee Ka Siong from the MCA was appointed a deputy minister for education. In a certain interview, instead of getting irritated over the fact that the MCA lost badly in the election, Dr Wee promised that the government would undertake to solve the problems facing Chinese primary schools. He first stated that the MCA would honour its promises made during the election concerning the building of more Chinese primary schools and the relocation of existing schools. He then said he was confident that the original campus of SJK (C) Damansara could reopen. He further said that he would undertake to instruct officials in his ministry that, henceforth, none of them, under any circumstances, should express the opinion that no new Chinese primary schools would be built.[45]

On another occasion, Dr Wee Ka Siong met up with representatives from the Dong Jiao Zong, a liaison committee of UCSCA and UCSTA, to discuss a very significant issue which concerned Chinese education. The issue was whether the Ministry of Education should, together with the Dong Jiao Zong, also set up a liaison committee to deliberate, from time to time, on problems which faced Chinese schools. It was agreed that such a liaison committee should be established. The agreement was epoch-making. Also, it was the first time a high official from the Ministry of Education discuss issues with people from the Dong Jiao Zong.[46]

In April 2008, just one month after the general election, the deputy minister for higher education, Dr Hou Kok Chung, visited the New Era College. He did this on his own initiative. It was observed earlier in the chapter that, during the time of electioneering in the general election, six national Chinese educational organizations had issued a set of five demands to promote the interests of Chinese education for the various contending political parties in the election to honour. One of these was that the New Era College and the Southern College should be upgraded to universities. And it may be noted now that, after the election, Dr Kua Kia Soong, principal of the New Era College, had expressed the sentiment that, because of the outcome of the election, there was now an opportunity for his college to become a university. Dr Hou Kok Chung's visit to the New Era College was, precisely, to discuss the elevation of the status of the college. Dr Hou undertook with Dr Kua that a committee would be put in place to help the college acquire the desired promotion.[47]

A little earlier in this chapter, we have noted that, in 2007, the Barisan Nasional-led government made public a 2006–2010 Education Development Blueprint. This document was supposed to guide the development of education in the country from 2006 to 2010. As seen, it was not favourable to Chinese education. Now, because of the outcome of the 2008 general election, would the Barisan Nasional-led government revise this document? The answer came in the middle of the year, just three months after the election, when the Ministry of Education set up a group to draw up what came to be known as a Mini Education Development Blueprint to be attached to the 2006–2010 Education Development Blueprint, whose purpose was to develop a plan for schools that were partially assisted by the government, including Chinese and Tamil primary schools, to be converted into fully-assisted schools. When transformed, they would get the same amount of financial support from the government as the fully-assisted institutions.[48] The plan would be a great boon to Chinese and Tamil primary schools as these had always been, above everything else, short of funds. Following hot on the heels of the setting up of the mini blueprint group was the convening in October of a roundtable conference of representatives from the various partially-assisted schools, with officials from the Ministry of Education, to explore problems faced by those schools so that solutions could be devised to have such problems overcome. The government was demonstrating a benign attitude.[49]

Were Chinese educationists happy with the favourable turns of events? Not quite, it seemed. Why? It was soon pointed out that in July, the minister for education, Hishammuddin, stated that whichever partially-assisted schools that wished to be converted to fully-assisted schools must, in the first instance, surrender the ownership of their land to the Ministry of Education. The Dong Jiao Zong soon notified all Chinese primary schools in the country not to give up the ownership of their land, their buildings, or other properties. Otherwise, the sovereignty of their management committees would be compromised.[50] UCSCA, on its own, further pointed out that, back in 2000, the then minister for education, Musa Mohammed, had already laid down the condition that, on conversion, the partially-assisted schools had not only to surrender their land to the government, but that their management committees would also be abolished and that they would henceforth be managed in the same way as National Primary Schools, which were Malay-medium schools.[51] Moreover, as seen from past experience, even when a partially-assisted school got converted, it was not certain that it could obtain all the money it expected from the government. Chinese educationists went on to say that if the government were serious about helping Chinese and Tamil primary schools, it should not lay down any condition for conversion.[52] And, to top it all, it was argued that in all the education laws that had been enacted so far, there had never been a distinction made between partially and fully-assisted schools. That such a differentiation had now emerged was due to the fact that there was a "Guideline on the Expansion and Rebuilding of Schools", adopted in 1998, which enabled officials in the Ministry of Education to launch an innovation. In doing this, the officials were making a law beyond the laws. The creation had the effect of setting up their ministry against the management committees of all the schools.[53]

It was also seen earlier on that the requirement by the Ministry of Education to have mathematics and science in Chinese primary schools taught in English, in addition to their being taught in the mother tongue, was very unpopular with Chinese educationists. In schools of other language streams, the two subjects were taught solely in English and not in the mother tongues. This policy also infuriated educationists of the other language streams.[54]

In view of the discontent of the educationists, the Ministry of Education in 2008 convened a series of roundtable conferences to discuss whether the practice of having mathematics and science in schools taught in English should be continued. In August the same year, the second of such conferences was held. Most of the participants at the conference voted for a discontinuation of the practice. But they all agreed that English was an international language and that the standard of students in this language should be raised by upgrading the teaching of the subject.[55] In December, the experts met again for a fifth time. On this occasion, there was still no decision made on whether or not to continue with the practice. The conference was only able to adopt a set of seven options of what could be done to be presented to the Cabinet for it to deliberate and act. The seven options were:[56]

(1) Continue with the standing policy.

(2) At the primary level, the two subjects should be taught in the mother tongue. Only at secondary level should they be taught in English.

(3) From Primary 1 to Primary 3, the two subjects should be taught in the mother tongue. Only from Primary 4 onwards should they be taught in English.

(4) At primary level, all subjects should be taught in the mother tongue. At secondary level, the National Language, that is Malay, should be the main medium of instruction.

(5) At primary level, let each school choose its own medium of instruction.

(6) From Primary 1 to Primary 3, the two subjects should be taught in the mother tongue. From Primary 4 to Primary 6, they should be taught in both the mother tongue and English. At secondary level, the two subjects should be taught only in English.

(7) From Primary 1 to Primary 3, the subject science should be abolished as a separate subject. It should be merged with other subjects and taught through those subjects.

The ball was now in the court of the government.

By January 2009, when the new school year began, the government was still unable to make up its mind on what it should do regarding the issue. This greatly upset both teachers and students in Chinese primary schools. Consequently, on 11 January, UCSCA, UCSTA, together with six other Chinese organizations, met and resolved to take all necessary steps to persuade the government to permit Chinese primary schools to revert to teaching students mathematics and science in the mother tongue, as well as to allow the examination of these two subjects to be conducted in the mother tongue.[57]

By March, Malay educationists also became agitated. They formed a Gerakan Memansuhkan Pengajaran-Pembelajaran Sains dan Matematik dalam Bahasa Inggeris (GMP) [Alliance for the Abolition of Teaching Mathematics and Science in English] which, on 7 March, was able to assemble a crowd of 5,000 people, including not only Malays, but also Chinese, Indians, and Aborigines, and get them to march from the National Mosque to the Royal Palace. The force of the demonstration was enhanced by the participation of Samad Said, a winner of a national prize for literature. The demonstrators presented a memorandum to the *Yang di-Pertuan Agong*, which appealed for the repeal of the policy of teaching mathematics and science in English.[58]

The Alliance had found that in the Primary Six Examination for the year 2008, only 46.6 per cent and 31.1 per cent of all the examinees could answer questions in English on mathematics and science respectively. The rest found English beyond their grasp.[59]

UCSCA, UCSTA, and the other six Chinese organizations did not participate in the demonstration as organizations. But they soon secured a common platform with the Alliance on the issue in dispute with the government. The two sides agreed on:[60]

(1) Calling on the government to give up the policy of teaching mathematics and science in English in primary schools of all language streams;
(2) Calling on the government to revert to the practice of teaching the subjects in the various mother tongues. Examinations were also to be conducted through the mother tongues; and

(3) The need for the teaching of the English language in schools should to be strengthened and upgraded.

The government might take some time before it could decide on the course of action.

It will be remembered that for Chinese educationists, there was also the issue of the reopening of the original campus of SJK (C) Damansara. And we noted just a little earlier on that the new deputy minister for education, Dr Wee Kia Siong, said in an interview that he was confident the campus would eventually reopen. In January 2009, with the beginning of the new school year, it was indeed reopened. But the permission was granted only because a very small Chinese school in Perak was closed down in exchange.[61]

Because of the outcome of the general election, the Barisan Nasional-led government has somewhat taken, and probably will continue to take, steps to adjust and amend its treatment of Chinese schools. Immediately after the election, the opposition, that is, the PKR, the DAP, and the PAS, or the Pakatan Rakyat, as was expected of it, also instituted measures in the states that had come under its control, to benefit Chinese schools.

First, one may take a look at Penang. In Penang, consequent to the election, the DAP led in forming the new state government. It set up a coordinating committee to assist an existing committee in the Executive Council that looked after education in the state pertaining to Chinese education. This coordinating committee was led by Zhang Ying, the newly elected member of parliament for Bukit Mertajam, and consisted of school management committee members, school teachers, and school alumni from the various Chinese educational organizations in the state as members. The coordinating committee was expected to help substantially in the development of Chinese education in Penang.[62]

Next, the DAP-led government increased financial assistance given to independent Chinese secondary schools in the state. Beginning in 2004, each of the independent Chinese secondary schools in the state had been given an annual grant of 30,000 ringgit by the then state government. In 2006, the amount granted was increased to 40,000 ringgit. Now in 2008, the DAP administration raised the annual amount further to 50,000 ringgit. The gesture of the DAP administration made the Chinese community happy. The Malaysian Chinese Schools' Old Boys' Association applauded its move and called on the governments of other states, which have also independent Chinese secondary schools, to emulate the good example of the DAP and generously extend grants to those schools.[63]

Perak came under the control of the Pakatan Rakyat as a whole. Many Chinese schools in that state were burdened with huge debts of rent which they could not settle. The new administration reduced their liability to only one ringgit each, which was a highly significant move. The initiative was immediately followed by Penang, Kedah, and Selangor, with possible and necessary adjustments. Even Johor, which was run by the Barisan Nasional, was affected. It also made the same offer to the Chinese schools under its purview.[64]

Kedah was led by the PAS. After the general election, the new *mentri besar* or chief minister made a public announcement that his government would give help to the Chinese schools in the state. He explained that in education, as in other matters, the state government had to depend on the central government for grants. If money was forthcoming, his government would do its best to help Chinese schools develop, including rendering assistance to independent Chinese secondary schools. He also made the statement that his administration would treat schools of all language streams with equality.[65]

Trouble at the New Era College

2008 was significant not only for the general election, but also for a development which could for quite some time to come, have Chinese educationists in the country divided amongst themselves. What happened concerned the New Era College, one of the highest centres of Chinese education in the country.

It had been the practice in the New Era College for teaching and other staff of any grade in the college to be hired or dismissed by the principal of the college. However, in April 2008, the chairman of the management committee of the college, Dr Yap Sin Tian, announced that the management committee had made the decision that henceforth the engagement and dismissal of academic and administrative staff at senior levels of the college would become the responsibility of a special human resources unit that would be established in due course. The announcement took the whole existing staff, the principal, the heads of the various academic departments, and senior administrators, by surprise and had them completely upset. Then, to add insult to injury, two months later, the management committee had another meeting, and the principal, senior administrative staff, and heads of the various academic departments who had turned up to attend the meeting, as was customary, were told to leave the meeting and absent themselves. This had the effect of stirring the conflict between the two sides.

Furthermore, the principal of the college, Dr Kua Kia Soong, was soon also to lose his job.[66]

Under the call of previous leaders of the Dong Jiao Zong, a committee of four men was soon set up to try to reconcile the two parties. The committee came up with a number of proposals for the management committee of the college to consider. They found, however, no listening ear. A few months later, two very influential Chinese educationists in the country, Sim Mow Yu and Zhang Ya Shan, appealed to the management committee to have Dr Kua Kia Soong reinstated as the principal of the college for the good of Chinese education, but their plea was ignored.[67]

In November, it was announced that a Dr Pan Yong Zhong had been engaged to become the new principal of the college. The challenge that lay ahead of Dr Pan would be whether or not he was able to earn the acceptance of the supporters of Dr Kua Kia Soong in the college, namely, the existing teaching and administrative staff, as well as the members of the students' union. It might take some time for the college to recover its health.[68]

The outcome of the general election in 2008 is a watershed development in the politics of the country. The relative weakening of the Barisan Nasional and the relative strengthening of the opposition is of historic significance. The event bodes well for the future of Chinese education. It may be surmised that in order to win back the voters it had lost in the general election, the Barisan Nasional will, as time passes, have an increasingly conciliatory attitude towards Chinese education, and the opposition, in order to hold onto the voters it had gained in the election, will, in the years ahead, do more and more for Chinese education. There could be some kind of competition between the two sides in this matter.

Notes

1. UCSCA, *Ma Lai Xi Ya Hua Wen Jiao Yu*, No. 8 (Kajang, 2008) (hereafter UCSCA, op. cit. 1), p. 89.
2. SMJK Conforming Executive Committee, *Directori SMJK Conforming* (Kuala Lumpur, 2006), pp. 240–44.
3. UCSCA, op. cit. 1, pp. 90–91. (37 in the peninsula, 14 in Sarawak and 9 in Sabah.)
4. Liao Wen Hui, *Hua Xiao Jiao Zong Ji Qi Ren Wu* (Kajang, 2006), p. 89; various Chinese newspapers, 11 December 2005.
5. Ibid.
6. UCSCA, *Dong Zong 50 Nian* (Kajang, 2004), pp. 616–21.
7. *Sin Chew Daily*, 28 October 2007.
8. *Sin Chew Daily*, 9 October 2007 and 28–29 October 2007.

[9]   *Oriental News*, 4 December 2007.

[10] UCSCA, op. cit. 1, pp. 24 and 31; *Oriental News* & *Sin Chew Daily*, 11 October 2007.

[11] UCSCA, op. cit. 1, p. 30; *Oriental News*, 11 October 2007.

[12] *Oriental News*, 28 January 2008.

[13] *Guang Hua Ri Bao, Nanyang Siang Pau* and *Oriental News*, 6 May 2007.

[14] Ibid.

[15] *Sin Chew Daily*, 11 October 2007; UCSCA, op. cit. 1 (Kajang, 2008), pp. 30–31.

[16] UCSTA, *2006 Nian Gong Zuo Bao Gao Shu* (Kajang, 2007), pp. 154–55.

[17] Ibid.

[18] Ibid.

[19] *Oriental News*, 22 June 2007.

[20] *Nanyang Siang Pau*, 12 June 2007.

[21] UCSTA, op. cit., pp. 157–58 and 162–63; *Oriental News*, 25 July 2007.

[22] *Nanyang Siang Pau*, 4 July 2007.

[23] *Guang Hua Ri Bao*, 12 September 2007; UCSTA, op. cit., p. 155.

[24] *Sin Chew Daily*, 17 March 2007 and 25 November 2007, article by An Huan Ran.

[25] SMJK Conforming Executive Committee, op. cit., p. 244.

[26] *Sin Chew Daily*, 23 September 2007.

[27] *Oriental News*, 6 May 2007.

[28] *Oriental News*, 14 May 2007; *Guang Hua Ri Bao*, 19 August 2007.

[29] *Oriental News*, 14 May 2007.

[30] *Oriental News*, 20 September 2007; data supplied by the New Era College.

[31] *Nanyang Siang Pau*, 26 November 2007.

[32] *Oriental News*, 20 September 2007.

[33] UCSCA, op. cit. 1, p. 91; *Nanyang Siang Pau*, 20 January 2008.

[34] *Sin Chew Daily*, 11 January 2009; *Nanyang Siang Pau*, 20 January 2009.

[35] *Sin Chew Daily*, 22 July 2007; *Oriental News*, 13 October 2007; *Sunday Star*, 27 January 2008, pp. 23–24; *Nanyang Siang Pau*, 1.2.2008, p. A1.

[36] *Nanyang Siang Pau*, 4 January 2008.

[37] *Nanyang Siang Pau*, 31 December 2007.

[38] UCSCA & UCSTA (Dong Jiao Zong), *Dui <2006–2010 Nian Jiao Yu Fa Zan Da Lan Tu> Zong Ti Yi Jian Shu* (Kajang, 2001), p. 11.

[39] *Sin Chew Daily*, 22 July 2007; *Sunday Star*, 27 January 2008, pp. 23–24.

[40] *Oriental News, Nanyang Siang Pau, Sin Chew Daily*, 27 February 2008.

[41] Gerakan, *In 40 Years, What has Gerakan Achieved?* (Penang, 2008), p. 13.

[42] *Oriental News*, 21 February 2008.

[43] *Oriental News, Nanyang Siang Pau*, 29 February 2008.

[44] *The Strait Times* (Singapore) 10 March 2008; *Nanyang Siang Pau*, 10 March 2008.

[45] *Nanyang Siang Pau*, 28 March 2008.

46 *Oriental News*, 11 April 2008.
47 *Oriental News*, 12 April 2008; *Nanyang Siang Pau*, 14 March 2008 and 12 April 2008.
48 *Oriental News*, 24 December 2008.
49 Ibid.
50 *Nanyang Siang Pau*, 25 July 2008 and *Oriental News*, 24 December 2008.
51 *Oriental News*, 24 December 2008.
52 Ibid.
53 Ibid.
54 *Sin Chew Daily*, 30 August 2008.
55 *Sin Chew Daily*, 30 August 2008 and *Sunday Star: Focus*, 14 December 2008
56 *Oriental News*, 9 January 2009.
57 Ibid.
58 *Oriental News*, 8 March 2009 and *Berita Minggu*, 8 March 2009.
59 *Oriental News*, 8 March 2009.
60 *Sin Chew Daily*, 14 March 2009.
61 *Oriental News*, 1 August 2009.
62 *Oriental News*, 28 March 2008.
63 *Nanyang Siang Pau*, 29 March 2008.
64 *Nanyang Siang Pau*, 8 April 2008.
65 *Nanyang Siang Pau*, 30 March 2008.
66 Save-New-Era-College Editorial Board, *Writings on the New Era College Controversy* (Kuala Lumpur, 2008), pp 26–27; *Oriental News*, 16 June 2008; *STAR, Education*, 13 July 2008.
67 Save-New-Era-College Editorial Board, op. cit., pp 39–42; *Nanyang Siang Pau*, 16 June 2008.
68 *Oriental News*, 21 January 2009, A37.

GLOSSARY

I. GLOSSARY OF CHINESE NAMES OF ORGANIZATIONS, PERSONS, PLACES, SCHOOLS, ETC.

In Hanyu Pinyin	In Chinese Characters	English Transliteration or Translation	Authors' Translation
Ai Qun [Bao She]	愛群［报社］	unknown	Ai Qun Reading Room
Bai Hua	白話	Pai Hua	Conversational Language
Bai Jia Xing	《百家姓》	*A Hundred Surnames*	
Bao Huang Dang	保皇党	Reform Party	
Beijing	北京	Peking/Pekin	
Beijing Daxue	北京大学	Peking University	
Bin Cheng Hua Qiao Xue Xiao Lian He Hui	槟城华侨学校联合会	Unknown	Confederation of Chinese Schools in Penang
Bin Hua Nu Xiao	槟华女校	Unknown	Bin Hua Girls' School
Bin Lang Yu Di Yi Zi Zhi Xue Xiao	槟榔屿第一自治学校	Unknown	The Penang Island First Self-Governing School
Bu Zhu Qing Pin Qiao Sheng Hui Guo Sheng Xue Gui Cheng	补助清貧侨生回国升学规程	Unknown	Regulations on Financial Aid for Poor Overseas Students Returning to China for Further Studies
Chen Guo Jie	陈国杰	Unknown	
Chen Jia Geng	陈嘉庚	Tan Kah Kee	
Chen Qing Jia	陈庆佳	Unknown	
Chen Shou Min	陈寿民	Unknown	

In Hanyu Pinyin	In Chinese Characters	English Transliteration or Translation	Authors' Translation
Chen Xin Zheng	陈新政	Unknown	
Chong De [Xue Xiao]	崇德［学校］	Unknown	Chong De School
Chou An Hui	筹安会	Unknown	Work-for-Peace Society
Chou Zhen Hui	筹赈会	Relief Fund Committees	
Chun Qiu	《春秋》	*Spring and Autumn Annals*	
Ci Xi Tai Hou	慈禧太后	Empress Dowager	Empress Dowager Ci Xi
Cui Ying Shu Yuan	萃英书院	Chiu Eng Si I	
Da Cai [Xue Xiao]	达才［学校］	Tat Choi School	
Da Lian	大连	Dalian	
Da Xue	《大学》	*Great Learning*	
Dong Jiao Zong	董教总	Unknown	UCSCA & UCSTA liason committee
Fu Zhu	辅助		Supplementary
Fujian Nu Xiao	福建女校	Fukien Girls' School	Fujian Girls' School
Fujian [Province]	福建［省］	Hok Kian Province	
Gong Yi [Shu Bao She]	公义［书报社］	unknown	Gong Yi Reading Room
Gu Guang Xing	顾光兴	Unknown	
Guang Han [Shu Bao She]	光汉［书报社］		Guang Han Reading Room
Guang Xi	广西	Kuangsi	
Guang Xu	光绪	Kuang Hsu	
Guangdong	广东	Kwangtung	
Guangzhou	广州	Canton	
Guo Yu	国語	Mandarin/ National Language	
Guomindang	国民党	Kuomintang	
Hai Wai Bu	海外部	Unknown	Overseas Department
Hainan	海南	Hainan	
Han Jiang [Zhong Xue]	韩江［中学	Unknown	

In Hanyu Pinyin	In Chinese Characters	English Transliteration or Translation	Authors' Translation
Hua Lian [Xue Xiao]	华联[学校]	Unknown	Hua Lian School
Hua Nan Nu Xiao	华南女校	Unknown	Hua Nan Girls' School
Hua Qiao Jiao Yu Hui Yi	华侨教育会议	Unknown	Overseas Chinese Education Conference
Hua Qiao Jiao Yu Hui Yi Bao Gao Shu	《华侨教育会议报告书》	Unknown	*Report on the Overseas Chinese Education Conference*
Hua Qiao Jiao Yu Hui Zan Xing Gui Cheng	华侨教育会暂行规程	Unknown	Temporary Regulations for Overseas Chinese Education Associations
Hua Qiao Jiao Yu Ji Jin Guan Li Wei Yuan Hui Zu Zhi Tiao Li	华侨教育基金管理委員会組织条例	Unknown	Rules Governing the Organization of Management Committees of Overseas Chinese Education Foundations
Hua Qiao Jiao Yu Wei Yuan Hui	华侨教育委員会	Unknown	Overseas Chinese Education Commission
Hua Qiao Jiao Yu Xie Jin Hui	华侨教育协进会	Unknown	Overseas Chinese Education Promotion Association
Hua Qiao Jiao Yu Zong Hui	华侨教育总会	Unknown	General Overseas Chinese Education Association
Hua Qiao [Nu Xue]	华侨[女學]	Unknown	Hua Qiao Girls' School
Hua Ren Jiao Yu Ji Jin	华仁教育基金	Unknown	Hua Ren Education Foundation
Hua Tuan Su Qiu	华团诉求	Unknown	Appeals of the Chinese Organizations
Hua Wen Du Li Zhong Xue Jian Yi Shu	《华文独立中学建议书》	Unknown	*Proposals for Independent Chinese Secondary Schools*

In Hanyu Pinyin	In Chinese Characters	English Transliteration or Translation	Authors' Translation
Hua Xiao Dong Shi Lian He Hui Zong Hui	华校董事联合会总会	United Chinese School Committees' Association	
Hua Xiao Jiao Shi Hui Zong Hui	华校教师会总会	United Chinese School Teachers' Association	
Huangpu Jun Guan Xue Xiao	黃埔军官学校	Whampo Military Academy	
Ji Nan Da Xue	暨南大学	Chi Nan University	
Ji Nan Xue Tang	暨南学堂	Unknown	Ji Nan School
Jian Jue Fan Dui Hong Yuan Xue Xiao Ji Hua	《坚决反对宏愿学校计划》	Unknown	*Firmly Oppose the Vision School Plan*
Jiang Jie Shi	蒋介石	Chiang Khai-shek	
Jiao Yu Bu	教育部	Unknown	Ministry of Education
Jiao Yu Bu Hua Qiao Jiao Yu She Ji Wei Yuan Hui Zu Zhi Tiao Li	教育部华侨教育设计委员会组织条例	Unknown	Ministry of Education Overseas Chinese Education Planning Committee: Rules of Organization
Jinan	济南	Unknown	
Jing Fang Nu Xiao	静芳女校	Unknown	Jing Fang Girls' School
Kang You Wei	康有为	Kang Yu Wei	
Kong Jiao Hui	孔教会	Confucius Society	
Kuang Qi Fang	邝其芳	Unknown	
Li Ji	《礼記》	*Book of Rites*	
Li Yuan Hong	黎元洪	Unknown	
Liang Shen Nan	梁燊南	Leong Sin Nam	
Lin Wen Qing	林文庆	Lim Boon Keng	
Lin Yi Shun	林义顺	Lim Nee Soon	
Ling Shi Guan Li Hua Qiao Xue Wu Gui Cheng	领事管理华侨学务规程		Regulations Governing the Management of Overseas Chinese Schools by Consuls
Liu Shi Ji	刘士骥	Unknown	

In Hanyu Pinyin	In Chinese Characters	English Transliteration or Translation	Authors' Translation
Lun Yu	《论語》	*Analects*	
Ma Lai Xi Ya Hua Wen Du Zong Jiao Yu Gai Ge Gang Ling	《马来西亚华文独中教育改革纲领》		*An Education Reform Plan for the Independent Chinese Secondary Schools of Malaysia*
Ma Lai Ya Hua Qiao Jiao Yu Hui	马来亚华侨教育会	Unknown	Malayan Overseas Chinese Educational Association
Mao Zedong	毛泽东	Mao Tze Tung	
Meng Zi	《孟子》	*Book of Mencius*	
Min Quan Zhu Yi	民权主义	Principle of People's Sovereignty	
Min Sheng Zhu Yi	民生主义	Principle of People's Livelihood	
Min Zu Zhu Yi	民族主义	Principle of Nationalism	
Mu Yu Jiao Yu Xuan Yan	《母語教育宣言》	Unknown	*Manifesto on Mother Tongue Education*
Nan Hua Nu Zhong	南华女中	Unknown	Nan Hua Girls' High School
Nan Hua [Xue Xiao]	南华[学校]	Unknown	Nan Hua School
Nan Yang/ Nanyang	南洋	Nanyang	
Nan Yang Hua Qiao Chou Zhen Zu Guo Nan Min Zong Hui	南洋华侨筹赈祖国难民总会	Unknown	Nanyang Overseas Chinese General Association for the Relief of Refugees in the Fatherland
Nan Yang Hua Qiao Jiao Yu Hui Yi	南洋华侨教育会议	Unknown	Nanyang Overseas Chinese Education Conference
Nan Yang Nu Zhong	南洋女中	Nanyang Girls' High School	
Nan Yang Xin Jia Po Hua Qiao Ge Jie Lian He Hui	南洋新加坡华侨各界联合会	Unknown	Union of Various Overseas Chinese Professions, Singapore, Nanyang

In Hanyu Pinyin	In Chinese Characters	English Transliteration or Translation	Authors' Translation
Nanjing	南京	Nanking	
Pei Cai [Xiao Xue]	培才[小学]	Unknown	Pei Cai Primary School
Pei Feng [Xue Xiao]	培风[学校]	Pay Fong School	
Pei Zhi [Nu Xue]	培智[女学]	Unknown	Pei Zhi Girls' School
Pi Li Hua Qiao Jiao Yu Hui	霹雳华侨教育会	Unknown	Perak Overseas Chinese Education Association
Ping Min [Xue Xiao]	平民[学校]	Unknown	Ping Min School
Ping Zhang Hui Guan	平章会馆	Ping Chang Association	
Po Ping [Xue Xiao]	柏屏[学校]	Unknown	Po Ping School
Po Rong [Xue Xiao]	柏荣[学校]	Unknown	Po Rong School
Pu Yi	溥仪	Pu Yi	
Qian Zi Wen	《千字文》	*Millenary Classic*	
Qiao Min Zi Di Hui Guo Jiu Xue Gui Cheng	侨民子弟回国就学规程	Unknown	Regulations Governing the Return of Overseas Students to China to Study
Quan Guo Wei Hu Hua Jiao Xing Dong Lian Luo Xiao Zu	全国维护华教行动联络小组	Unknown	All-Nation Protect Chinese Education Action Liason Group
Ri Xin [Xue Xiao]	日新[学校]	Jit Sin School	
San Min Zhu Yi	三民主义	San Min Chi I/ Three People's Principles	
San Min Zhu Yi Jiao Yu Shi Shi Gang Yao	《三民主义教育实施纲要》	Unknown	*Principles of Enforcement of San Min Zhu Yi Education*
San Zi Jing	《三字经》	*Trimetrical Classic*	
Shandong	山东	Shantung	
Shang Wu Yin Shu Guan	商务印书馆	Commercial Press	
Shanghai	上海	Shanghai	
Shen Ting	沈亭	Unknown	

In Hanyu Pinyin	In Chinese Characters	English Transliteration or Translation	Authors' Translation
Shenyang	沈阳	Shenyang	
Shi Jing	《詩经》	*Book of Odes*	
Shu Jing	《书经》	*Book of History*	
Si Shu	《四书》	*Four Books*	
Song Jiao Ren	宋教仁	Unknown	
Song Wang Xiang	宋旺相	Song Ong Siang	
Sun Yi Xian	孙逸仙	Sun Yat Sen	
Tianjin	天津	Tientsin	
Tong De [Shu Bao She]	同德［书报社］	Unknown	Tong De Reading Room
Tong Han [Xue Xiao]	同汉［学校］	Unknown	
Tong Meng Hui	同盟会	Tung Meng Hui/ Alliance Society	
Tou Jia	头家		Proprietor/Shop Owner
Wang Jing Cheng	王景成	Unknown	
Wang Jing Wei	汪精卫	Unknown	
Wang Yong Nian	汪永年	Waung Yoong Nien	
Wen Yan	文言		Classical Language
Wu Jing	《五经》	*Five Classics*	
Wu Xian Zi	伍宪子	Unknown	
Wuhan	武汉	Wuhan	
Xi Zhou [Xiao Xue]	喜洲［小学］	Unknown	Xi Zhou Primary School
Xiamen	廈門	Amoy	
Xiamen Da Xue	廈門大学	Unknown	
Xiao	孝	Filial Piety	
Xiao Jing	《孝经》	*Canon of Filial Peity*	
Xie He [Xue Xiao]	协和［学校］	Union School	
Xin Hua [Xue Xiao]	新华［学校］	Unknown	Xin Hua School
Xin Jia Po Hua Qiao Jiao Yu Zong Hui	新加坡华侨教育总会	Unknown	General Association of Overseas Chinese Education, Singapore

In Hanyu Pinyin	In Chinese Characters	English Transliteration or Translation	Authors' Translation
Xin Jia Po Nan Yang Hua Qiao Zhong Xue	新加坡南洋华侨中学	The Chinese High School	Singapore Nanyang Overseas Chinese High School
Xin Jia Po Zhong Hua Zong Shang Hui	新加坡中华总商会	Singapore Chinese Chamber of Commerce	
Xin Ke Cheng Biao Zhun Jiao Ke Shu	新课程标准教科书	Unknown	New Curriculum Standard Textbooks
Xin Ke Cheng Biao Zhun Shi Yong Ke Ben	新课程标准适用课本	Unknown	New Curriculum Standard Textbooks Suitable for Use
Xin Ke Cheng Biao Zhun Tong Yong Ke Ben	新课程标准通用课本	Unknown	New Curriculum Standard Textbooks for General Use
Xin Min Shu Ju	新民书局	Unknown	New People Book Company
Xing Hua Ge Jie Kang Di Hou Yuan Hui	星华各界抗敌后援会	Unknown	Singapore Chinese All-Groups Anti-Enemy Back-up Society
Xing Hua Shu Ju	兴华书局	Unknown	Rebuild China Book Company
Xing Hua [Xue Xiao]	兴华[学校]	Sin Hua School	
Xing Zhong [Xiao Xue]	兴中[小学]	Shing Chung Primary School	Xin Zhong Primary School
Xing Zhong [Xue Xiao]	兴中[学校]	Unknown	Xing Zhong School
Xing Zhong [Zhong Xue]	兴中[中学]	Unknown	Xin Zhong Secondary School
Xue Bu	学部	Ministry of Education	
Xun Ren [Xue Xiao]	循仁[学校]	Unknown	Xun Ren School
Yan Yuan Zhang	严元章	Unknown	
Yang Cheng Cai	杨诚财	Unknown	
Yang Zheng [Xue Xiao]	养正[学校]	Unknown	Yang Zheng School

In Hanyu Pinyin	In Chinese Characters	English Transliteration or Translation	Authors' Translation
Yi Jing	《易经》	*Book of Changes*	
Ying Shu Hua Qiao Xue Wu Wei Chi Chu	英属华侨学务维持处	Unknown	Office for Upholding Educational Matters of Overseas Chinese in British Possessions.
Ying Xin [Xue Xiao]	应新[学校]	Unknown	Ying Xin School
Ying Yong Wen	应用文	Unknown	Language for Practical Purposes
You Lie	尤列	Unknown	
You Xue Qiong Lin	《幼学琼林》	*Odes for Children*	
Yu Cai [Xue Xiao] (Ipoh)	（怡保）育才[学校]	Yuk Choy [School] (Ipoh)	
Yu Cai [Xue Xiao] (Singapore)	（新加坡）育才[学校]	Unknown	Yu Cai School (Singapore)
Yu Dong Xuan	余东旋	Eu Tong Sen	
Yu Hua Xue Xiao	育华学校	Unknown	Yu Hua School
Yu Pei Gao	余佩皋	Unknown	
Yu Qiao [Xue Xiao]	育侨[学校]	Unknown	Yu Qiao School
Yu Ying [Xue Xiao]	育英[学校]	Unknown	Yu Ying School
Yu Zhi [Shu Bao She]	育智[书报社]	Unknown	Yu Zhi Reading Room
Yu Zhi [Xue Xiao]	育智[学校]	Unknown	Yu Zhi School
Yuan Shi Kai	袁世凯	Yuan Shi Khai	
Zhang Bi Shi	张弼士	Unknown	
Zhen Hua [Xue Xiao]	振华[学校]	Unknown	Zhen Hua School
Zhen Ying [Xue Xiao]	振英[学校]	Unknown	Zhen Ying School
Zhong	忠	Loyalty	
Zhong Hua Confucian [School] (Penang)	（槟城）孔圣中华[中学]	Chung Hua Confucian School (Penang)	
Zhong Hua Gong Hui	中华公会	Unknown	Chinese Association

In Hanyu Pinyin	In Chinese Characters	English Transliteration or Translation	Authors' Translation
Zhong Hua Nu Xue	中华女学	Chung Hwa Girls' School	
Zhong Hua [Shu Bao She]	中华[书报社]	Unknown	Zhong Hua Reading Room
Zhong Hua Shu Ju	中华书局	Chung Hwa Book Company	
Zhong Hua [Xue Xiao] (Mentakab)	（文德甲）中华[学校]	Unknown	Zhong Hua School (Mentakab)
Zhong Hua [Xue Xiao] (Penang)	（槟城）中华[学校]	Unknown	Zhong Hua School (Penang)
Zhong Hua [Xue Xiao] (Raub)	（劳勿）中华[学校]	Unknown	Zhong Hua School (Raub)
Zhong Le Chen	钟乐臣	Unknown	
Zhong Ling [Xue Xiao]	钟灵[学校]	Chung Ling [School]	Zhong Ling School
Zhong Yong	《中庸》	*Golden Means*	
Zhuang Xi Quan	庄希泉	Unknown	
Zun Kong [Xue Xiao]	尊孔[学校]	Unknown	Zun Kong School

II. GLOSSARY OF CHINESE NAMES OF ARTICLES, AUTHORS, BOOKS, AND PERSONAL MEMOIRS

Authors	Titles in Hanyu Pinyin	Authors and Titles in Chinese Characters	Titles in Our Translation
Bai Xiao Bao Liu Yuan Xiao, Zeng Qu Fen Xiao Wei Yuan Hui	*Ba Gen Liu Zhu 500 Tian* (Kuala Lumpur, 2002)	白小保留原校, 争取分校委员会: 《把根留住 500天》	*Protect the Root of Chinese Education During These 500 Days*
Foo Wan Thot	*Foo Wan Thot Hui Yi Lu* (manuscript)	胡万鐸: 《胡万鐸回忆录》	*The Memoirs of Foo Wan Thot*
Hua Zhong Xiao Zhang Li Shi Hui	*Ma Lai Xi Ya Guo Min Xing Hua Wen Zhong Xue Zhi Nan* (Kuala Lumpur, 2006)	华中校长理事会 《马来西亚国民型华文中学指南》	*Directory SMJK Secondary Conforming Schools, Malaysia*
Kua Kia Soong	*Ma Lai Xi Ya Hua Jiao Fen Dou Shi* (Kuala Lumpur, 1991)	柯嘉逊: 《马来西亚华校奋斗史》	*A History of the Struggle of Chinese Schools in Malaysia*
Kuang Qi Fang	*Ma Lai Xi Ya Hua Wen Xiao Xue Jia Jiao Xie Hui de Zhu Zhi yu Gong Neng* in *Ma Lai Xi Ya Hua Wen Jiao Yu*, 2007, No. 7 (Kajang, 2007)	邝其芳: 《马来西亚华文小学家教协会的组织与功能》	*The Organization and Functions of Teacher-Parent Associations of Chinese Primary Schools in Malaysia*
Liao Wen Hui	*Hua Xiao Jiao Zong Ji Qi Ren Wu* (Kajang, 2006)	廖文辉: 《华校教总及其人物》	*UCSTA and its Personalities*
Lim Lian Geok	*Feng Yu Shi Ba Nian*, Vol. 1 (Kuala Lumpur, 1988)	林连玉: 《风雨十八年》上集	*18 Years of Adversity,* Vol. I

Authors	Titles in Hanyu Pinyin	Authors and Titles in Chinese Characters	Titles in Our Translation
Lim Lian Geok	*Feng Yu Shi Ba Nian*, Vol. 2 (Kuala Lumpur, 2001)	林连玉：《风雨十八年》下集	*18 Years of Adversity*, Vol. II
Lin Kai Zhong	*Jian Gou Zhong de Hua Ren Wen Hua* (Kuala Lumpur, 1999)	林开忠：《建构中的华人文化》	*The Making of Chinese Culture*
Loot Ting Yee	*Wo Men de Zhe Yi Tiao Lu* (Kuala Lumpur, 1993)	陆庭谕：《我们的这一条路》	*This Road of Ours*
Min Zhen Xing	*Jing Yi Zhuan Qi* in *Nanyang Siang Pau*, 3 April 2007	闵振馨：《敬益传奇》	*The Legend of Lim Keng Yaik*
Mok Soon Sang	*Ma Lai Xi Ya Jiao Yu Shi, 1400–1999* (Kuala Lumpur, 2000)	莫顺生：《马来西亚教育史，1400-1999》	*A History of Education in Malaysia: 1400–1999*
New Era College	*1998 Nian Gong Zuo Bao Gao Shu* (Kajang, 1999)	新纪元学院：《1998年工作报告书》	New Era College: *1998 Annual Report*
Shen Ting	*Wo Yu Pi Li Dong Lian Hui* [author's memoir]	沈亭：《我与霹雳董联会》	*I and the Perak General Association of School Committees*
Sim Mow Yu	*Shi Zai Huo Bu Mie* (Kuala Lumpur, 1996)	沈慕羽：《石在火不灭》	*When There Is Stone, The Fire Will Not Die Out*
Tan Liok Ee	"Da Ma Ban Dao Hua Wen Jiao Yu de Fa Zan" in UCSTA, *Jiao Zong 33 Nian* (Kuala Lumpur, 1987)	陈绿绮：《大马半岛华文教育的发展》	*The Development of Chinese Education in Peninsular Malaysia*

Authors	Titles in Hanyu Pinyin	Authors and Titles in Chinese Characters	Titles in Our Translation
Tang Chee Yee & Mok Soon Sang	*3-M Xiao Xue Xin Ke Cheng: Jiao Xue Gai Lun* (Kuala Lumpur, 1983)	邓梓仪、莫顺生：《3-M小学新课程：教学概论》	*Primary School New Curriculum: Teaching and Learning*
UCSCA	*Dong Zong 50 Nian* (Kajang, 2004)	《董总50年》	*Dong Zong's 50 years*
UCSCA	*Feng Yun Ji Dang Yi Bai Ba Shi Nian* (Kajang, 2001)	董总：《风云激荡180年》	*180 years of Lashing Wind & Rain*
UCSCA	*Hua Guang Yong Yao* (Kuala Lumpur, 1993)	董总：《华光永耀》	*The Light of Chinese Education Shines Forever*
UCSCA	*Jian Jue Fan Dui "Hong Yuan Xiao Xue Ji Hua"* (Kajang, 2000)	董总：《坚决反对宏愿小学計划》	*Oppose Firmly the Vision Primary School Plan*
UCSCA	*Jiao Yu Gai Ge Gang Ling* (Kajang, 2005)	董总：《教育改革纲领》	*Guidelines for Education Reform*
UCSCA	*Ma Lai Xi Ya Hua Wen Jiao Yu*, No. 8	董总：《马来西亚华文教育》第8期	*Chinese Education in Malaysia*, No. 8
UCSCA	*1999 Nian Dong Jiao Zong Mu Yu Jiao Yu Xuan Yan* (1st draft) (Kajang, 1999)	董总：《1999年董教总母语教育宣言》（初稿）	*1999 Declaration of the Dong Jiao Zong on Mother Tongue Education* (1st draft)
UCSCA & UCSTA (Dong Jiao Zong)	*Dui <2006–2010 Nian Jiao Yu Fa Zan Da Lan Tu> Zong Ti Yi Jian Shu* (Kajang, 2007)	董教总：对《2006-2010年教育发展大藍圖》总体意見書	*Overall Comments and Suggestions on the <2006–2010 Education Development Blueprint>*

Authors	Titles in Hanyu Pinyin	Authors and Titles in Chinese Characters	Titles in Our Translation
UCSCA & UCSTA (Dong Jiao Zong)	*Jian She Yu Fa Zan* (Kajang, 2000)	董教总：《建设与发展》	*Construction and Development*
UCSCA & UCSTA (Dong Jiao Zong)	*Zui Hou Fang Xian* (Kajang, 2003)	董教总：《最后防线》	*The Last Line of Defence*
UCSTA	*Hua Wen Jiao Yu Shi Liao* (Kuala Lumpur, 1984), mid. vol.	教总：《华文教育史料》，中册	*Chinese Education: Historical Records,* mid. vol.
UCSTA	*Hua Wen Jiao Yu Shi Liao,* (Kuala Lumpur, 1984), last vol.	教总：《华文教育史料》，下册	*Chinese Education: Historical Records,* last vol.
UCSTA	*Hua Wen Zhong Xue Gai Zhi Zhuan Ji* (Kuala Lumpur, 2000)	教总：《华文中学改制专辑》	*Conforming Chinese Secondary Schools: A Special Compilation*
UCSTA	*Jiao Zong 33 Nian* (Kuala Lumpur, 1985)	教总：《教总33年》	*Jiao Zong's 33 Years*
UCSTA	*1985 Nian Quan Guo Hua Wen Xiao Xue Diao Cha Bao Gao* (Kuala Lumpur, 1986)	教总：《1985年全国华文小学調查报告》	*A 1985 Survey of Malaysia's Chinese Primary Schools*
UCSTA	*Tiao Zan Yu Hui Ying* (Kuala Lumpur, 2001)	教总：《挑战与回应》	*Challenge and Response*
UCSTA	*2002 Nian Gong Zuo Bao Gao Shu* (Kajang, 2002)	教总：《2002年工作报告书》	*2002 Annual Report of the Jiao Zong*
UCSTA	*2006 Nian Gong Zuo Bao Gao Shu* (Kajang, 2007)	教总《2006年工作报告书》	*2006 Annual Report of the Jiao Zong*

Authors	Titles in Hanyu Pinyin	Authors and Titles in Chinese Characters	Titles in Our Translation
UCSTA, Secretariat	*Lim Lian Geok Gong Min Quan An* (Kuala Lumpur, 1989)	教总秘书处：《林连玉公民权案》	*The Case of Lim Lian Geok's Citizenship*
UCSTA, Secretariat	*Lim Liang Gong An* (Kuala Lumpur, 1987)	教总秘书处：《林梁公案》	*The Debates between Lim [Lian Geok] and Leong [Yu Koh]*
Yang Pei Gen	*1996 Jiao Yu Fa Ling Hui Da Lu* (Kajang, 1998)	杨培根：《1996教育法令回答录》	*The Education Act of 1996: Questions and Answers*
Yang Pei Gen	*Ma Lai Ya Zhi Chun*, in *Oriental News* (*Dong Fang Ri Bao*), 2006	杨培根：《马来亚之春》	*Spring in Malaya*
Zhen Gong	*Hua Jiao Chun Lei: Lim Fong Seng* (Kajang, 2006)	甄供：《华教春雷：林晃昇》	*Spring Thunder in Chinese Education: Lim Fong Seng*
Zheng Liang Shu	*Ma Lai Xi Ya Hua Wen Jiao Yu Fa Zan Shi*, vols. 1–4 (Kuala Lumpur, 1998–2003)	郑良树：《马来西亚华文教育发展史》第一至第四分册	*A History of The Development of Chinese Education in Malaysia*, Vols. 1–4.
Zhu Ke Li	*Hua She Yan Yi* in *Nanyang Siang Pau*, 2006–2007	朱可立：《华社演义》	*Chinese Society: An Epic Story*

III. GLOSSARY OF CHINESE NAMES OF NEWSPAPERS IN THE NOTES

In Hanyu Pinyin	English Transliteration or Translation	In Chinese Characters	Authors' Translation
Dong Fang Ri Bao	*Oriental News*	东方日报	
Guang Hua Ri Bao	*Kwang Hwa Jit Poh*	光华日报	
Tong Bao		通报	
Xing Bin Ri Bao	*Sing Pin Jit Poh*	星槟日报	
	Chung Kuo Pao (China Press)	中国报	
	Nanyang Siang Pau	南洋商报	
	Sin Chew Jit Poh (Sin Chew Daily)	星洲日报	

BIBLIOGRAPHY

Government Documents

Federation of Malaya. *Annual Report on Education* [for the years 1948 to 1955]. Kuala Lumpur: Government Publications, 1948–55.

———. *Education Act* [1961] (No. 43 of 1961). Kuala Lumpur: Government Publications, 1961.

———. *Education Ordinance* [1952] (No. 63 of 1952). Kuala Lumpur: Government Publications, 1952.

———. *Education Ordinance* [1957] (No. 2 of 1957). Kuala Lumpur: Government Publications, 1957.

———. *First Report of the Central Advisory Committee on Education* (Council Paper No. 29 of 1950). Kuala Lumpur: Government Publications, 1950.

———. *Registration of Schools, 1950.* Kuala Lumpur: Government Publications, 1950.

———. *Report of a Mission Invited by the Federation Government to Study the Problems of the Education of the Chinese in Malaya: Chinese Schools and the Education of Chinese Malayans.* Kuala Lumpur: Government Publications, 1951. Commonly known as the Fenn-Wu Report.

———. *Report of the Committee on Malay Education.* Kuala Lumpur: Government Publications, 1951. Commonly known as the Barnes Report.

———. *Report of the Education Committee, 1956.* Kuala Lumpur: Government Publications, 1956. Commonly known as the Razak Report.

———. *Report of the Education Review Committee, 1960.* Kuala Lumpur: Government Publications, 1960. Commonly known as the Talib Report.

———. *Report of the Special Committee Appointed by the High Commissioner in Council to Consider Ways and Means of Implementing the Policy Outlined in the Education Ordinance, 1952, in the Context of Diminishing Financial Resources of the Federation, 1954* (Council Paper No. 67 of 1954). Kuala Lumpur: Government Publications, 1954. Commonly known as the White Paper of 1954.

———. *Report of the Special Committee Appointed on the 20th Day of September, 1951 to Recommend Legislation to Cover All Aspects of Educational Policy for the Federation of Malaya.* Kuala Lumpur: Government Publications, 1952.

Kementerian Pelajaran Malaysia. *Kurikulum Baru Sekolah Rendah*. Kuala Lumpur: Government Publications, 1981.

————. *Laporan Jawatankuasa Kabinet Mengkaji Pelaksanaan Dasar Pelajaran*. Kuala Lumpur: Government Publications, 1979.

Malayan Union. *Annual Report on Education in the Malayan Union for the Period 1st April 1946 to 31st December 1946*. Appendix XV: Council Paper No. 53 of 1946. Kuala Lumpur: Government Publications, 1947.

————. *Annual Report on Education* [for 1947]. Kuala Lumpur: Government Publications, 1947.

Malaysia. *Education Bill* [1995]. Kuala Lumpur: Government Publications, 1995.

————. *Fourth Malaysia Plan*. Kuala Lumpur: Government Publications, 1981.

————. *Universities and University-Colleges Act 1971 (Act 30)*. Kuala Lumpur: International Law Book Services, 2002.

Ministry of Education. *Educational Statistics of Malaysia, 1958–1967*. Kuala Lumpur: Government Publications, 1968.

The Straits Settlements. *Straits Settlements Annual Report, 1884*. Singapore: Government Publications, 1884.

Timbalan Menteri Pendidikan. Circular TMP 9.3/1 (38). 8 June 1989. Kuala Lumpur: Kementerian Pendidikan Malaysia, 1989.

Personal Memoirs

Foo Wan Thot. *Foo Wan Thot Hui Yi Lu* (manuscript).

Shen Ting. *Wo Yu Pi Li Dong Lian Hui*. Perak: n.p., n.d.

Newspapers

Chung Kuo Pao (China Press)
Dong Fang Ri Bao (Oriental News)
Kwang Hwa Jit Poh (Guang Hua Ri Bao)
Nanyang Siang Pau
New Straits Times (Malaysia)
Sin Chew Jit Poh (Sin Chew Daily)
Sing Pin Jit Poh (Xing Bin Ri Bao)
The Star
The Straits Times (Singapore)
Tong Bao
Utusan Melayu

Articles

Chen Tian Qi. "Chinese School Statistics, 2007". In UCSCA, *Ma Lai Xi Ya Hua Wen Jiao Yu*, No. 8. Kajang: UCSCA, 2008.

Kuang Qi Fang. "Ma Lai Xi Ya Hua Wen Xiao Xue Jia Jiao Xie Hui de Zhu Zhi yu Gong Neng". In UCSCA, *Ma Lai Xi Ya Hua Wen Jiao Yu*, No. 7. Kajang: UCSCA, 2007.

Lee, Molly N.N. "Educational Reforms". In *Reflections: The Mahathir Years*, edited by Bridget Welsh. Washington: Southeast Asia Studies Program, SIAS, 2004.

Min Zhen Xing. "Jing Yi Zhuan Qi". *Nanyang Siang Pau*, 3 April 2007.

Tan Liok Ee. "Da Ma Ban Dao Hua Wen Jiao Yu de Fa Zan". In UCSTA, *Jiao Zong 33 Nian*. Kuala Lumpur: UCSTA, 1987.

Tunku Abdul Rahman. "As I See It". *The Star*, 25 March 2007, Special III.

Yang Pei Gen. "Ma Lai Ya Zhi Chun". *Dong Fang Ri Bao*, 2006.

Zhu Ke Li. "Hua She Yan Yi". *Nanyang Siang Pau*, 2006–07.

Books

Alis Puteh. *Language and Nation Building*. Petaling Jaya: Strategic Information and Research Development, 2006.

Bai Xiao Bao Liu Yuan Xiao, Zeng Qu Fen Xiao Wei Yuan Hui. *Ba Gen Liu Zhu 500 Tian*. Kuala Lumpur: [Bai Xiao Committee], 2002.

Baker, Jim. *Crossroads: A Popular History of Singapore & Malaysia*. Singapore: Marshall Cavendish International, 1999.

Cartens, Sharon A. *Histories, Cultures, Identities: Studies in Malaysian Chinese Worlds*. Singapore: Singapore University Press, 2006.

Chai Hon Chan. *Education and Nation Building in Plural Societies: The West Malaysian Experience*. Canberra: Australian National University, 1977.

Cheah Boon Kheng. *Malaysia: The Making of a Nation*. Singapore: Institute of Southeast Asian Studies, 2002.

―――. *Red Star over Malaya*. Singapore: Singapore University Press, 1983.

Chelliah, D.D. *A History of Educational Policy of the Straits Settlements, 1800–1925*. Kuala Lumpur: Government Press, 1947.

Crouch, Harold. *Government and Society in Malaysia*. Singapore: Talisman Publishing Pte Ltd, 1996.

Gerakan. *Gerakan: In 40 Years, What Has Gerakan Achieved?* Penang: Gerakan, 2008.

Hooker, V.M. *A Short History of Malaysia*. Crows Nest, NSW, Australia: Allen & Unwin, 2003.

Hsu, Immanuel C.Y. *The Rise of Modern China*. Kuala Lumpur: Oxford University Press, 1975.

Ibrahim Saad. *Pendidikan dan Politik di Malaysia*. Kuala Lumpur: Dewan Bahasa dan Pustaka, 1977.

Khoo Boo Teik. *Beyond Mahathir*. New York: Zed Books Ltd, 2003.

Kua Kia Soong. *Ma Lai Xi Ya Hua Jiao Fen Dou Shi*. Kuala Lumpur: [Selangor Chinese Assembly Hall], 1991.

―――. *May 13*. Selangor: Suaram Komunikasi, 2007.

————. *New Era Education*. Kajang: New Era College, 2005.

————. *A Protean Saga: The Chinese Schools of Malaysia*. Kuala Lumpur: UCSCA, 1985.

Lee Ting Hui. *Chinese Schools in British Malaya: Policies and Politics*. Singapore: South Seas Society, 2006.

————. *The Open United Front: The Communist Struggle in Singapore, 1954–1966*. Singapore: South Seas Society, 1996.

Liao Wen Hui. *Hua Xiao Jiao Zong Ji Qi Ren Wu*. Kajang: UCSTA, 2006.

Lim Lian Geok. *Feng Yu Shi Ba Nian*, vol. 1. Kuala Lumpur: LLG Cultural Development Centre, 1988.

————. *Feng Yu Shi Ba Nian*, vol. 2. Kuala Lumpur: LLG Cultural Development Centre, 2001.

Lin Kai Zhong. *Jian Gou Zhong de Hua Ren Wen Hua*. Kuala Lumpur: [Hua She Research Centre], 1999.

Loh Kok Wah. *The Socio-Economic Basis of Ethnic Consciousness: The Chinese in the 1970's*. Kuala Lumpur: Persatuan Sains Sosial Malaysia, University of Malaya, 1984.

Loot Ting Yee. *Wo Men de Zhe Yi Tiao Lu*. Kuala Lumpur: Oriengroup Sdn. Bhd., 1993.

Mahathir Mohamad, Dr. *Malaysia Melangkah ke Hadapan*. Kuala Lumpur: Dewan Bahasa dan Pustaka & ISIS, 1991.

Means, Gordon P. *Malaysian Politics*. London: Hodder and Stoughton, 1970.

Milne, R.S. and Diane K. Mauzy. *Malaysian Politics under Mahathir*. New York: Routledge, 1999.

Mok Soon Sang. *Ma Lai Xi Ya Jiao Yu Shi, 1400–1999*. Kuala Lumpur: LLG Cultural Development Centre, 2000.

————. *Nota Ulangkaji dan Latihan PTK, Bahagian I, Kompetensi Umum (Teras dan Profesional)*. Kuala Lumpur: Multimedia-es Resources Sdn. Bhd., 2007.

————. *Nota Ulangkaji & Latihan P.T.K. Bahagian II, Kompetensi Khusus (P&P)*. Puchong: Multimedia-es Resources Sdn. Bhd., 2008.

————. *Pendidikan di Malaysia*, Edisi ke-7. Selangor: Kumpulan Bulliman Sdn. Bhd., 2006.

New Era College. *1998 Nian Gong Zuo Bao Gao*. Kajang: Kolej New Era, 1999.

Ooi Jin Bee. *Land, People and Economy of Malaya*. Oxford: [Oxford University Press], 1963.

Ratnam, K.J. *Communalism and the Political Process in Malaya*. Kuala Lumpur: University of Malaya Press, 1963.

Ruslan Zainuddin, et al. *Kenegaraan Malaysia*. Petaling Jaya: Fajar Bakti Sdn. Bhd., 2005.

Ruslan Zainuddin. *Sejarah Malaysia*, Edisi ke-2. Selangor: Fajar Bakti Sdn. Bhd., 2006.

Save-New-Era-College Editorial Board. *Writings on the New Era College Controversy*. Kajang: New Era College, 2008.

Shahril et al. *Pendidikan di Malaysia*. Kuala Lumpur: Utusan Publication, 1993.

S. Husin Ali, ed. *Kaum, Kelas dan Pembangunan, Malaysia*. Kuala Lumpur: Persatuan Sains Sosial Malaysia, University of Malaya, 1984.

Shu Yun-Tsiao and Chua Ser-Koon, eds. *Malayan Chinese Resistance to Japan, 1937–1945: Selected Source Materials*. Singapore: Cultural & Historical Publishing House, 1984.

Sia Keng Yek. *SRJK(C) dalam Sistem Pendidikan Kebangsaan: Delima dan Kontroversi*. Kuala Lumpur: University of Malaya, 2005.

Sim Mow Yu. *Shi Zai Huo Bu Mie*. Kuala Lumpur: UCSTA, 1996.

SMJK Conforming Executive Committee. *Directory SMJK Conforming*. Kuala Lumpur: Hua Zhong Xiao Zhang Li Shi Hui, 2006.

Song Ong Siang. *One Hundred Years' History of the Chinese in Singapore*. Singapore: University of Malaya Press, 1967.

Tan Liok Ee. *The Politics of Chinese Education in Malaya, 1945–1961*. New York: Oxford University Press, 1997.

Tan Teng Jin et al. *The Chinese Malaysian Contribution*. Kuala Lumpur: Centre for Malaysian Studies, 2005.

Tang Chee Yee and Mok Soon Sang. *3-M Xiao Xue Xin Ke Cheng: Jiao Xue Gai Lun*. Kuala Lumpur: Media Distribution Sdn. Bhd., 1983.

Turnbull, C.M. *A History of Singapore, 1819–1975*. Kuala Lumpur: Oxford University Press, 1977.

UCSCA. *Dong Zong 50 Nian*. Kajang: UCSCA, 2004.

UCSCA. *Feng Yun Ji Dang Yi Bai Ba Shi Nian*. Kajang: UCSCA, 2001.

———. *Hua Guang Yong Yao*. Kuala Lumpur: UCSCA, 1993.

———. *Jian Jue Fan Dui "Hong Yuan Xiao Xue Ji Hua"*. Kajang: UCSCA, 2000.

———. *Jiao Yu Gai Ge Gang Ling*. Kajang: UCSCA, 2005.

UCSCA and UCSTA. *Dui <2006–2010 Nian Jiao Yu Fa Zan Da Lan Tu> Zong Ti Yi Jian Shu*. Kajang: UCSCA and UCSTA, 2007.

———. *Jian She Yu Fa Zan*. Kajang: UCSCA and UCSTA, 2000.

———. *1999 Nian Dong Jiao Zong Mu Yu Jiao Yu Xuan Yan* (1st draft). Kajang: UCSCA and UCSTA, 1999.

———. *Zui Hou Fang Xian*. Kajang: UCSCA and UCSTA, 2003.

UCSTA. *Hua Wen Jiao Yu Shi Liao*, mid. vol. Kuala Lumpur: UCSTA, 1984.

———. *Hua Wen Jiao Yu Shi Liao*, last vol. Kuala Lumpur: UCSTA, 1984.

———. *Hua Wen Zhong Xue Gai Zhi Zhuan Ji*. Kuala Lumpur: UCSTA, 2000.

———. *Jiao Zong 33 Nian*. Kuala Lumpur: UCSTA, 1985.

———. *1985 Nian Quan Guo Hua Wen Xiao Xue Diao Cha Bao Gao*. Kuala Lumpur: UCSTA, 1986.

———. *Tiao Zan Yu Hui Ying*. Kuala Lumpur: UCSTA, 2001.

———. *2002 Nian Gong Zuo Bao Gao Shu*. Kajang: UCSTA, 2002.

———. *2006 Nian Gong Zuo Bao Gao Shu*. Kajang: UCSTA, 2007.

UCSTA Secretariat. *Lim Lian Geok Gong Min Quan An*. Kuala Lumpur: LLG Cultural Development Centre, 1989.

————. *Lim Liang Gong An*. Kuala Lumpur: LLG Cultural Development Centre, 1987.

Wong Hoy Kee and Ee Tiang Hong. *Education in Malaysia*, 2nd ed. Kuala Lumpur: Heinemann (Asia) Sdn. Bhd., 1975.

Wong Weng On, James. *From Pacific War to Merdeka*. Kuala Lumpur: Strategic Information Research Development, 2005.

Yang Pei Gen. *1996 Jiao Yu Fa Ling Hui Da Lu*. Kajang: UCSCA, 1998.

Yap Sin Tian. *The Chinese Schools of Malaysia: Towards the Year 2000*. Kuala Lumpur: Ye Shi Enterprise, 1992.

Yu Shu Kuen et al. *Nanyang Nian Jian*. Singapore: [Nanyang Bao She], 1951; *Six-Year Education Plan*.

————. *Nanyang Nian Jian*. Singapore: [Nanyang Bao She], 1951; *Ten-Year Education Plan*.

Zakaria Hj. Ahmad, ed. *Government and Politics*, vol. 2. Kuala Lumpur: Archipelago Press, 2007.

Zhen Gong. *Hua Jiao Chun Lei: Lim Fong Seng*. Kajang: UCSCA, 2006.

Zheng Liang Shu. *Ma Lai Xi Ya Hua Wen Jiao Yu Fa Zan Shi*, vols. 1–4. Kuala Lumpur: UCSTA, 1998–2003.

INDEX

ABOUT THE AUTHOR

Lee Ting Hui was born and raised in Malaysia. He started working life as a teacher in a Chinese primary school in a small town there. Later he switched to teach in one of the largest Chinese secondary schools, the Yoke Choy High School in Ipoh. When he came to Singapore from Ipoh, he taught in the Chung Cheng and the Chinese High Schools at different times, the two premier Chinese secondary schools on the island. After graduation from the University of Malaya, he taught in the Chinese Department of the same university, and later, he also taught in the History Department of the Chinese-medium Nanyang University. He also worked in the Political Study Centre and in the Ministry of Education in Singapore where he trained Chinese primary and secondary school principals and teachers as well as students in general politics.

Lee is conversant with Chinese culture which is the basis of Chinese education and is a much decorated poet in the Chinese language. He was at one time the Secretary-General of the All-World Society for Chinese Poetry. He also led Chinese literary activities in Singapore, being the President of the Singapore Chinese Writers' Association for a number of years, for which he was awarded the BBM by the President of Singapore.

Lee's earlier publication in the field of Chinese education is *Chinese Schools in British Malaya: Policies and Politics.*

www.ingramcontent.com/pod-product-compliance
Lightning Source LLC
Chambersburg PA
CBHW021853020426
42334CB00013B/306